"You Have No Rights Here"

A true story about one American's thirty-three months in a Middle East prison

ان ه ق و ق ح ك د ل س ي ل

Paul B. Ciceri
Illustrations by Dale Amlund

©2007 Paul Ciceri
Published by Conch Republic Press

All rights reserved. No portion of this book may be reproduced, stored in a retrieval system, or transmitted in any form, by any means, including mechanical, electronic, photocopying, recording, or otherwise, without the prior written permission of the publisher, except in the case of brief quotations embodied in critical articles or reviews written for inclusion in a magazine, newspaper, Internet, or broadcast. For information about obtaining reproduction rights, please contact the publisher.

While this is a work of nonfiction, the names and personal characteristics of several peripheral characters may have been changed or omitted in order to protect their privacy. In these instances, any resemblance to persons living or dead is entirely coincidental and unintentional.

Publisher's Cataloging-In-Publication Data
(Prepared by The Donohue Group, Inc.)

Ciceri, Paul B.
   "You have no rights here" : a true story about one American's thirty-three months in a Middle East prison / Paul B. Ciceri ; illustrations by Dale Amlund.

p. : ill. ; cm.

   Transliterated title: Ah yas adyak haakwa heena.
   ISBN-13: 978-0-9788679-0-4
   ISBN-10: 0-9788679-0-4

1. Ciceri, Paul. -- Imprisonment. 2. Prisoners -- Ab͞u Zaby (United Arab Emirates) -- Biography. 3. Americans -- Ab͞u Zaby (United Arab Emirates) -- Biography. I. Amlund, Dale. II. Title.
HV9781.5 .C53 2007
365.4/092   2006908567

Publishing Consultant: Sylvia Hemmerly
Book Design: Publishing Professionals, Port Richey, FL
Cover: Paul Ciceri and Sylvia Hemmerly; Files by William Dennison
Illustrations: Dale Amlund
Book Shepherd: Sylvia Hemmerly

Printed in Canada
08 07 06 05 5 4 3 2 1

Dedication

My father died six months before my release from prison. During his last two years he struggled for my release, hoping that with his failing health I might be set free on humanitarian grounds. He stood firmly with me during my ordeal at Al Wathba as he had throughout my entire life. He was a great friend with whom I could share my feelings and I miss him profoundly. His last words to me were, "I love you. Keep up the good work."

I love you too, Dad, and I dedicate this work to you.

Table of Contents

Preface vii
Acknowledgments ix
Time Line xi

1   Days to Remember 1
2   Going to the Middle East 4
3   The Summer of '98 9
4   Greece in September 1998 11
5   A Moment to Remember 16
6   The Arrest 20
7   Mina Jail 32
8   Arrival at Al Wathba Prison 45
9   The Prison 55
10   Block 3 62
11   First Visit from the Embassy 68
12   Settling In 73
13   The First Few Weeks in Block 3 79
14   Return to the Public Prosecutor 87
15   Reality Sets In 92
16   Word from Home 100
17   Getting the Message Out 105
18   Meeting with My Lawyer 109
19   The First Holidays Behind Bars 112
20   Ramadan Prison Style 126
21   The Year of Reckoning Begins 131
22   The Trial 139
23   Police on the Rampage 146
24   Politicians Feign Interest 149
25   The Defense 156
26   Waiting for the Verdict 159

27	The Verdict Is In	165
28	The Aftermath	170
29	The Appeal	176
30	The First Long Hot Summer	180
31	A Visit from my Brother	192
32	Coal in My Christmas Stocking	206
33	Next Year	213
34	The Warden Hates Us	222
35	My Guardian Angels	229
36	Springtime Hopes	232
37	God Bless Sheikh Mohammed	239
38	Contact with my Father	244
39	A Tough Summer	250
40	Sheikh Mohammed Does It Again	255
41	A Year of Blessings	264
42	The Worst Possible News	267
43	England Hears about Al Wathba	274
44	Another Opportunity Missed	278
45	Light at the End of the Tunnel	282
46	My Last Easter in Captivity	288
47	Counting Down	292
48	Something's Up	296
49	June 6, 2001	300
50	The Agonizing Wait	305
51	Day 1000	312
52	Goodbye to Al Wathba	317
53	Freedom	323
54	The Journey Back	329
Addendum A	Photographs and Documentation	335
Addendum B	Poem: A Better Person	355
Addendum C	A British View of Things	361
Addendum D	Poem: The Noise	371
Addendum E	Count Down	381

Preface

As I begin this journey of writing about my experiences in an Arabian prison, I realize that it was exactly three years ago that this episode of my life began. Just as those who witnessed the assassination of President Kennedy, saw the Challenger spacecraft explode shortly after lift-off from Cape Canaveral, or watched the World Trade Center towers attacked and destroyed will never forget those moments in time, I will never forget the ordeal that began at 11:30 p.m. Arabian time on the night of October 7, 1998.

This is a story about the human spirit and the will to survive. Half a world away from America, I faced each day with the determination to go on, to maintain my dignity as a human being and as an American, and to use well the time of my imprisonment. For thirty-three months I held out hope of release, and what a miracle it was to finally be set free on the American Independence Day!

Every day I think about the people I left behind. Perhaps in some way, my raising the consciousness of life in places like Al Wathba prison among the citizens of the world will help speed the release of those still held captive. In many ways this is their story too.

Paul Ciceri
October 7, 2001

Acknowledgments

My family, especially my brother Richard, daughter, Jennifer, and former wife, Susanne, spearheaded the effort for my release with relentless determination. All of them have my deepest gratitude and I am proud to call them 'family'.

Tom Hennessy, an American resident of Abu Dhabi, gave up many weekends over the thirty-three months of my imprisonment to stand for hours in the blazing Arabian sun in the hope of getting a five-minute visit with me. He was an angel who thought this was merely "the Christian thing to do." I will never forget.

Numerous friends and acquaintances buoyed my spirits by writing me, providing moral support to my family, raising money for my defense fund, and sending care packages of books and magazines. I am blessed to have such friends.

Ambassador Kattouf and staff *of the American Embassy in Abu Dhabi*, especially *Charles Glatz* and *Jamal Bafagih*, fought diligently for my release, assisted my family and friends by answering questions, and exchanged pertinent information with them. They were in the courtroom for my trial, visited me on a regular basis or when I needed immediate assistance, and kept in close contact with the prison manager and other staff in pursuit of my well-being. It is good to know that as Americans we have such dedicated public servants available around the world to help us in times of need.

Dale F. Amlund, Professor of Theater Arts design at Rollins College in Winter Park and a friend for over twenty-five years, provided the illustrations for this book. I value his ongoing friendship and admire his creative talents.

Julia Gabell edited my manuscript and shared her insights and expertise with openness and respect for my opinion. She helped me step back to view my work with an unbiased eye and develop *You Have No Rights Here* into a book of which I am proud.

Sylvia Hemmerly, whose extensive knowledge of the publishing industry and her timely shepherding, have been invaluable in bringing this work of love to fruition. Without her encouragement I might have limited this story to the few who were involved. My book speaks of angels and she is another one that God sent my way.

James McCarthy, who has held numerous positions in teaching and mental health counseling services in the United States and the United Kingdom, graciously spent hours exploring with me my feelings after my release. He supported my idea of writing this book and encouraged me to take time for myself in order to make it happen. At each step of the way he listened to my stories, understood my frustrations, shared my hopes, and made me feel that I was on the right course.

Jon Reames, a friend of many years, warmly welcomed me into his home when I returned to Orlando to sort out what I wanted to do with my life after my release from Al Wathba. Having that safe haven was a vitally important step in my return to life back in the United States.

Time Line

February–March, 1997	Interviewed for and accepted position with ELS Language Centers, Middle East
April, 1997	Attended ELS Language Centers Management Academy for two weeks in Santa Monica, CA
May 6, 1997	Left for the Middle East
May 8, 1997	Arrived in Abu Dhabi, United Arab Emirates
	Met with Dr. Patrick Fitch, Managing Director and Sheikhs Shaya and Khalid bin Ahmad al Hamed, owners of ELS Language Centers, Middle East
May 9, 1997	Assumed position as Director of ELS Language Centers in Kuwait
Late July, 1997	Won bid for contract to teach English to Kuwait military personnel
August, 1997	Recruited teaching personnel in Canada, U.S., and England
September 11, 1997	Beginning of teaching contract with the Military
March, 1998	Appointed Director of Marketing for ELS Language Centers, Middle East
August 7, 1998	American Embassies bombed in Dar es Salaam, Tanzania and Nairobi, Kenya
September 25, 1998	Began 2-week vacation in Greece
September 27, 1998	Went to Canada for 10 days to attend Mother's funeral
October 5, 1998	Arrived back in Greece
October 7, 1998	Arrested by Customs agents at Abu Dhabi International Airport
October 12, 1998	Taken before Public Prosecutor to review charges
	Transferred to Al Wathba prison
	First contact since arrest with American Embassy personnel
October 13, 1998	Assigned to Block 3 in Al Wathba
October 14, 1998	First face-to-face meeting with consular officials from American Embassy
October 28, 1998	First contact with family members via Embassy staff
November 2, 1998	Second meeting with the Public Prosecutor
November–December, 1998	Visits to Abu Dhabi by former Presidents George Bush and Jimmy Carter and former Secretary of Defense William Cohen

December 1, 1998	Meeting with attorney
December 23, 1998	Christmas visit from Embassy staff
January 3, 1999	First visit to Shariah court. Postponement of trial
February 14, 1999	First court session
March 6, 1999	Second court session
April 12, 1999	Third court session
May 1, 1999	Fourth court session. Sentence of 4 years imposed.
May 3, 1999	Transfer to Block 8 in Al Wathba
May 16, 1999	Appeal filed
June 14, 1999	First appeals court session. Trial postponed.
July 5, 1999	Second appeals court session. Appeal withdrawn.
Mid July–Mid August, 1999	Assigned to prison clinic
October 30, 1999	Visit from brother and Embassy officials
November 1, 1999	Brother and Embassy officials met with Sheikh Diyab bin Zayed al Nahyan, head of the Diva Court
November 2, 1999	Second visit from brother
Mid December, 1999	Prisoners sentenced for drugs cases isolated from rest of prison population
January 31, 2000	Ambassador Kattouf makes appeal for release to Royal Family
May, 2000	Sheikh Mohammed of Dubai releases all prisoners with drug related sentences
June 14, 2000	Telephone conversation with my father
November 1, 2000	Cast vote for November U.S. general election
November, 2000	Sheikh Zayed bin Sultan al Nahyan, President of the UAE returns to the UAE after recovering in the United States for a kidney transplant
December 24, 2000	Clandestine Christmas service for Christians in the block
December 30, 2000	Embassy informs me of my father's death
December 31, 2000	Ambassador Kattouf makes another appeal for clemency
June 6, 2001	Abu Dhabi announces the release of 6000 prisoners in honor of Sheikh Zayed's recovery
July 3, 2001	Day 1000 Advised in meeting with Warden and Embassy staff of my release
July 4, 2001	Transferred from Al Wathba prison to Abu Dhabi airport
July 5, 2001	Arrival in Toronto, Canada

1

Days to Remember

THE SCORE WAS TIED 9–9. It was the seventh game of the World Series between the Pittsburgh Pirates and the New York Yankees and it was now the bottom of the ninth with the hometown Pirates coming to bat.

The place was Forbes Field in Pittsburgh.

It was Thursday afternoon, October 13, 1960 and the large Longines clock in left field indicated 3:36 p.m.

Statistically, the Yankees had dominated the Series. They had out-hit the Pirates 91–60, led in runs 55–27, and scored ten home runs compared to the Pirates' four. They had more than doubled the Pirates' RBIs 54–26. All three Yankees wins had been by lopsided scores while the Pirates wins had come in at 1 or 2-point victories.

But the stubborn Pirates had held on and this game had everyone on the edge of his seat. The Pirates had grabbed an early 4–0 lead with two runs in each of the first two innings. The score held until the fifth inning when the Yankees scored their first run, then added four more in the sixth, eventually extending their lead by two more in the eighth. Down 7–4, the Pirates had only two innings in which to rally and pull out an upset. Their biggest scoring inning of the Series came in the bottom of the eighth with a five-run outburst. The fans were ecstatic now that the boys in black and yellow were leading 9–7 with only one inning left. The deafening roar in the park, however, subsided when the Yankees scored two more in the top of the ninth to tie the score 9–9.

But the partisan hometown crowd knew that this was the big chance to win the Series and the noise built as the Yankees took to the field for the bottom of the ninth. This was a legendary Yankees team. It included baseball greats like Mickey Mantle, Bobby Richardson, Bill (Moose) Skowron, Tony Kubek, and Yogi Berra. And the coach was none other than Casey Stengel. This was one hell of a team to beat and the Pirates had a chance to make history.

Just one run from winning the World Series and the pressure was enormous! Tension gripped the Pirates' bench as players pondered their downslide at the top of the inning and realized how close they now were to becoming World Champions. It was Bill Mazeroski's turn to bat and someone yelled, "You're up!" Deep in concentration Mazeroski slowly selected his bat and walked to home plate.

The crowd was on its feet as the noise reached a fever pitch. The first ball came and Mazeroski watched it whiz by. It was a fastball, high and inside. He gathered his thoughts and once more hunkered down to face the pitch—something he had done hundreds of times throughout the season. The second pitch was on its way and it was high in the zone.

Mazeroski saw it as *his* ball and swung hard. There was a crack as ball met bat and the crowd went wild. Mazeroski took off for first base and headed for second, hoping for a double if his slam was uncatchable. All he heard was a deafening roar; couldn't understand what his first-base coach yelled as he rounded the turf. At second, he glanced at the left field umpire who extended one finger high over his head, rotating it in a circular motion. The sign of a home run!

The ball had cleared the 12-foot, left-center wall to the right of the Longines clock—3:37 p.m. And the Pirates had won the 1960 World Series with that hit in the bottom of the ninth in the seventh game.

It was perhaps the most dramatic moment in World Series history. No one in the stands would ever forget that afternoon.

Two hundred miles from Forbes Field, I had been watching that game on television, hoping that the Pirates would beat those damn Yankees. The noise of that ball connecting with the bat and the sight of it sailing over the left field wall became embedded forever in the memory of this fifteen-year-old. What a game, what a series, what a hero! An event and a day to remember forever!

There would be several other such moments in my life: the afternoon on October 16, 1962, when we sat on edge while the U.S. and Russia jockeyed for position at sea, and the Russian ship carrying missile parts bound for Cuba was finally turned back by U.S. ships; the afternoon of November 22, 1963, when President Kennedy was assassinated in Dallas; the twelfth day of January, 1969, when the New York Jets led by Joe Namath beat the highly-favored Baltimore Colts to win Super Bowl III in Miami; the morning of January 28, 1986, when the Challenger spacecraft exploded less than a minute after lift off from Cape Kennedy with a loss of all seven crew; and finally, the morning of September 11, 2001, when the world watched in disbelief as two hi-jacked planes flew into the World Trade Center.

To that list I can now add the events of Wednesday, October 7, 1998, a day that would begin a 1000 day ordeal for me in the notorious Al Wathba prison in the desert outside of Abu Dhabi in the United Arab Emirates.

2

Going to the Middle East

FOR MANY YEARS I HAD had a desire to work outside North America and had pursued several leads for jobs in Europe and the Middle East. Though all my attempts had been unfruitful thus far, I still hoped to use my skills in marketing, finance, and business management to add some international experience to my resume.

One night in February 1997 while I was in Orlando, I met a man who wore a convention badge with the acronym "TESOL" printed in large letters. Curiosity got the best of me and upon inquiring about the meaning of the letters, I was told they stood for "Teachers of English to Speakers of Other Languages." The man was in Orlando for a convention of persons involved in teaching English all over the world. He himself had been a teacher in Saudi Arabia for sixteen years.

The following day I was able to convince one of the security staff to let me enter the convention area simply to peruse what was available in one of the rooms set aside for job networking. Easels were set up for listings of job opportunities in the English-language teaching field, so I took some time looking for the parts of the world to which I wanted to relocate. Since I didn't have the credentials for teaching, I narrowed the opportunities to six and submitted copies of my resume for each one.

The next day I repeated my conversation with the guard and sought out the postings for assigned interviews. My name appeared on one list and I put my name down for the earliest possible session. It turned out to be one of the most interesting job interviews of my life. I learned about the explosion of English-teaching positions throughout the world and the availability of career opportunities overseas; the interviewer, Dr. Patrick Fitch, asked questions that were not only relevant to selected teaching positions, but were also targeted to embrace related experience in marketing and management. Dr. Fitch, who would later become my manager in the Middle East, told me that he had selected me for the interview, not because of any qualifications in the education field, but because of my marketing experience with IBM, my one-time position as a stockbroker, and the fact that I had owned my own business. Marketing experience was essential because he was hiring personnel for positions as school directors, and the success of the schools depended on the resourcefulness of the marketing efforts in attracting students.

He explained the mission of a company called ELS Language Centers, an American company that operated twenty-five schools in the United States and Canada and franchised schools throughout the world. Dr. Fitch was the Managing Director for two sheikhs in Abu Dhabi who held the franchise rights for the Middle East and North Africa. Seven Centers were already in operation and future plans were to expand throughout the region.

Six days later in a follow-up meeting, I was offered a position as Director of the Kuwait Center. Two days later I accepted.

For the next month I arranged to close down and sell my Massage Therapy practice and prepare to go to the Middle East. But prior to that I was off to Los Angeles to take part in an ELS Management Academy, a two week program designed to bring together and train newly-appointed management personnel for all the schools worldwide. My class included people who were going to Centers or who owned Centers in Colombia, Argentina, Malaysia, Japan, and Indonesia.

The class was well run by the executive staff of ELS Language Centers and at the end of two weeks I was excited about taking on my new responsibilities as Center Director in Kuwait. Although to date this project had been financially unsuccessful, before I left for the Middle East the President of the Company told me that he was expecting me to "save" the Center. That was my mission and I was ready.

So on Tuesday, May 6, 1997, I was off for the Middle East. As the plane approached Kuwait, I remember peering down on huge expanses of land where there were no lights or signs of habitation in the vast desert regions. Over Kuwait, the dark of night was punctuated by the vent fires burning at each of the hundreds of pumping oil wells. One could only imagine the scene six years earlier when all the wells had been set ablaze by the retreating Iraqi troops. Coincidentally, I arrived at my destination on May 8, the first day of the Islamic New Year.

After meeting with my staff and sizing up the challenge that faced me, it was time to get to work. I made a concerted effort to attract children who had just begun their summer break and soon the Center was thriving. A push had to be made to locate teachers for the numerous classes. It was gratifying to see our classrooms full and to witness the eagerness shown by staff to provide a great learning experience for the children. Everyone pitched in and by July the Center, for the first time in its history, had had a profitable month. We were on our way.

Throughout the summer the school was a very busy place, and while the staff took control of maintaining the program, I looked for new resources to ensure our Center's success after the children had returned to their regular school program. With the support of my staff and Dr. Fitch, we bid on the largest English-language teaching contract in the country, and in late July we were awarded the contract to teach the country's military personnel. Because of the delay in finalizing this agreement, we had only six weeks in which to recruit thirty-three teachers, locate accommodations for them, secure lease vehicles, and arrange for entry visas.

Thus began a routine of sixteen-hour days. I made quick trips to the United States, Canada, and England to recruit teachers. The task was made even more challenging by the fact that the military personnel overseeing the selection of our staff showed bias against us because I strongly believed they had had a stake in the company that previously had held the contract. Even when I challenged them on that belief they denied any connection After much wrangling, we were up and running by late September. We leased an entire apartment complex, secured the use of three vans and four cars, and spent days at the Ministries of Defense, Immigration, and Education getting all the paperwork approved for the new staff. In addition, we had to arrange for transportation and contracts for each of the new staff members. The project had been a superb team effort, and by the time we were operational, our Center had become the largest ELS Language Center worldwide, a tribute to all those who had worked so tirelessly during the five months since my arrival in Kuwait.

We continued to face new challenges that were unique to our situation. Saddam Hussein continued to threaten Kuwait by amassing troops along the border and by making verbal assertions that Kuwait was rightly the property of Iraq. Because of the widespread uncertainties, some of the teachers faced enormous pressure from family and friends to leave the Middle East. Several packed up and left on late-night flights without any advance notice; others took leaves during the most serious times of Iraqi threat. I attended several meetings at the United States Embassy where the latest developments with Iraq were discussed. We were told what preparations we should make for the evacuation of our staff and their dependents; precautions that we as foreigners should take to ensure our safety were reviewed. We were given contingency evacuation plans to guarantee that every American would be warned as quickly as possible in case of imminent danger. Fortunately, the United States military still had a large presence in Kuwait, and with their threat of further retaliations against Iraq, the tension was diffused to the point that none of our contingency plans had to be implemented.

In March 1998 I was promoted to Director of Marketing for our system of Centers throughout the Middle East and North Africa. My major responsibility was to assist the Center Directors in attracting students to their program and in maximizing their Centers' profitability. The job required traveling to all our Centers on a regular basis, and because it primarily entailed international travel, there was always work to be done in securing appropriate visas well ahead of time for each trip. I became a frequent user of the Abu Dhabi airport and was very aware of immigration and customs checks that went on at the airport for incoming passengers.

I enjoyed the challenges of my position as Dr. Fitch and his colleagues had allowed me to draw on my varied experiences in marketing, finance, and management. I also had the freedom to be as creative as I wanted in achieving the results that we were looking for. The opportunity for travel to foreign countries and the chance to learn about new cultures added to the satisfaction I got from the job. At the same time I was enjoying Abu Dhabi as a place to call home, though in retrospect it was that way because I was only there for short periods. On March 16 in an e-mail I wrote "I think I'll be in Abu Dhabi for a while . . . at least 1–2 years or so. Unlike Kuwait there is a life here . . . lots to see and do . . . excellent restaurants and culture . . . and even bars. It's a great place . . . a good experience."

In six months my opinions would change dramatically.

3

The Summer of '98

SEVERAL YEARS EARLIER I HAD become acquainted with a fellow from the Far East through a travel club to which I belonged. He had come to the United States on a holiday and had visited with my partner and me for several days. He was a school teacher and spent his summers traveling the world.

Over the years we had been in contact from time to time via the Internet. Then, in early May of 1998, he told me he was traveling in Europe for the summer and asked if I wanted to meet him there for a few weeks. Since it had been my intention to vacation in Greece in late September, and since that fit in beautifully with his plans, we agreed to meet in Athens on September 25 and travel to the island of Mykonos.

On August 7, 1998, the American Embassy compounds in Dar es Salaam, Tanzania and Nairobi, Kenya were bombed resulting in the loss of two hundred and twenty-four lives including twelve Americans. Through my contacts at the ELS Language Center in Kuwait I had been told that one of my acquaintances from the American Embassy in Kuwait had recently transferred to Nairobi and that both he and his son had been killed in the explosion there. The bombings quickly became a personal issue for me.

In the aftermath of the explosions, U.S. military forces retaliated by blowing up a pharmaceutical plant in Sudan and by bombing suspected terrorist strongholds in Afghanistan. At most, it was a token response that did not deter the terrorists as was proven by the September 11, 2001, attacks on New York City and Washington D.C.

Regardless of the fact that we had been attacked, many people throughout the world, especially those in the Middle and Far East, saw our retaliation as just another bully act by the world's superpower. That was the feeling shared by my friend whom I would meet in Greece in September.

We finalized plans to meet in Athens. I would be traveling from Abu Dhabi and he would be coming from Rome.

4

Greece in September 1998

OUR ARRANGEMENT WAS TO MEET in Athens on September 25 and that same evening catch a flight to Mykonos where we had hotel reservations for seven days. The second week we had planned to return to Athens and explore areas of Greece north of there.

The scheduled arrival times for our flights were within forty minutes of each other late on that Friday afternoon. Both flights landed close to schedule, so I was waiting for my friend when his Singapore Airlines flight flew in from Rome. Since he had been traveling for almost two months, he had collected souvenirs along the way and had excess baggage that was extremely heavy. We sought out and finally found a facility for storing part of his luggage for the week we would be in Mykonos.

After an easy transfer to the terminal serving domestic routes, we settled in to wait for our departure. A celebration of sorts was in order for our having met again, so I set off to buy each of us a beer and find out if there was a special area where one should sit while drinking alcoholic beverages. The bar attendant I approached was a friendly, outgoing person and in a rather loud voice said, "Honey, this is Greece. You can do whatever you want here!" Everyone within earshot thought that was rather funny and laughter rippled around us. This lightheartedness helped me to get into the spirit of being on holiday in a country far more liberal than the one from which I had just come.

The Olympic Airways flight from Mykonos was on a twin-engine prop plane. Even though I had a confirmed seat and my friend was still wait-listed, we were able to board with no problems and had an enjoyable trip over the Aegean to our destination. Our hotel, the elegant Elysium situated on top of one of the surrounding hills, provided us an excellent view over the town and harbor areas. Everything should have been perfect. Still, my friend did not seem as happy to see me as our several telephone conversations had indicated. It was my first premonition that something wasn't the way I had expected it to be.

The next morning while we ate breakfast on the outside terrace overlooking the sea, a second "out of character" incident occurred that made me uneasy about our next two weeks together. I am usually quite open to striking up conversations with people in relaxed situations. Since I hadn't had much contact with other Americans for several months, I exchanged pleasantries with a fellow at the next table whose accent clearly indicated he was from Texas. It was a normal friendly conversation that lasted for only a few minutes. When I turned back to my friend, he made a rather biting comment: "Americans are all the same," he said. "You people talk so loud that you want everyone to hear you because you think you are so important." I was taken back because the comment was so unwarranted and so unexpected. I brushed the incident aside, but I couldn't help feeling that things were just not right.

We spent that day lounging by the pool and walking around the town photographing the things that Mykonos, as well as most of the Greek Islands, is noted for: the harbors, white-painted buildings, narrow streets, easily-identifiable architecture, and beautiful boats and water. It was an idyllic day in an idyllic setting. When we returned to our room later in the afternoon, the friendliness I had experienced earlier that day began to dissipate and he seemed distant and annoyed. Again, I was quite amazed by his reaction as it was so out of character. I didn't make an issue of it.

The following morning we rented a motor scooter and toured the entire area. I was elected to drive, and we crisscrossed the island taking unmarked roads here and there to explore various remote sections of the land. It was a rather quiet tourist time, so we didn't encounter much traffic anywhere. We did manage to spend a few hours on several of the beaches for which Mykonos is famous.

We returned to our hotel around 5:00 p.m., and as we walked through the lobby, the desk clerk told me he had a message for me. Only two people knew where I was. One was my brother in

Toronto (I always let family know where I would be when I took extended trips) and the other was my secretary back in Abu Dhabi. Without looking at the note, I knew that it was bad news. My mother who had been in failing health had died that morning.

Trying to reach someone at Olympic Airways, either at the Mykonos airport or at the national toll-free number, was an exasperating experience. The calls were never answered by a person though, finally, I was able to ascertain from the recordings that there was a flight to the mainland later that evening. So I packed my things and left for the airport hoping there would be seats available on some flight. Fortunately, with the help of my travel agent in Abu Dhabi, I got bookings for the following day from Athens to Toronto via Rome. I left my friend in Mykonos. I had prepaid the room, so he planned to stay on and visit some other islands for the remainder of the week. He would then head back to Athens where I would contact him via his cell phone when I knew what my future plans would be.

As expected, my mother's death was a sad time in my life. Her love and support had seen me through many a hard time, but I knew that she had been spared a painful, agonizing death. I stayed with my father for the ten days I was in Canada and we were able to communicate our feelings of grief, talk about what he would do without my mother in his life, and share our faith and hopes for the coming days.

Leaving Dad was very difficult. My mother and father had been together for fifty-eight years of married life and I knew the coming months would be a lonely time for him. It was an emotional drain knowing that I would be heading back to the Middle East half a world away. When it came time for me to leave for the airport to head back to Athens, I saw tremendous sadness on my father's face and heard it in his voice.

He said, "Well. I guess it's that time." He gave me one of our traditional warm meaningful hugs and we kissed as fathers and sons do. Then he said, "I love you, son. Keep up the good work."

"I love you, too, Dad," I told him. "I will try. I'll talk with you soon." And I was off.

I contacted my friend in Athens and told him I had made reservations at the Best Western Main Gate hotel and that he should meet me there on October 5. That left us with less than two days to share time in Athens, but it also got me back to the city so I could catch my scheduled flight back to Abu Dhabi on Wednesday, October 7.

I arrived in Athens late on Monday afternoon. My friend was waiting for me in the hotel room as planned and he told me about all he had done during the past ten days. Our remaining time was short. Just one night. He would be leaving the next day and I would catch my plane the day after.

Now that I was back, he was excited to have a companion with whom he could take in Athens at night and do some partying. Actually, that was the last thing I wanted to do at that moment. I was tired from the long trip, angry with Alitalia for not accommodating me with a special "grievance fare," and very distressed over my mother's death and the thought of leaving my father by himself. After several attempts to persuade me didn't work, my friend told me he had something that would take my mind off things and would pick me up. He showed me a small vial of cocaine and offered to share it with me so we could go and have a good time in spite of all that had happened. I reluctantly agreed and we did go out to see the sights of Athens that night.

The next day we spent most of the morning walking the streets of Athens and shopping for souvenirs. As the day wore on, my friend became increasingly irritable and commented rather crisply that he "hated children" when some youngsters were making noise in a school yard next to where we had stopped for a snack. My attempt to quell his annoyance by mentioning how happy they seemed met with biting sarcasm. Then the conversation quickly moved to the recent news about U.S. retaliation for the bombings of our Embassies in Africa. He went off on a tirade about Americans being warmongers. What we had done, he stated, was totally uncalled for. This was a continuation of the anti-American sentiment that he had displayed earlier in our trip, but now he seemed to direct his hostility toward me as an American. Because the bombings had become a personal issue for me with the death of my friend and his son (I later learned the information I was given about their deaths was untrue), I stood my ground and said that we should have retaliated even more. What had been a pleasant morning deteriorated as my friend and I got into a heated exchange and I witnessed our friendship dissolve.

We headed back to our hotel with barely a word spoken between us. I kept my distance as he collected his belongings from the closets and bathroom and prepared to leave for the airport. I helped him carry his bags to the bus stop and said goodbye realizing that I would likely never see him again.

That night I wandered through downtown Athens off the beaten paths that tourists usually follow. That left me with one more morning to explore Athens before I had to catch my flight back to Abu Dhabi. So I was up early, walked to the Acropolis, and was at the main gate just prior to its opening for the day. At the beginning of our two-week trip I had bought a new camera, so I spent the entire morning strolling around the Acropolis taking pictures and experimenting with its various settings and features. It was a beautiful morning and I was both enthralled and saddened by my experience. When one contemplates all that was the majesty of Greece, one cannot help but be awed by the beauty and magnificence of the surroundings. On the other hand, when you see the ruins of what once was, you can only feel sorry that wars and greed destroyed the grandeur of this former hilltop structure.

I was so taken in by the majesty of what was left that I didn't realize I had overstayed the time I had allotted to tour the site. I rushed back to my hotel room and prepared to gather my belongings and get to the airport. Since it was the end of my trip and I knew I'd have to wash everything when I got home, I hastily placed my clothes in my bag, brushed my teeth and put my toothbrush and toothpaste in my toiletry bag. Other toiletries that I would normally have placed in there, I simply tossed into bags with my clothing knowing that within hours I would be home and could sort them out. I hurriedly left my room, checked out, and was soon in a cab heading towards the airport.

Little did I know that my life of freedom was about to come to an abrupt end.

5

A Moment to Remember

NOT ONCE DURING MY STAY IN Athens had I seen the smog that so often envelops the city. Fortunately, the skies had been clear during the entire time of my stay allowing for great views of the surrounding hills from the city and spectacular views of the city from the Acropolis.

After checking out of the hotel, I had a fairly easy taxi ride to the Athens airport. There was some traffic congestion but nothing compared to the stories of gridlock and long delays that I had heard. Gulf Air, Flight 42 was scheduled to depart Athens for Bahrain at 3:10 p.m. and I had arrived two hours early to allow plenty of time for security checks and check-in procedures.

Bahrain is the major hub for Gulf Air, so most long-distance international flights to and from the Gulf connect there. The international departures terminal in Athens was very congested. Unlike many major airports, there were no dedicated check-in counters for each airline. As soon as one plane was boarded, the gate was used by the next airline in line. Typical of flights to and from the Gulf States, there were always many expatriates traveling between their homelands and the Gulf States where they work. These persons generally carried excessive amounts of luggage and this flight proved to be no exception. With the small area set aside for check-in, there was much confusion and jostling for position in line. I usually avoid this hassle and approach the check-in desk only after most people have been cleared and the lines are short. That was the case that afternoon and boarding was uneventful.

The four-hour flight to Bahrain went smoothly and I enjoyed a good conversation with some vacationers who were returning to Australia after a visit to Greece. We arrived on schedule in Bahrain and it was an easy process to proceed through the transit area to the boarding area for the last leg of my journey to Abu Dhabi.

Gulf Air, Flight 2 was boarded on time for an 8:10 departure and I was happy that everything was going so well on my return home. It had been a long day and a difficult trip emotionally, and I was looking forward to being home, getting a good night's sleep, and going to the office the next morning. My flight was scheduled to arrive in Abu Dhabi at 10:25 local time, only a one hour and fifteen minute flight. That would give me ample time to clear customs and immigration, get my car, and be home by 11:30.

But then things started to change. A flight heading for Bahrain with passengers who planned to transfer to our flight to Abu Dhabi was behind schedule, and a decision was made to hold our plane until those passengers and their luggage were boarded. So we sat for an extra fifty minutes. It was with some relief that we finally left Bahrain because it was getting late and all I wanted to do was get home.

The flight to Abu Dhabi was a routine one and we landed at the gate just forty-five minutes behind the scheduled arrival time. It was now 11:10 p.m. in Abu Dhabi. As I had done over twenty times before, I headed for the immigration area where, to my surprise and delight, the lines were short. I would be home sooner than I had thought.

Getting through immigration was uneventful. I had a ten-year unlimited entry visa for the United Arab Emirates and numerous entry and departure stamps in my passport for that country, so I was cleared through immediately. Then it was on to the baggage claim just a few feet away where I would retrieve my two checked bags, clear customs and head home.

It was a surprise that my bags were already waiting on the carousel for me to pick up. No one else was in the luggage area so it appeared that, aside from those traveling with carry-on bags, the remainder of the passengers were transiting on other flights to different locations. Things seemed to be going exceptionally well because normally I would have waited another twenty minutes for my luggage to appear.

There were four customs agents waiting at different counters to check people through, so I lugged my three bags, a green backpack, a brown suitcase, and a black suitcase to the closest check point. I was seconds away from disaster!

With the confidence that I always project in approaching the customs agents, I carried my luggage to the counter and handed the agent my passport. More often than not, when I had previously presented my American passport at the same counter, the agents had simply glanced at the passport and asked if I had anything to declare. This time, as usual, I replied "No." Then he asked a question I had never been asked before.

"Where did you come from?" he inquired.

I replied, "Bahrain."

His response was, "No, before Bahrain."

I replied, "Athens."

And then he said something that sent a chill up my spine.

"Ah, yes," he remarked in a tone that indicated he had been expecting my arrival. "Open the black bag."

Only one other time, when I had indicated I had something to declare, had I been told to open up one of my bags. Without hesitation, because I had nothing to hide, I began to unzip the black suitcase. Before I could finish, the customs agent interrupted.

"No, not that one. It's this one," he said pointing to my green backpack.

It's this one echoed through my mind and I felt twinges of fear and anxiety as I tried to understand the meaning of his words. I thought, *What does he mean, 'it's this one'?*

As soon as I had unzipped my backpack, he instructed me to stand away. There on top were my camera and some calendars I had bought with pictures of Mykonos. It was immediately obvious that he was looking for something specific as he rustled through my belongings. After what seemed like eons but were only seconds, he pulled out my black toiletries bag and said, "This is it." Immediately, I understood that he really *had been* looking for a black bag and that initially he had erred in asking me to open the black suitcase. It was the black toiletries bag that he wanted! *Why? What was going on here?* My feeling of uneasiness increased.

The toiletries bag was rectangular and running the length of the top side along the center was a zipper. Each end folded over to allow the bag to compress or expand easily. He laid the bag on the desk and told me to open it. Nervously I did so, revealing only my toothbrush and toothpaste. Normally it would have been filled with other items, but in my haste to pack I had thrown the remaining articles into the suitcases. So I was relieved, for apparently what he was looking for wasn't there.

I said, "There's just a toothbrush and toothpaste."

"I don't think so," he said motioning again for me to stand back. With that he put his hand into the bag and reached under one of the folded ends. When he withdrew his hand, he was holding the vial that had contained the cocaine that my friend had shared with me in Athens two days earlier!

Panic and shock immediately overtook me. In a split second my mind processed what I had seen and I knew I was in a very difficult situation. Through my confusion I heard him ask, "What is this?"

I could tell that the vial was empty except for a few grains of cocaine stuck to the inside surface so all I could think to say was, "It was some medicine my doctor had prescribed but you can see I've finished it."

He ignored my explanation and said, "Let's have a look." He proceeded to take off the cap, rubbed his finger along the rim of the bottle, and put his finger to his mouth. "This is cocaine. Close your bags. Bring them with you and follow me."

I felt an electric shock shoot through my body and I thought, *Should I just make a run for it?* But as quickly as the idea came, it was replaced by the knowledge that running would only make matters worse. I could never get away and would most likely be shot in the back. I suspected that this was the beginning of a nightmare, though I never imagined the length and depth to which it would go. It was 11:30 p.m. on Wednesday, October 7, 1998, and I knew I would be late getting home.

6

The Arrest

THE CUSTOMS OFFICER ESCORTED ME into a room just beyond the baggage claim. It was a large room that contained cubicles and other areas that were totally enclosed. He led me into one of the cubicles, a cramped space that was empty except for two chairs. At that moment, as nervous and frightened as I was, I rationalized that he would merely search me to make sure I had no other drugs with me and then let me go. After all, the quantity of cocaine in the container was so minimal that one couldn't even hope to get a "buzz" from it. I was an American. Surely they would release me in a short time and I'd be on my way to my apartment.

As we walked into the room, several other customs agents stopped by the entrance to have a look at the catch of the day—an American!

In the Middle East, almost without exception, the local and Western expatriate population has servants to watch their children, cook their meals, do their laundry, drive them from place to place, walk their animals, and perform sundry other duties that they deem worthy of a slave. I call them 'slaves' because they are paid a mere pittance, and are exploited with impunity. They usually come from the Indian subcontinent or poorer Asian countries and many of them (women mostly) are sexually molested by their local Arab employers.

The first thing the customs agent did was to summon his "assistant" and tell him to bring me a cup of tea. It is customary to serve tea whenever someone visits an office on business-related matters, and I wanted to believe that this official was being nice to me because he knew that this was a routine inspection and hoped I would speak well about my treatment when I was released in a short time. Because of my business and social dealings with Arabs, however, I had a nagging suspicion that the agent was merely playing "nice cop" so that I would open up and admit to having all the drugs that I was supposed to have with me.

There we were in the cubicle area. He sat on a chair that had one armrest missing and looked as if it were going to collapse at any moment; my bags were placed on the floor next to him. I sat on an equally dilapidated secretarial chair holding a cup of tea the size of a demitasse that one would get when ordering an espresso.

Once I had finished the tea, it was time for the inspection to begin. He ordered me to take off all my clothes. As I removed each item, he inspected it. First my shirt. Then my shoes. Then my socks. Then my pants. Now I was down to my underwear and he ordered me to remove that too. Once that was done, he instructed me to turn around and bend over. I think he actually took pleasure in my discomfiture, considering the look in his eyes and the smirk on his face. He sliced through my embarrassment by saying, "You have a really nice athlete's body. Why do you deal in drugs?"

"I don't deal in drugs," I said. "Don't you see what's happened here? What you found in my bag wasn't mine! It was planted there on purpose and you knew that, didn't you?"

He didn't reply to my question but motioned for me to put my underwear back on. Each time he glanced at the ring that I was wearing on one pierced nipple, I felt another surge of uneasiness since any kind of body piercing is forbidden in Islam.

Then the next phase of humiliation began. He picked up my clothes one piece at a time and inspected them. He looked at my shirt and dropped it to the floor. He did the same with the socks. Then, as he picked up one shoe, he pulled out a knife and began cutting at the heel to make sure it wasn't hollow and concealing drugs. He cut the lining inside the shoe to check there. He did the same with the second shoe. When he picked up my pants, he examined them for hidden pockets and then began to cut the waistband looking for drugs there. I felt violated—as if I was being raped from two feet away. There I was, sitting on a chair in my underpants with my clothes now heaped on the floor beside him. My captor was in control and I was very, very nervous.

"I need to contact my lawyer and the American Embassy," I said.

"Not now," he responded without hesitation. His tone was decidedly less friendly than it had been up to that point. "Now let's look at what you've got here."

He went through the contents of my bags one item at a time examining the clothes thoroughly. Other personal items he put aside in a pile. Just as he had cut the shoes and pants I was wearing, so now he cut the shoes and other articles of clothing in my luggage. When he held up my camera and started to search for the way to open the film storage slot, "Please don't open that," I said. "I just took pictures at the Acropolis in Athens this morning, and if you expose them, the pictures will be lost."

To my surprise he responded, "Okay."

Now anyone knows that a camera case is a common place for someone to hide drugs, and I wondered at that moment why he didn't persist in opening it up. Was he playing with me? Was he just going through the motions of doing his job? Did he really know there were no drugs among my things, and was he just trying to scare me? Why did he agree to abandon the camera check so quickly?

When my two suitcases and backpack were empty, he looked at them carefully searching for signs of hidden items. My most valued suitcase was the brown one. It was genuine leather and I had bought it months earlier on a trip to Florence, Italy. He saw the look of horror on my face as he took his knife and started to cut the lining. "I'm sorry," he said, "but I'm just doing my job. Do you have anything you want to tell me?" He had read my expression as one of two things: I was either distraught that he was cutting my suitcase or I was petrified that he was on the verge of finding more drugs. Since the former was the case, the feeling of abuse intensified.

I sensed that he was becoming upset that he could find no more drugs. I wondered why. It was obvious earlier that he had known about the vial of cocaine and where it was stashed in my bags. As he became more agitated, I began to feel more and more distressed. It now occurred to me that perhaps more cocaine had been planted in my bags, and he simply hadn't found it where he expected it to be. On the other hand, I also thought that maybe he was just playing this up, knowing all along that the only indication of drug use was the vial with a trace amount of cocaine. I sorted through various possibilities in a matter of seconds. I was tired, confused, apprehensive, and thoroughly frightened.

Now it came time to go through the non-clothing items that he had piled on the floor beside him. He stood and walked out of the cubicle, but was back in seconds with a waste paper basket. First, he picked up a large tube of *Crest* that had hardly been used. He turned it upside down over the basket and began to squeeze. As he did so, I again had the feeling that I was being raped. He was taking something of mine and rendering it worthless, albeit a tube of toothpaste. He emptied its contents and tossed the tube into the basket. He did the same with containers of shampoo and conditioner, body lotion, and most importantly to me because it was rather expensive, a container of body-massage oil.

Again he responded to the look on my face and asked, "Is there anything you want to tell me?"

I said, "All I can tell you is that I have no drugs in my bag and you're wasting your time and mine by destroying my property." I was still sitting in my underpants; he looked at me and responded with a controlling and menacing scowl.

Next, he grabbed a container of white powder that had the appearance of cocaine and inspected it as though he had just struck pay dirt.

In Abu Dhabi I had religiously used the weight room facilities in my apartment building to work out. It is very common for people who exercise rigorously to supplement their diet with vitamins, protein and carbohydrate drinks, and other body enhancers that come in powder, liquid, pill, or spray form. Whenever I travel, I make it a point to take my supplements with me. I explained that I was a certified personal trainer, having worked with the athletes at the summer Olympic Games in Atlanta just two years earlier. It was my business to know about legal supplements and how they can be used to enhance performance. I also made the point of explaining that in no way were they considered drugs, but in most cases were natural products sold in health food and nutrition stores.

So here he was, holding a vial of what I'm sure he hoped was more cocaine. "That's Creatine," I said.

"What's that?" he asked.

"It's a substance used by body builders to enhance the results of their exercise routine by providing the body with nutrients necessary for the building of muscle mass," I replied. "It is very common for athletes in America to use this product. It comes in this powder form, but you can also buy it in capsules or in a spray that permits easy absorption under your tongue. You can even buy it here in Abu Dhabi. You can see it in the windows of sporting good stores on Al Hamdan Street."

He looked at me, remembering, I think, the comment he had made about my body earlier and shrugged. He didn't put the container back with my clothes but began another pile. I knew he wasn't going to let that pass easily; that he was going to save it for later testing.

I had taken some supplements in pill form with me as well. Rather than pack the containers of each product, I had separated a small number of pills from each and wrapped them in plastic to save space in my bags. Considering the current situation, it looked appallingly suspicious as he started to examine the various packets I had with me. There were supplements called DHEA, Retibol, and Treboxil among others. I tried to explain the purported benefits of each to him, but I knew he either didn't understand or didn't care as he put them with the container of Creatine.

We had planned on our trip to do some hiking in the Greek Islands and on the mainland, so I had taken with me a snake bite kit. It contained nothing more than a sharp-edged instrument for cutting around the area of a bite, some suction cups for drawing out venom, and a liquid antidote in a vial. To a customs agent searching for drugs, it raised numerous red flags, so it, too, went into the pile with the powder and the pills.

My Swiss Army knife was the next thing he thought worthy of further examination. It also went on the new pile. Then he picked up my dog tags.

"Are you in the military?" he asked.

"No," I replied. "When I go hiking, I usually wear these since I don't carry other ID with me. If anything should ever happen to me, the person who finds me would know who I am and where I am from." He accepted that response and put my dog tags back on the pile with my clothes.

By now we had been in that cubicle for an hour. I was totally under his control with nowhere to go. There was nothing I could do but suffer the humiliation he inflicted on me. I was angry, but that anger was overridden by a dread of something worse to come. *What was going to happen after this?*

Then he picked up the Halloween treats I had bought for my secretary's children. They were plastic pumpkin men, figures with a pumpkin body and arms and legs and a head attached to it. The body was filled with small chocolate candies like Smarties or M&M's covered in a hard shell of various colors. He looked at those items, and after I explained what they were, he put them on the pile with my clothes without even opening them up to verify that what I said about the contents was true.

Next, he took the calendars I had bought in Mykonos. They were still sealed in plastic wrap so he removed the coverings and flipped through the pages of each. Satisfied that there was nothing sinister there, they, too, went with my clothes.

Finally, he was done. I was still sitting there in my underwear with my three slashed bags tossed in a pile at my feet. My clothes and some other items were in another pile. The items he wanted to look at further were in a third pile.

"Put your clothes on and put your other clothes back in the bags," he directed. He left the cubicle for a few minutes and returned with a plastic bag. In that he placed all the items that he wanted to keep. When I was finished dressing and repacking my bags, he said, "Bring your bags and follow me." I told myself that we were almost done and that he'd be sending me home soon.

We walked to the adjoining offices where the officer in charge of the shift was located and where the other agents congregated when activity was slow. Right now, I was the only traveler there and no one was in the baggage claims area. It was 12:50 on the morning of October 8.

I sat down in a chair opposite the official's desk as he pulled out what appeared to be an incident report on which he would write down all the details of what had just transpired. The agent who had searched me now spoke Arabic to his manager and he began to complete the documents. The other agents gathered in a small area just around the corner from where the manager was filling out the form. Occasionally, they would look at me, one would say something, and they would laugh. The big joke escaped me at the time.

Completion of the document seemed to take forever. Hopefully, I thought that once he finished with this form the nightmare would end and I would be free go on my way. After all, I was an American, and this country depended on us for military support. The amount of cocaine that concerned them was miniscule. While the manager was filling in the form, the customs agent who had inspected my luggage told me to go around the corner where other agents waited to take my picture. When I turned to do what I was told, I was flabbergasted by what I saw. All of the items that the agent had placed in the plastic bag earlier were spread out on a table to make it look as if they had just been confiscated in a major drug bust. There were the pills, the Creatine powder, my Swiss Army knife, and the cigarette roller. The latter I had bought for a friend who worked at one of the advertising agencies that did print advertising for us. He loved to roll cigarettes from fresh tobacco, and on my last visit to his office I had noticed that the roller he was using wasn't working well. The new roller was to be a surprise for him. One of the agents picked up a Polaroid camera and motioned for me to sit behind the table. I knew that it was time for a "we gotcha" picture.

It is a common practice in that part of the world that pictures of drug dealers and users, along with the drugs with which they were apprehended, appear in the newspaper. Knowing that, I had a horrible image of my face appearing on some front page—surrounded by paraphernalia that made it look as if I were one of the world's major drug lords. I couldn't let that happen. By now I was very tired, so I told them in no uncertain terms that I would not let them take my picture with all the items on the table.

"Those things are not drugs, and you're making it look like they are," I shouted angrily. "I won't let you take my picture with them,"

The agents were stunned for a moment. There was absolute silence as all heads turned toward me. Then, the officer who had earlier searched my luggage said, "Okay, we need your picture, but we'll take everything but the cocaine vial away." To that I reluctantly agreed. After the picture was taken, I realized what it was for. There on the wall in their meeting area was a collection of photos of others who had come before me. It was their "Wall of Fame." This, apparently, wasn't the source of the pictures that appeared in the newspapers. Momentary relief!

I resumed my seat in front of the manager who was still completing my paperwork. To his side, two policemen held a spoon over a cigarette lighter and on the spoon was one of the DHEA pills that they had taken from my luggage. This was their crude way of testing whether the pill was a drug, though I'm not sure what they expected the pill to do. When there was no reaction to the heat, they just shrugged and terminated their test with disappointment written all over their faces.

"I want to make a telephone call to the American Embassy," I said again.

When the manager responded with an emphatic, "No! You have no rights here," a cold chill traveled up my spine. Finally, he put his pen down, slipped the form into a manila folder, and told me that it would just be another minute. Things were quiet again, and I sat there hoping that he would tell me to get on my way.

After ten or fifteen minutes, the door to the office opened and a police officer appeared with what I thought were handcuffs but which were actually leg shackles. My heart missed a beat at that point, because I realized that things were going to get worse before they started to get better. The officer and the manager of the customs area chatted in Arabic for a few minutes, and then I was directed to go with the officer. Before we did so, however, the officer put the shackles on my legs and told me to follow him. I was able to put my bags in a luggage cart and we started the long walk through the terminal to the airport police offices. Embarrassed and humiliated, I was thankful beyond words that the terminal was empty at that time of the morning. It was now 1:40 a.m.

I was led to a room that opened up directly to the airport apron on the ground level where there were several chairs. One was occupied by a well-dressed Indian businessman. He glanced at me, and I at him, but we said nothing. He looked as frightened as I felt. There I waited for what seemed like an eternity until a truck pulled up outside the room and the officer motioned me toward it. The vehicle, the size of a large pick-up, had a truck bed enclosed in wire mesh. Into this, I was obviously supposed to go.

Maneuvering with leg shackles took some doing, especially as I was trying to haul my luggage at the same time. I hoisted myself into the back, and for the first time in my life, felt the helplessness of being confined against my will.

After the door was closed and padlocked, the driver slid into the cab with a piece of paper in his hand. I assumed that this paper contained information about me and my case, and would likely explain what was to be done with me once I had been delivered to my destination. Thus, my first ride in the back of a police truck began.

As we left the airport, we passed my parked car and I wondered when I would see it again. Little did I know that I would never see it again! We continued down the main highway toward Abu Dhabi, the same route I would have taken earlier to return home. My spirits plummeted to an all-time low. Here I was, sitting like a caged animal for all the world to see as we passed by. Fortunately, it was the middle of the night and there wasn't much traffic.

Eventually, we arrived in Abu Dhabi where, ironically, we passed close to my apartment and then drove directly past my office. At that point, I knew that we were heading to the Khaldiya police station, a short distance from work and next door to Spinney's grocery store where I usually shopped. I kept thinking that this was simply a bad nightmare and that I would wake up either on the airplane or at home in my bed. After all, this kind of thing just didn't happen to me!

We stopped by a gate at the entrance to the police station, and the driver went to talk to someone about letting us enter. After a few minutes he drove inside the compound and parked the truck. It was obvious that this was our destination because he motioned for me to disembark and bring my bags with me. Since he did not speak English, we had had no verbal communication and I was in no mood to try my limited Arabic. Once we entered the police station, we had to climb two flights of stairs—leg shackles and my three bags in tow!

Finally, we got to a dark landing and stopped. No one was in sight and the silence was deafening. The policeman looked confused. Whomever he was supposed to meet apparently wasn't around, so he began searching from room to room. After the fifth try, I heard him talk briefly to someone, and shortly thereafter a person dressed in a disdasha appeared. His obvious annoyance indicated that he had just been awakened, and the scowl on his face said he didn't want to deal with processing me. The policeman handed him the paper that he had been given at the airport. The gentleman in the disdasha looked at it and frowned; then he tore it up and gave pieces back to the policeman. Angry words were exchanged and the policeman motioned for me to follow him. We returned to the truck and once again I was locked in the back. I could think of nothing except what was on that piece of paper. *Why did that man tear it up? Did that mean that I could be released now?*

The policeman was obviously furious and slammed the door to the cab as he got in. What was supposed to be a routine delivery of a criminal to the jail had now become an ordeal for him too.

We continued our drive through the streets of Abu Dhabi and this time we went right past my apartment building. It was now 2:45 in the morning and I had to be at the office at 8:00. I desperately hoped I would wake up soon from the nightmare.

Eventually, we wound our way to an area near the Zayed Sports Complex. I had never been inside, but I soon learned that this was the location of the Mina jail. As we drove into the complex, I noticed a sign that read "Drug Enforcement Agency" on the facing of a building. So this is where we were going! I figured that the driver didn't know where else to take me and thought that the people in the agency could decide what to do. Again, I stepped down with my bags and was escorted up another two flights of stairs in my shackles. It was 3:00 a.m. as I was led to a cluster of offices.

Once there, a plain-clothes officer motioned for me to sit. The policeman talked with him for a few minutes and then left. Now it was the turn of this officer to fill out a stack of paperwork for my case. I was asked a few simple questions and given some tea. Then I sat and waited. At one point the plain-clothes officer had to leave, so a uniformed officer came to watch over me. I told him that I wanted to make a telephone call to my Embassy. He ignored me and went to sit in his glass-walled office where he could work and still keep an eye on me.

There I sat for a long time staring into space and wondering how all this could be happening to me. By 6:00 a.m. I began to yawn for I had gone without sleep for twenty-four hours!

The officer came out of his office and said, "Paul, would you like to sleep for a while?"

"Yes, I'm very tired," I responded.

He stepped into a hallway and opened the door to a cell that was next to his office. He went in to fix up a bed for me, a bed made up of a few blankets on the concrete floor.

"You can sleep there," he said.

I wasn't about to argue. I was tired and sweaty; my clothes had been cut up and the blankets looked inviting. So I lay down and quickly fell asleep.

A few hours later I awoke to the sounds of loud talking. It was now 8:00 a.m. and it appeared that people were arriving for their regular duties. The plain-clothes officer noticed that I was awake and told me to come out and resume my place outside of his office. Again I said, "I want to make a call to the American Embassy."

He merely said, "Later."

Tea was being served all around, and I was offered one. Later the officer told me that he wanted a urine sample, and I happily agreed since I knew I wouldn't be released until I complied with all their demands. With that done, I resumed my place in the chair.

Around 10:00 a.m. I was moved to another room where there were four men, three in street attire and one in a disdasha. I was told they wanted to ask some questions and check my bags. I couldn't understand why there was all this fuss over a little bit of cocaine. For the next several hours these men went through my luggage again and tossed my clothing on the floor after each piece had been examined. It was difficult to understand some of their questions, but I answered to the best of my ability while my statements were transcribed by one of the men.

Frustrated, I told them again, "I want to call my office and the American Embassy. They are expecting me to be at work today and they will wonder where I am."

The officer who had been with me during the night said, "Someone is calling the Embassy now." I didn't know whether to believe him or not, but I hoped that it was true. Later I learned that this was a lie.

We remained in that room until 12:30. Now that the weekend was here, I was concerned that no one would know where I was and that my friends would worry. Once more I said, "I want to call my office and the Embassy." I took a piece of paper and pen from the desk and wrote down the name and telephone number of my manager. I said, "Call him. The offices close at 1:30 for the Middle East weekend and it's important that you call him before that time." One of the men took the piece of paper and nodded, giving the impression that he would make the call.

After the questioning was completed, they handed me the report that they had written out. It was in Arabic. I was told it was a transcription of what had transpired during the interview and that I had to sign it.

"I can't read it," I complained.

"It's just what you said," one officer assured me. Reluctantly, I signed.

"Where are the people from the American Embassy?" I asked after signing the form.

"They know you're here," the officer in charge replied. "They'll be here to talk with you." That offered me some consolation as I hoped I would be able to find out what was going to happen to me at this point.

When they ordered me to put my clothes back in the bag, I didn't even try to fold them for by now they were so rumpled that it didn't matter. After the bags were closed I was given a form to sign. Again it was in Arabic, but I was told it was a receipt for the three bags. "Why do I need a receipt? Are you going to keep the bags?" My question was met with a nod and grin, but no verbal response.

Three of the four men left the room, and as they turned to go, I reminded them again that someone should call my manager right away. The one who had the paper with the telephone number just nodded and left. I didn't feel confident that the call would be made.

No one from the Embassy had yet shown up. *Where were they?*

Once more I was alone with the plain-clothes officer whom I had met earlier that morning upon my arrival. Finally, a uniformed officer arrived and I was told to go with him. Now where was I being taken?

7

Mina Jail

I LEFT MY LUGGAGE IN THE ROOM where I had been interrogated and followed the officer. We went down the two flights of stairs and out the main entrance of the Drug Enforcement Agency offices. From there we crossed a small parking lot to another building that I couldn't identify since all the signs were in Arabic.

Once inside, we turned to the left where there was a desk with two uniformed policemen. My escort said something to them in Arabic and went away. Somewhere beyond the desk I could hear many people talking, but I could see no one. One policeman asked me to remove my belt and watch and anything that was in my pockets. I still had my set of keys, wallet, some coins, and currency from Canada, the U.S., Greece, and the UAE. He opened a drawer that was full of belts and he added mine to the collection. Next the items from my pockets were placed in a brown envelope on which he scrawled what I assumed was my name. That accomplished, I was directed to follow one of the policemen into a small adjoining room where I was fingerprinted and booked. Obviously I wasn't going home just yet.

Neither of the two policemen spoke English, so all directions were communicated with hand gestures. Eventually, one officer motioned for me to follow and we retraced our steps back past the desk toward the area where I had heard voices at the time of my arrival. Just a few yards beyond that, we came to what looked like a cell door. As soon as we approached, a throng of faces appeared at the entrance and the occupants started yelling at the policemen in several languages. *My God*, I thought. *This place smells and these people are practically in rags. It looks like the Black Hole of Calcutta.*

I was numb with apprehension and probably in shock from all that had happened so far. Facing all those people on the other side of the gate was like having someone punch me in the stomach. The policeman opened the gate and for a second I stood there thinking, *I'm not going in there.* Then the policeman shoved me and I was left without a choice.

The noise stopped. All eyes were on me. People stared with deranged expressions. I felt as if I were going to be attacked and stripped of my clothes; perhaps even raped. I scanned the sea of faces and there wasn't another westerner, let alone a light-skinned person, among them. I was an oddity and I heard people whispering, "American! American!" People drew closer and began touching me. It was as if I were tied helplessly in a den of vipers. I was paralyzed with fear and in total denial that this was really happening. I looked beyond the bodies that were closing in on me and saw people sitting on the floor on blankets. Most were disheveled, some had long unkempt hair, and it appeared that many were psychotic. And then the smell hit me. I was immersed in a pool of unwashed bodies reeking of urine and smoke. Paralyzed from the utter shock of what I saw and smelled, and repulsed by the touch of hands all over me, I stood motionless not knowing what to do. My overtaxed senses were too numb to comprehend or respond. All I could think was *this can't be really happening. I'm in hell. Please, God, let me wake up and let all this be just a bad dream.*

Suddenly, a hand grabbed mine and a voice said in English, "Come with me." I looked in the direction of the voice and saw a young man about thirty. When my eyes met his, he said, "Come. I'll help you." The mob parted so I could go with him, and all eyes turned to follow my every move. The man told me to take off my shoes and I put them on the floor beside those of everyone else. Then we walked into one of the rooms, stepping over people's bedding to a corner where we sat down. My rescuer told me that he had some blankets for me and that I could have a spot near him. I quickly assessed the dimensions of the room. It was an area about 12 feet by 20 feet. There were no beds; there was a toilet in one corner, and a few small opaque windows through which one could determine only if it was daytime or night. There seemed to be a hundred people huddled in this room that smelled like a sweaty armpit!

He told me his name was Kumar and he introduced me to a few of his friends. He explained that we were in the Mina (Me-nah) Police Station and that he and his friends were from India and had been in this room for seven months. As he described their plight, I observed more of what was going on around me. All eyes were still focused on me, just staring. I sensed that many of the people were not quite normal. They muttered to themselves, talking out loud to no one in particular, and staring into space. It was now 4:30 on a Thursday afternoon, but this was not my nice, clean, airy apartment. And why had no one from the American Embassy come to see me?

Kumar explained to me that he and his friends had been working together in the offices of a company that forwarded freight. They received shipments of various goods from other firms and then made sure that they were re-directed to their final destination either by truck or boat. In a routine inspection of the goods they had in transit, it was found that one container held a crate of rifles bound for Africa. The police, even before figuring out who was responsible, came through their offices and arrested everyone who was there. So he and his friends had been incarcerated, had never been charged with any crime, and had been sitting in this hole for over seven months. I could only think that I would have gone insane.

As we talked further, people who had been standing around slowly moved away and went about doing whatever it was they did. Some talked, some sat down and stared at nothing, some chanted verses from the Koran, some lay down to sleep, and some were involved in some unknown altercation. Those conversations were not in English, so I had no idea what they were upset about.

My new friend said that the police brought food to the block three times a day and that it would be distributed on large trays so people could eat in groups. He told me I could eat with him and his friends and that I shouldn't worry. He pointed to an older man who was sitting on his blankets six feet away and advised me never to step on his blankets. The fellow was psychotic and would lash out at anyone that touched his bedding.

In a short time I felt sleepy and told my friend that I needed to rest for a while. I'd had only about three hours sleep in the last thirty-six. So I lay down, said a short prayer for deliverance from this nightmare, and immediately fell asleep.

I was awakened by a loud commotion by the entrance gate. I looked over and realized that food had arrived and people were fighting to get their fair share. Inmates were organizing themselves into groups and Kumar gestured that I should come over to his blanket and join him and his friends. Soon the food was distributed and the groups settled down to eat. Each of us had a piece of flat, unleavened bread that was shaped like a small pizza crust and there was a communal bowl of something that looked like soup with a few chunks of vegetables floating in it. The procedure was that we should dip pieces of our bread into the liquid and eat. My new friends were very generous and insisted that I eat some of the vegetables floating in the very watery brew. I hadn't thought about food until that moment, but as soon as I tasted the first morsel, I realized that the last time I had eaten was on the plane flight from Athens to Bahrain over twenty-four hours earlier. I was famished!

I was mentally and physically exhausted after what had happened during the last eighteen hours, so right after dinner I again went back to my blankets and easily fell back to sleep. I awoke hours later to the sound of people at the front gate fighting over breakfast. I roused myself and joined my friends for a meal that consisted of another piece of bread and what looked like refried beans. I still had a ravenous appetite and devoured my share. I had been given a cup the night before and I used that to get some water from a tap in the hallway. I wondered about the quality of the water, but I realized that this was all there was and took my chances on drinking it.

After breakfast we sat down to talk. I learned more about the plight of the five Indians who had all been arrested for something they knew absolutely nothing about. They had merely worked in the office handling the paperwork that accompanied the goods that were received and shipped. No one from their embassy had been to see them and the police would not answer their questions about why they were being held. They had not yet seen a judge. That was frightening, and it occurred to me that likely none of my family, friends, or business associates knew where I was. Surely by now someone had realized that I was missing!

I was introduced to another fellow from the UAE. His English was good and I learned from him that he was going to be released the following day. I told him that I had to notify people on the outside of my whereabouts and that I needed help to get out of the jail. I asked him to call my manager at ELS. That was the only telephone number I knew. He said he would make the contact and that I should give the number to him early the next morning because releases occurred right after breakfast. I felt relieved knowing that I now had a means of getting in touch with someone who could help me.

The rest of the day I slept. In times of extreme stress one's body has a marvelous mechanism that allows one to withdraw and sleep easily. This was a merciful escape from the disgusting place I was in. I awakened in time for lunch that consisted of a stack of white rice on our tray and a piece of meat for each person. We sat around the tray, each one using his hands to dig into the pile of rice. I would later learn that this was the way these folks commonly ate, even at home, but I never could quite get into the routine of putting my hands into the common food bowl and licking my fingers between mouthfuls. I ate just enough to satisfy my hunger because the disgusting sights of eating this way soon curbed my appetite for more. After lunch I slept again, woke for a dinner that consisted of bread and more watered down soup, and then slept some more. For whatever my body was doing to allow me so much sleep, I was thankful.

Sometime in the middle of the night I awoke. It was quiet except for occasional whispers here and there. As the reality of being in this place settled in, I started mentally banging my fists on the wall and thinking, *Please, God, get me out of this place. This isn't where I belong. I didn't do anything wrong.* The nightmare was ongoing. *Why can't I wake up from this bad dream?* I lay awake for the rest of the night wondering what was going to happen to me and trying to make sense of what had transpired during the last forty-eight hours.

Saturday morning came and it was the first day of the work week. In Islamic countries Friday is the holiest day of the week, so it compares to Sundays in our Western culture. Breakfast was delivered. This time it was the usual bread, but with it this day we received two hard-boiled eggs each. I sought out the fellow who had promised to make the phone call for me when he was released. I gave him the number of my manager and he wrote it on his arm along with my name. He told me he would call and tell him where I was and that I needed help to get out. I also asked him to contact the American Embassy and tell them a man named Paul was being held at the Mina Police Station and needed their help. He assured me he would. At this point people started congregating near the entrance gate and a shouting match began between the prisoners and the policemen on the front desk. Eventually, the police came to the gate and began calling out names of those being released, those being transferred to the Central Prison, and those who were going to court. I listened for my name, but it was not called. However, when the fellow to whom I had given the telephone number was released, I felt a glimmer of hope.

I sat down on my blanket and wondered what would happen to me next. On one hand, I thought that the fellow would follow through, make the calls for me, and things would begin happening to expedite my release. But what if he didn't? Obviously, no one as yet knew where I was. All the assurances from the police that the Embassy had been alerted about my arrest were apparently lies. It was Saturday and I should have been to the office by now. Surely my co-workers must have been wondering what had happened to me.

At ELS Language Centers on that Saturday morning, people had become concerned when I didn't arrive for work. On Thursday when I hadn't shown up, they were worried, but thought that maybe I had gotten delayed somewhere along my route. By Saturday, however, they were convinced that something serious had happened. It was very out of character for me to be out of the office when I had said I'd be there. I had never missed a day of work and was usually the first to arrive each morning.

Belinda Campos, my secretary, placed a call to my father. It was 2:00 a.m. in Kitchener, Ontario on Saturday morning when my father was awakened from sleep. Belinda explained that I hadn't shown up for work and my father assured her that I had left six days earlier to return to Athens and that I had never indicated that I would be extending my stay in Greece. My father, in turn, contacted my brother Richard and informed him of my disappearance. Richard then contacted the United States Embassy in Abu Dhabi and sought their help in locating me.

The Embassy staff took the matter very seriously and began searching immediately. Cables were sent to the U.S. Embassies in Greece and Bahrain asking for their help in checking local hospitals for any recent admission of an American. Gulf Air was contacted and they ascertained that my tickets had been used, and that I, or someone using my ticket, had flown all segments of the return trip from Athens. Someone was dispatched to the airport to check to see if my car was still parked there. It was found, so it appeared that I had arrived in Abu Dhabi, but obviously hadn't left the airport in my car. I had left my key with Belinda, so she checked my apartment and found no sign that I had returned there. The Embassy staff then checked all hospitals and police stations in Abu Dhabi. No one had seen me. I was now more than two days overdue in arriving home. I was an American missing in the Middle East.

Later that Saturday morning a group of new people arrived at the Mina Jail and one of them, a young man from Sri Lanka, occupied the floor space next to me. He and a few other new arrivals were wearing the same outer clothing, and it seemed to me that perhaps these men were members of a sports team. When I asked, he responded by telling me that this was the standard prison uniform. I had to laugh at my own naiveté and the fact that I had been so far off in my assumption. He, as well as most Sri Lankans that I met during my time in the Middle East, spoke excellent English. He told me that he had just finished serving a two-year sentence at Al Wathba prison, the main prison of Abu Dhabi. He was now in the process of being released. A quiet thoughtful young man, he explained that he had been working as a housekeeper at one of Abu Dhabi's hotels. One day he had seen another housekeeper take money from one of the guest's rooms and had reported it to management. The police were called and by the time they arrived the other person had fled. He told me that they had needed someone to pay for the crime, so they had arrested him. That sounded far-fetched to me, but the young man seemed sincere and believable. Over the next several years I was to learn that his story was most likely true, insofar as people from Asian countries are arrested and put in prison without any due process as we know it in America. The philosophy among the police is that someone has to pay for the crime, and they go for the overkill by arresting people in groups and charging them all in the hope that they will somehow get the right person. This was graphically illustrated by the plight of the Indian fellow who had befriended me a few days earlier.

The Sri Lankan had told me his impressions of Al Wathba, a maximum-security prison set high on a hill in the desert outside Abu Dhabi and his tales were frightening. Prisoners were denied access to television and radio but were allowed visitors and a newspaper. He described a cold, dreary place where people were treated like cattle and left to pass their time in boredom. *That must be the most dreadful place on earth*, I thought, never dreaming for a moment that I would be sent somewhere like that.

On Saturday afternoon one of the Indians gave me a book to help pass my time. It was a book of two hundred Hadiths, a collection of the sayings, teachings, and doings of the Prophet Mohammed. I read through most of it and was surprised that what was said, for the most part, mirrored my Christian principles and morals.

Sunday was a repeat of Saturday: three meals, five prayers; some prisoners released, some new ones in; lots of talk, occasional fights. The rank smells in the air nauseated me and made sleep difficult. And still no one at the American Embassy, in my family, or among those with whom I worked had any idea where I was.

By Monday the fifth day I woke up in a state of agitation. I had been living in the same clothes for five days; I was unshaven, and felt filthy. After breakfast the police again called the names of those who were to be released or taken to court or to Al Wathba. Again my name wasn't among them.

I am usually a calm, soft-spoken person, but once in a while, like at that moment, I had had enough! I went to the front gate and began to shout for a policeman, demanding that I be allowed to make a call to the United States Embassy. The other inmates became very quiet and wondered what this Yankee was doing! One came over to me and said that he would help me get the guards to understand. When a policeman appeared, the inmate yelled in Arabic that I wanted to contact my Embassy immediately, and that I felt I had the right to do so. The policeman glared at me, muttered something in Arabic, and went away. I only hoped that he would do something. I went back to my bed, and the noise of many voices talking in many languages resumed.

About an hour later I heard someone calling, "American! American!" So I went to the gate where a policeman was telling me something in Arabic. When I asked someone what was going on, I was told that I should get my belongings, that the officer would be taking me out. Finally, I thought, I will be able to talk with somebody about what is going on with my situation. I went back to the room, said a quick goodbye to my Indian friends and wished them well. Then I was led outside and back up to the offices of the Drug Enforcement agency. There I was told to sign a form so I could pick up my bags, but no one would tell me what was going to happen after that. I was escorted outside to a white van by two policemen dressed in disdashas. When I realized I was leaving this place, I indicated that I had to go back to the police station to retrieve the other personal items that had been taken from me when I was booked.

With those in hand, we started driving away from the Mina Police Station and within minutes arrived at a building identified by a sign as the Sharia Courts. Now I knew that the law of the land is based on Islamic teachings and the law contained within the religion is called Sharia Law. As numb as I had been for the past five days because of the uncertainty of my situation I felt an even deeper fear as we pulled up to the courthouse. I left my luggage in the van and was escorted, shackled, through the courthouse. To have people stare at this American walking in chains was indeed one of the low points of my life.

After a short walk, we arrived at an office. The police knocked, and when the door opened, I could see a man in a disdasha at a desk and two other people sitting nearby. The man behind the desk motioned for me to come in and indicated that the shackles be removed. The two policemen who accompanied me did not enter, but remained at the door. One of the men sitting near the desk stood and told me that I was there to give a statement. That was not what I wanted to hear. *Where the hell was my Embassy?* For the second time in a few days, I reacted with a verbal tirade that I'm sure reverberated throughout the hallways. I shouted that I wouldn't give any statements until I had talked with an attorney or my Embassy. I loudly declared that the treatment I had received was against all international norms. But, as I later learned, the UAE had never ratified one of the Vienna conventions that dealt with the treatment of arrested persons, so they were under no obligation to follow its dictates. I was a prisoner in their country and there wasn't a thing I could do about it!

I must have been quite a sight. My clothes were rumpled from having lived and slept in them for five days; my hair had not been properly combed, and I had neither shaved nor washed with anything but cold water during that entire time. The officers could tell that I was distraught. One man sitting by the desk told me I would be allowed a telephone call after I had given a statement. After more defiance on my part that was met only with an indifferent response, I reluctantly agreed to answer questions and give a statement. Once I calmed down, the door was closed and I sat facing the three officials. This was the Public Prosecutor's office and these men wanted to know what had happened.

The Public Prosecutor who sat behind the desk spoke no English, so any communication he had with me was through a second man from the Indian subcontinent who was an interpreter. The third man, a Lebanese, was there to record the questions and answers.

The Public Prosecutor reached into a drawer and pulled out a brown envelope that had been previously sealed. He opened it and withdrew a smaller brown envelope from which he extracted my American and Canadian passports. The interpreter asked me why I had two passports and said it was illegal to have more than one. I clarified that it indeed *was* legal to have two, and that the Canadian government had made it a matter of policy that once you are a Canadian, you are always a Canadian even if you take on the citizenship of another country. That is exactly what I had done since I had become a naturalized United States citizen fifteen years earlier. The Prosecutor then dumped the contents of the envelope on his desk. There was the vial that had contained the cocaine, all the pills and powders I had taken as dietary supplements, my Swiss army knife, the cigarette rolling machine, and the vial of anti-snake venom that had been part of my snake-bite kit.

The vial that had contained the cocaine was empty. It was explained that laboratory tests showed that the contents were indeed cocaine and that my urine analysis had tested positive for the use of cocaine. I told them that this was not a surprise since I had told the customs officers at the airport I had used cocaine in Greece. With that statement I got a nod from them all that seemed to say, "Okay, so you were telling the truth." The interpreter then declared that everyone in the United States uses cocaine all the time because he had lived in Miami and knew that to be true. I found his statement quite amusing and laughed out loud. I told him that his opinion was baseless. Perhaps in Miami he and his friends had used cocaine, but that certainly was not the norm in the United States. When he asked me if I had ever used cocaine before, I told him I had about ten years previously at a New Year's party. But, I assured them, I had never used cocaine in the UAE. We talked about my trip to Athens and the argument I had had over the United States' retaliation for the bombings of the embassies in Africa two months earlier. I made it very clear that I had not put the vial in my bags and that I could think of only two persons who might have done that: the friend with whom I had traveled in Greece or someone from the hotel in Athens. The hotel management, as well as my friend, knew my itinerary because my passport was being held in their vault and they had a copy of my airline ticket.

We then moved on to the powder. When asked what it was, I assured them that it was Creatine and that it could be bought in any of the sports stores in Abu Dhabi. They said nothing and then asked about the DHEA tablets. I explained what they were for and told them I had purchased them at a GNC store on a recent trip to Jeddah, Saudi Arabia. That was the truth, but I figured that if they were sold in Saudi Arabia of all places, then they must be accepted in other Gulf countries. The translator said he knew of GNC from his time in the United States. The discussion then moved on to the knife and the vial of anti-snake venom. After I explained why I had these items with me, the discussion ceased. Likewise, I explained why I had bought the cigarette rolling machine and they recorded my comments, or at least I think they did.

The interrogation had lasted seventy-five-minutes. When we were done I was asked to sign what had been written. I told them I had no idea what had been written and that I couldn't sign it. Very clearly and icily I was told that if I didn't sign it, there would be no telephone call. My blood turned cold and I quickly churned through the consequences that signing or not signing might entail. I concluded that I should sign because I knew that there were people who were very concerned about my welfare and that I had to let them know where I was. Also, this was possibly my only chance to get word to my Embassy to try to do something to help me. But, as I would later learn, it was the wrong decision.

The man who had recorded the discussion offered me the telephone. I said a quick prayer that my manager would be in his office to take my call because his was the only telephone number I knew and I was aware that I would only have one shot at making a call. I dialed the number and my manager was on the line quickly.

He said, "Paul where are you? The Embassy, your family, and I have been looking for you for days."

"Kamal, I'm with the Public Prosecutor. I've been arrested for possession of drugs."

"God, no!" he exclaimed—and from the way he said it, it sounded as if it was the worst thing I could have done. "What can I do to help you?"

"Call the Embassy and let them know where I am," I said. As soon as the words were out of my mouth, the door opened and the two policemen who had accompanied me in the van strode across the room. One grabbed the telephone out of my hand and forcibly steered me toward the doorway. There was quite a commotion as he dragged me across the room. Outside a cluster of people who had been waiting to see the Public Prosecutor watched it all. I asked the man who had given me the phone to tell my manager where I was, and saw him talking on the telephone as I was removed from the room.

My legs were again shackled and I was led back through the hallways past curious onlookers and out to the waiting van. The van was windowless in the back, but I could see out the front through a wire mesh that separated me from the two policemen. Once I was in, they slammed the doors behind me, slid into their seats, and we left. Frightened and totally distraught, I could not imagine where we were going now. Somewhere in the deep recesses of my mind I kept thinking: *This is no way to treat a visitor to a foreign country.*

I stared out the front window looking for signs of our destination. We wound through a maze of side streets and then out onto the main road to the airport. Rationalizing this, I told myself that we were heading to the airport so that I could pick up my car or the policeman could put me on the next plane out of the country. Either way would be a relief.

For a while we drove on that highway, but then we exited onto another roadway I had never been on before. We passed some businesses and residential areas, and once those thinned out, we found ourselves riding outside the city in the desert. It appeared that we were in for a long haul because the policeman in the passenger seat opened his newspaper and began to read. When he had turned a few pages, I noticed an advertisement for our Abu Dhabi ELS Language Center. I tried to make conversation by telling him that this was an ad that I had placed, but I'm not sure that he really understood.

We kept driving and the traffic thinned. I was depressed by all that had happened and figured that now they were taking me into the desert where they would kill me and nobody would ever find me. I felt helpless and hopeless. But then I saw a sign that took my breath away, and I knew things were getting even worse. The sign was for Al Wathba Prison. *My God, my God! I'm going to prison. Unimaginable! Unbelievable! This isn't really happening. Oh, please, God, let me wake up now!*

I couldn't move. I thought I would have a heart attack and die right there in the van.

8

Arrival at Al Wathba Prison

I HAD NEVER HEARD OF AL WATHBA PRISON before that night in the Mina Jail. Surely it had been mentioned in the newspaper many times, but the stories related to crime and prisoners had never interested me.

There it was in the distance. Positioned ominously on a hilltop in the middle of the desert—a fortress with walls that seemed to reach high into the sky! It was late in the afternoon now, and as on the day I was arrested, I didn't notice any signs of hunger even though I had not eaten since early that morning. As we approached the prison, I tried to take in all that was happening. It was as though my senses had become so overloaded that I was a robot and moved without any remembrance of the past hours. In my state of shock I was totally focused on the next five seconds and constantly wondered what they were going to bring.

Nobody will find me here was my terrified reaction.

The driver stopped the van at the guardhouse outside the entrance to the prison. He produced a paper and the guard examined it. Some words in Arabic were exchanged and we were motioned to move forward. Straight ahead was the inner prison compound. My vision through the front window of the van was limited, and now I couldn't even see the top of the walls. Movies that feature prisons always picture huge main entrances to the complex and this prison was no exception to that. The doors loomed ever larger and the gates to hell opened wide in front of me.

As we approached the entrance, the driver swung the van to the left and stopped in front of what appeared to be an administrative office. He went inside and a few minutes later, the doors on the side of the van were opened. There stood the driver and two uniformed policemen. They looked at me, said some words to each other in Arabic, and smiled in a way that said, "The catch of the day has arrived." Still shackled, I disembarked and slowly climbed the few stairs to the entranceway, a piece of luggage in each hand and my backpack in place. As I did so, I moved both bags to one hand, and with my free hand reached inside my shirt and removed the ring that I had been wearing through my left nipple.

I was directed to a room via a left jog from the main hallway. It was a narrow room about 6 feet wide and 15 feet long with a few chairs positioned against one of the longer walls. Opposite was a counter that separated an area where several uniformed policemen worked at desks. Around them were numerous filing cabinets, and beyond the place where they worked was a more extensive area where I saw luggage stacked on floor-to-ceiling shelves. From movies I had seen, I recognized this as the place where I would have to turn in my personal effects and my luggage.

The two policemen who had driven me to the prison escorted me to the counter and spoke with one of the other policemen in Arabic. After their conversation had ended, one turned to me and uttered his first word in English: "Okay?"

My feelings of utter helplessness were expressed in rage as I screamed at him, "No, I'm not okay! You guys are fucking liars. Everything you told me was a lie." In an even louder voice I proclaimed, "I haven't even done anything illegal and you brought me to a prison. Goddamn bastards!" Through my duress I heard only frantic, frenzied words; it was as if it weren't Paul who was yelling, but some demon trapped inside him, wailing from the depths of his soul. Although the policemen had never shown any indication that they understood English, they had the wherewithal to know that I wasn't exchanging pleasantries, and one of the policemen flinched at my tirade. They turned and walked out. I wasn't going to see them again until the night of my release thirty-three months later. And that was also to be the last time that any raging outbursts came from me. The demon died.

As they turned to leave I noticed for the first time that there were four young boys sitting on the chairs in the room. My eyes caught theirs, and I could see that they were shocked to silence by what had just happened. I was jarred back to the moment when a policeman behind the counter said, "Pockets, pockets." I looked at him. He was holding a small brown envelope into which it was obvious that I was to put the contents of my pockets and also any body jewelry. I laid these items on the counter and he took one at a time and listed its description in Arabic on a form. When he was finished, the envelope contained an assortment of things: Greek, UAE, Canadian, and American currencies in bills and coins; my nipple ring; a set of three keys (apartment, car, office); my dog tags, wristwatch, and credit card case; Florida driver's license, Kuwait driving license, and a piece of paper with telephone numbers of friends and family.

When he finished writing, he took a copy of the receipt and stapled it to the brown envelope. He then pointed to my bags and said something in Arabic that I did not understand. I guess the young boys realized I didn't know what he was saying, and one told me that I should take my toothbrush and toothpaste and some underpants and shirts out of my bag. I opened one bag, searched through the disorganized mess of crumpled clothes, and retrieved three pairs of underpants and a few T-shirts. The boy told me that would be enough, so I closed my bags and placed the three of them on the counter. The policemen then added an entry on the receipt form to indicate that I had also left three suitcases with him. He gave me my copy and indicated an empty chair where I took my place. I looked at the boy who had translated for me and I thanked him.

Shortly afterwards, a policeman came, removed my shackles, and motioned that I should follow him. We retraced our earlier steps and came back again to the main entrance hall. He led me past a few offices and then through a door to the outside. We were now on the prison side of the massive door that earlier had loomed before me like the gates of hell. It was nearly evening and the sun cast long shadows from the walls of the prison across the inner yard. We walked 100 yards to another building, then climbed a few steps, and went inside. Inside, just beyond the door, he stopped, pulled out his keys, turned to the right, opened a cell door, and motioned me to enter. In my listless, robotic state, I numbly followed his direction and stepped in.

I quickly surveyed my surroundings. The room was about 10 feet by 15 feet with a 12-inch wide concrete seat stretching along three walls. Two barred entrance doors were situated on the fourth wall. There were no beds. The floor area was packed with people squatting on blankets. Most of the people resembled those with whom I had shared the room at Mina Jail, but there were a few others who were better dressed than the rest and looked as if they might have been business people. I found an empty spot and sat down without saying a word. As I glanced around, I noticed that all eyes were on me in the deafening silence.

It was the first chance I had had to take inventory of my situation since early that morning. I was still wearing the same clothes that I had worn when I was arrested, and I must have been quite a sight with my unkempt hair and unshaven face. I felt mentally exhausted and realized that I was also ravenously hungry. All that I had eaten that day had been a piece of bread and two hard-boiled eggs at breakfast.

Finally one of the other prisoners asked, "You're British?"

I responded, "No, I'm an American."

Everyone understood what I had said because the pronunciation of the word 'American' in English isn't much different from the pronunciation in Arabic. For the next thirty-three months prisoners and policemen would ask me over and over again, "You're British?" and I would reply, "No, I'm an American." It was indeed rare for an American to be in prison at Al Wathba and throughout most of my stay there, I was the only one. It was more common for British citizens to be in jail, and at any one time there were usually four to eight.

I learned that this was the transit cell. It was the place where prisoners who were brought to Al Wathba during the day were detained. Early the next morning, those in custody were processed and repositioned among the various blocks that held the general prison population. We were informed that in the morning they would fingerprint us, shave our heads, take our clothes and shoes, and issue prison uniforms. They would give us four blankets to be used as our bedroll during our stay at Al Wathba. A blood sample for HIV testing would be taken along with our picture, and ID cards would be issued. Basically, they were going to take away our individuality as much as possible in order to exercise their power and control over us. I didn't feel much like talking. I just sat by myself considering all that we had been told and realizing that I couldn't give up. I had to keep a positive attitude toward getting out of this place. It was about 7:00 in the evening now and hunger consumed me.

About an hour or so later a policeman came to the door and said, "American, come! Embassy." I felt an immediate surge of relief knowing that the Embassy had found me. *Had they come to get me out? Was the ordeal over?* I followed the guard back out to the courtyard, and we walked to the administrative office where I had been processed earlier that day. At the desk he pointed to a telephone. My hopes plummeted. The Embassy wasn't there waiting to see me.

A consular officer, Justine Sincavage, was on the telephone, and after telling me who she was, she asked how I was doing. Of all the things I could have said to her about the treatment I had received, I responded, "They are going to shave my head in the morning." It may sound now like a really stupid response, but at that moment the thought of having my head shaved left me feeling desperate. Once that was done, it meant that I really was a prisoner—just a number amid the mass of humanity hoarded into Al Wathba. Justine told me that she could tell I was distressed by the tone of my voice, and assured me that the Embassy was now aware of my situation. My family had been notified of my whereabouts and would soon have contact with me. She indicated that I should simply go along with procedures in the prison and that someone would be out to visit with me on Wednesday, the normal day for embassy visitations at the prison. I felt both a sense of relief that the Embassy had found me and a deep depression because it appeared I wasn't going to get out of that place for at least several days.

When I returned to the transit cell, everyone wanted to know if I was going to be released. I just told them, "No, I'll have to wait a while."

In a short time most of the men had settled down and the cell was quiet. As tired as I was, I couldn't sleep and my mind replayed all that had transpired that day. I was too apprehensive to rest, so I stood on the concrete seat and stared down a long hallway. At the far end a policeman guarded our section. He looked at me and then started walking toward me. When he arrived at the gate, he said something in Arabic that I did not understand. As soon as he realized I did not know what he was saying, he told me in French that I should not stand on the bed. I was amazed: first, because he spoke French and second, because I didn't consider the bench where I was standing, a bed. *Where else*, I thought, *would a 12-inch stoop be considered a bed?* When I replied in French, I think he was more amazed than I. He smiled and said he hoped I slept well.

It was the first decent comment and gesture that any policeman had made to me in days, and I thought that maybe they weren't all bad. I learned later that the policeman's name was Mohammed and he was from Mauritania. He was the first "in-shape" policeman I had seen there, and it was obvious he had the build of an athlete. It would turn out that Mohammed would be there for the duration of my stay at Al Wathba, and whenever I encountered him in the prison, he always had a smile and a "Bonjour" for me.

So I lay down on my blankets, still in the same clothes I had worn for days, and slept. It was Monday night, October 12, 1998.

Morning came early, as it would every day at Al Wathba. People rose prior to sunrise to wash and prepare for the first of the five daily prayers that are incumbent upon Muslims to perform. The earliest risers shouted and banged on the cell door to get the attention of the guards to come take them to the bathroom. The guards responded with yelling of their own and an impatience that kept everyone on edge.

Prayers were recited in the cell, and after that, things became quiet as everyone settled down to sleep again or became lost in their own thoughts. A little while later at the change of shift the morning activity increased. Policemen walked by our cell in all directions, talking and laughing with one another and preparing for the duties of the day. It was not long before I realized that the main entrance to the prison housing complex was next to our cell. During the course of my stay at Al Wathba, I would walk by that transit cell many times on my way to and from court appearances.

Suddenly there was a clamor at the end of the long corridor facing into our cell. Several policemen had gathered there, conversing loudly among themselves. Then the talking turned to shouting as I heard individual names being called out. One by one, prisoners appeared at the end of the hallway and gathered there in a group. I was told that these were the detainees who were going to appear in court that day. Some wandered over to our cell to talk to their friends, but that action was met with loud shouts from guards who moved them further down the hallway. After all the prisoners going to the courts were accounted for, they were marched past our cell and through the adjacent door to the outside. There, I was told, they would be shackled and put into trucks for the ride to Abu Dhabi. It wouldn't be long before I would be part of that ritual.

The door to the outside constantly opened and closed due to the activities of the morning. I could hear the drone of trucks pulling up near the building, the metallic clink of shackles, and the bellowing commands of the guards.

All these were first time sights and sounds for me, and I sat on the bench taking it all in, hardly saying a word to anyone. I remembered an episode of *Nightline* where Ted Koppel had spent a night or two in a prison so that he could better relate to what actually went on inside the walls. I hoped that my stay would be as short as his. I had already seen enough.

Eventually, some prisoners carrying a huge pot and a large coffee urn appeared with their guards. It was time for breakfast. Before they let us out of our cell, however, I saw a group of other prisoners gather around the pot and dish out a portion of its contents. I was told that those prisoners were from another cell located just around the corner at the end of the long hallway. They lived permanently in a cell positioned directly along the main artery that led into the heart of the building. These were the obviously effeminate gay prisoners and part of their punishment was to be housed where there was a lot of traffic so they could be constantly taunted and verbally abused.

We were allowed to leave our cell to walk down the hallway and get our share of food. In the pot was a white creamy liquid in which there appeared to be small noodles. I was given a dirty plate, and after rinsing it the best I could, I took some of the food along with a piece of bread similar to that we had received at the

Mina police station. The meal was very sweet-tasting, and having not eaten since the previous morning, I devoured it. We were also given a cup of tea that didn't taste like tea but was something sweet that resembled caramel in both taste and color.

The guards made sure that we didn't use the time to socialize by urging us back to our cell as soon as the last of us was given his serving. Other prisoners told me to ignore them because generally we would have five to ten minutes to eat. One by one we moved back to our cell and waited for our fate to unfold. It was 7:00 in the morning.

Around 8:30 activity picked up outside. A man dressed in white arrived with a policeman, and they began the preparations for our processing into the prisoner community. This man, I was told, was the barber and he was setting up in a room off the hallway close to our cell. The block became quieter as each person contemplated this next step in the controlled process of robbing us of our individuality. One by one they called us out of the cell and led us to the room to have our hair sheared off. One man with whom I had spoken was a businessman in Abu Dhabi like me, but he was an Arab. When his name was called, he talked to the guard and from the exchange I could tell that he was trying to get out of having his hair cut. The dispute grew angrier, but finally the conversation stopped and he remained in the cell as another took his turn to have his hair cut. Eventually, another policeman of higher rank arrived and talked with the man again about having his hair cut. That tussle ended in an apparent deadlock and the policeman left, only to return soon with an officer. As the prisoner talked with the policeman, my name was called, and like a lamb being led to slaughter, I took my place on the shearing stool. Within twenty seconds my hair had been cropped to within one quarter inch of my scalp. I felt naked and humiliated.

After the haircut, we were ushered into the next room. There, two sets of our fingerprints were taken, after which we were allowed to wash off the ink with cold water. Even with warm water and soap, the ink used for fingerprinting is difficult to get off. With cold water only, our hands remained ink-stained.

Then we moved down to a counter at the end of the hallway. There we were each issued four blankets, a plastic cup, two sets of uniforms and a brown sack that resembled a gunny sack. The uniform was in two pieces. The pants were blue and had a drawstring tie around the waist. The top was the same color blue, but on the back there was a red stripe that ran the width of the back and was about 4 inches high. Some were just a plain red bar, but some had white Arabic numbers formed by stitching white thread. The top slipped over the head and there was one button that fastened on the shoulder to keep it snug around the neck. We were told to put our own shirts, pants, shoes, and socks in the brown bag and to get into our uniforms. Everyone else was obviously better prepared for this situation than I, because they all wore sandals and those they were allowed to keep. I was the only one now bare-footed. A policeman wrote our name on a tag for each bag and the end was knotted closed. This was obviously a routine these policemen followed every day since they were clearly bored and showed their impatience by yelling at us to move faster and faster so they could get past this major inconvenience.

As we finished up, the man who had balked at getting his hair cut joined us. He had lost his battle to save his hair. Once everyone was dressed in his prison uniform and our clothes were in sacks, we were ordered to follow several policemen past rooms that I was told were for solitary confinement. We also went past the cell that housed the gay prisoners with whom we had shared breakfast. We were led up two flights of stairs that opened to a hallway that was about 12 feet wide and looked as if it extended at least one quarter mile. After being positioned approximately 10 feet apart, we were directed to place our belongings on the floor along each wall. Next to these packets we then sat, silent and unable to talk with one another.

A short time later we were ordered to get up, leave our possessions behind, and follow a policeman. We straggled behind him down a side corridor to a cramped area where we were directed to wait outside a room with an open door. One by one we were called into the room. There, a machine was set up to take our picture and within seconds produce an identification card. My turn came and my identification card was handed to me. It contained my picture and information that included my name, prisoner number, date of entry into the prison, and the crime that I had allegedly committed. On the back side, one of the policemen had written the number three in Arabic. This was to be my block number. Adjacent to that was a room where blood samples were taken for HIV screening. The people in authority had a real paranoia about HIV and AIDS, and their way to deal with anyone who tested positive was to isolate them from the general prison population, regardless of whether the person showed any outward signs of being infected or not.

Once that process was completed, we followed the policemen back to the corridor where we had left our belongings. Our clothes that had been left in neat piles were now strewn all over the corridor. Another act of humiliation and control! We were ordered to gather our belongings together and reclaim them. With the little we had, arguments broke out among the prisoners over what belonged to whom, but eventually everyone was satisfied that he had his own things and we formed a line along one wall and sat down. The fellow next to me wanted to know what block I was going to. When I told him, he said that Block 3 was a pretty good block. I didn't know how one block could be any better than another, but over the following months I would soon learn about these differences.

We were then taken in groups toward our respective blocks. There were three of us assigned to Block 3, my new residence for the next seven months.

9

The Prison

BLOCK 3 WAS KNOWN AS A TRANSIT BLOCK in that it was a block that housed people who had not yet received their sentence from the court. At any given time, it could house prisoners convicted of anything from overstaying a visa to theft to drinking alcohol to being a drug smuggler to murder. People charged with almost any crime were housed together in Blocks 1, 3, or 4. Those charged with incest or rape were confined to Block 5, and to identify them they had to wear green uniforms while everyone else wore blue.

Al Wathba prison was purportedly built by the Germans as a high security prison to accommodate approximately nine hundred prisoners. Throughout my time there, it actually housed about two thousand. Two electrified walls were topped with barbed wire. Guard houses were positioned above the walls at each of the four corners. Buried in the ground were horizontal steel sheets to prevent burrowing by the prisoners. At night rifle-toting guards with dogs patrolled the area between the two walls, and throughout the complex cameras were positioned on walls and on roof tops to record all outside activity. There were also cameras inside the blocks to register movements in the corridors.

The prison housed the men in four towers; the women and younger men and teenagers were held in another tower. The four identical towers that housed the male prisoners were square structures, each three stories high with an inner courtyard. The upper two stories were built as living quarters and the lowest story was left open to the courtyard.

Each block had a corridor that ran around the perimeter of a courtyard which was enclosed by a concrete wall with horizontal cut-outs. The walls were formed so that the base of the walls could be used as a bench for sitting. Along the corridor there were rooms of various sizes that were meant to house anywhere from one to six people depending on the number of beds. In my experience I saw the smaller rooms house up to four people and the largest up to thirty-four. The beds (for those who had them) were concrete slabs with grooves running across the width. There were no mattresses or sheets or pillows. Prisoners could use their blankets any way they wanted: for padding between them and the concrete, for a cover when sleeping, or as a pillow. Some open shelves were available for personal items and clothes. One corner of the block had a doorway that connected it to the main corridor, and the opposite corner had a stairway that connected the three levels. Access to it was always locked. Usually six toilets were available in each block and two of those doubled as showers. The toilets were holes in the floor, and small water hoses were provided for cleansing oneself.

All the rooms, except for those designed for one person, had barred windows. At the entrance of each there was a 2-inch steel door with a small window about 3 inches high across its width. The doors remained unlocked so that the prisoners could move freely around the block. Initially, guards had been stationed inside each block and the prisoners had been locked in their rooms. That changed when some inmates died from the extreme heat that built up in the rooms during the summer. From that point on, the doors were left unlocked and the guards were stationed just outside the blocks. Running along the outside perimeter of the blocks was a walkway about 3 feet wide. This was used by the police to randomly check on activities in the rooms without having to enter the blocks. Generally one room in each block was set aside as a mosque. Here, books such as *The Koran* and other religious books were stored and prisoners could come to pray or read.

Because the prison population had become so large, two extra blocks were added to the original eight and were created out of the open space on the lowest level in two of the towers. The work was done by the prisoners themselves, and as a result, the two blocks were not as professionally built as the original ones. When hallways were cleaned, water would collect in puddles because the slope of the floor wasn't adequate to provide proper run off. The bathroom areas also had sections of standing water because of the poor drainage. The openings in the walls adjacent to the courtyard were smaller than those in the initial construction of the other blocks; thus, the two new blocks were dark and permanently in the shadows cast by the upper stories. Those blocks had no benches on which to sit, nor did they have beds and shelves like the other blocks. The rooms were basically empty boxes. Because of this, those blocks were the two to which no one wanted to be assigned. Later in my stay at Al Wathba, these were also the blocks which the prison manager designated for all drug offenders, and I would spend my last eighteen months in one of them.

When Al Wathba was first opened, food was delivered in bulk to the blocks and then further distributed among the prisoners from there. Since some men hoarded food hoping to resell it, unsanitary conditions resulted causing people to get sick. Eventually, prison officials decided to have the inmates come to a common area to eat and prohibited the taking of any food back to the blocks. The lowest level of the two other towers was converted to an eating place. Prisoners built tables and benches from concrete blocks and topped them with tiles for easy cleaning. To this section the men would come, a block at a time, to pick up food already prepared on trays.

The complex had a clinic area that was staffed during the daytime by one or two doctors and several nurses. At all times there was at least one nurse on duty. A few days a week there was a dentist, and at longer intervals, perhaps once every second week, a dermatologist and a psychologist would visit. As part of the clinic, a section on the second floor was set aside for sick prisoners who were kept out of the general prison population. Those who had physical disabilities such as broken limbs, severe back problems, or impairments that made mobility difficult were also housed in this area that had beds sufficient to accommodate about twenty-four people.

There was a library that contained a collection of books in Arabic and English, and to a much lesser extent, in Hindi and Urdu. Generally, the Arabic books were supplied by the prison, but it was rare when new books were added to the collection. All the English books were contributed by the inmates. Prisoners were allowed to have approved books brought to them, and for the most part when a prisoner had read his books, he donated them to the library. It was very rare for an Arabic reader to do this. As a result of the generosity of the English readers, the English language section of the library rapidly became as large as the Arabic section with the number of English books numbering about seven hundred. Still, the collection was very small. Once a week, a few people from each block were allowed to go to the library and select books for other block mates. The general prisoner population, except for a few, were not allowed to go to the library themselves to sit and read or do research. I would eventually become one of the privileged few who were allowed library privileges.

Next to the library was an artists' studio. This was set up for propaganda purposes to show outsiders who came to visit the prison that inmates were treated well and that creativity was allowed to flourish in the program. Initially, the studio was used by only one long-term prisoner who created paintings, sculptures, and some signage for the prison. He was released during my stay there and eventually three other prisoners were allowed to use the facility.

Just as the artists' studio and the library were used to show the outside world what a wonderful place Al Wathba prison was, there was also an area set aside for classrooms. These were used to teach Arabic, English, basic Mathematics, and Islam. Prisoners with an interest were brought to these classes several mornings each week. Only a few had a genuine desire in coming to learn anything; rather, the classroom was a place to get out of the stifling summer heat or a place to meet friends from other blocks. Prison officials provided no textbooks for the students or for professional teachers, but reluctantly, from time to time, would provide notebooks and pencils. Quite often the prison was visited by people from the police department, Ministry of Justice, the Public Prosecutor's office, and international organizations such as the United Nations' and Human Rights' organizations. On those days additional people were brought to the school, mostly all against their will, to make the classes look full and give the appearance that the prison management was very concerned about the welfare and education of those incarcerated. Eventually, I would become a teacher in this educational component, and even though we knew the whole thing was a charade, we still played along because it was better to be there than to stay in the blocks.

There was a recreation building where once a week prisoners could go, on a block by block basis, to exercise for an hour. It was a large room with a roof and walls whose upper half was covered by wire mesh that allowed ventilation. The men were permitted to play soccer (football), volleyball, shoot basketballs at nets, or engage in a game of table tennis. Some just came to watch and to get out of the block; others used the occasion to do some jogging. For most of the prisoners soccer was their favorite sport, and it was a great way for the men to exercise and to vent a little of their frustration at being imprisoned in such a depressing place. Unfortunately, the facility was not maintained. A third of the lights had burnt out and had never been replaced, while over the years the asphalt floor had buckled and broken in several places. As a result, there were many foot and leg and upper body injuries when prisoners stumbled and fell. All sports activities took place simultaneously and side by side, so balls of one sport were constantly crossing through or into the territory of another. Years before my arrival, the complex had had a weight room and an area for gymnastics, but that had been deemed too extravagant for prisoners.

Some prisoners were allowed to go outside, but still within the walls of the prison, to produce concrete blocks and paving stones. A small manufacturing facility was devoted to developing products that would improve the prison surroundings. Concrete blocks were fashioned and used to build tables and benches in the eating areas; paving stones were produced and laid over the original blocks in each of the four courtyards and over damaged concrete floors. A few detainees were allowed to tend a garden where vegetables used in the preparation of meals for the policemen were grown.

All of the prison uniforms were made on the premises, and several days a week selected prisoners worked in the mornings to cut and sew the material that produced them. Others worked in a carpentry shop where they attended to simple repairs throughout the prison and also fashioned small items that were sold outside the prison.

The men in each block were responsible for keeping their block clean. Usually, one or several persons were assigned to the bathroom areas and hallways. In return for that work, other prisoners would usually give a pack of cigarettes gotten during visitation to those people who did the work for them. The common areas like the courtyards, eating areas, main hallways, and walkways on the perimeter of the blocks were hosed and cleaned down each day by inmates assigned on a rotating basis.

Each of the blocks, except for the two on the ground floor, had speakers in them that were used solely for broadcasting chants from the Koran every morning. I guess that the prison officials thought that maybe some proselytizing would have a positive effect on the prisoners. I never met anyone, Muslim or otherwise, who thought the broadcasts were anything but boring and annoying.

One section of the prison was set aside for female prisoners and another for young men and teenagers. These inmates were usually confined to their blocks, and food was brought to them rather than risk their close association with the general prison population. The young men were forced to attend classes several mornings each week, and eventually I had the opportunity to teach them English. The only contact these young men had with the rest of the inmates was that they got to use the sports facility with other prisoners who attended classes at the school.

In addition to the classrooms in the school area, there was one room with a stage area surrounded by bench-seating for about two hundred persons. This could be used for presentations or lectures and was devoted primarily to religious purposes. All Muslims were brought there once a week on a block by block basis for a sermon on Islam. The police responsible for these lectures would come to the block and spend a considerable amount of time rounding up Muslims to attend. Very few wanted to be there voluntarily, and the police would move from room to room forcing people to go either by hitting them with a cane or writing down their names so they would not be allowed visitations. The men would pretend that they did not understand Arabic, that they were of a religion other than Islam, or that they were sick. Some even hid behind doors or in the lavatory or shower stalls to avoid being caught in this ridiculous cat and mouse game. If you were known to be of another faith you were not bothered.

For those who were not Muslim, there was an opportunity to attend Islamic studies classes several mornings each week. These

I attended for six months and, like the other classes, it gave us a chance to get out of the blocks for a short time and to meet prisoners from other blocks. Very few who attended did so because they had a genuine interest in studying Islam with the intent to convert to the religion.

Scattered throughout the prison complex were rooms designated for solitary confinement. These were generally used for men who had gotten into fights, had had altercations with the police, had tried to smuggle food from the eating areas back to the blocks, or had been caught with contraband items such as knives, needles, or radios. It was easy to violate any number of prison rules that seemed to change on a daily basis. These rooms were also used to house those whose sentences included solitary confinement, those who tested HIV positive, those who were members of the UAE military working in sensitive or commanding positions, and those who were considered too dangerous to be among the general prison population.

10

Block 3

THE POLICEMAN ESCORTED THE THREE of us toward Block 3. As we approached, we turned a corner and there, about twenty feet away, was the entrance to the place where we would be housed. People were gathered at the door, many shouting at the police in Arabic. I didn't know at that time what all the shouting was about but it became commonplace during my stay, and I soon learned that the shouting represented many things: trying to get to see the doctor, reporting a fight, complaining about the overcrowding, wanting to know why someone hadn't been called to court, asking to speak to an officer or the manager about a personal problem, and on and on. The sight reminded me of what I had experienced at the Mina Police Station.

    The guards barked a few orders and the inmates moved back from the gate so that we could enter. Everyone quieted when they realized there was a Westerner among that day's group of new prisoners and a few asked in English, "Where are you from?" Word spread throughout the complex within minutes when it was learned there was an American among the detainees, and the rest of the inmates gathered around to have a look. Finally, the foreman of the block introduced himself and told the three of us to put our belongings down and he would find a place for us. One of the men who came to Block 3 with me recognized some people he knew, and right away they found him a place in their room. He left to join them. A few minutes later a young Indian fellow came to me and said that his friends wanted me to move into their room. He helped me with my things and showed me to one of the larger rooms that had six beds, but housed twenty-one people. All were Indian or Sri Lankan in the room, and most spoke or understood English. I felt comfortable and safe as each welcomed me into their group and directed me to a spot on the floor where I could put my blankets.

Sudi was the name of the fellow who had come to greet me. He shared one of the small rooms with another person named Saratch and he introduced me to him. They had been friends outside of prison and when I asked them why they had been arrested, I was stunned when they answered, "Murder." I didn't really know what to say, though I tried to look nonplussed. Sensing that I was tongue-tied, they volunteered the circumstances of what had happened. They had been with some friends one evening and at one point two of them had started to fight. During an exchange of punches, one of them fell, knocked his head, and eventually died of his injuries. On the day I met them, they had been in prison for two years with no sign of an imminent decision in their case.

Everyone in the room wanted to know why I was there and I related the circumstances. I think I repeated the same story fifty times as people from the block came by to introduce themselves and tell me how much they loved America.

Sudi gave me a bar of soap and a small box of Tide for washing my clothes. At the same time one of my roommates presented me with a pair of flip flops. It is customary that sandals be worn everywhere outside of the rooms, but they are left at the entrance to the room before entering. That was not only an attempt to keep the rooms as clean as possible, but it was also a part of the customs of many of the Asian and Arab countries.

Soon it was time for our block to go to lunch, so I joined my roommates in line as we walked down to the lower level to where we would eat. This was the first time I had witnessed the chaos that reigned when the prisoners had to queue up for any reason. The Arabs, particularly, ignored any sense of order and would walk to the front of the line or stand four or five abreast despite orders to the contrary from the police. On that first Tuesday, and most Tuesdays thereafter, the luncheon meal consisted of white rice topped with a little watery sauce, a piece of fatty mutton, a few shavings of carrot and cabbage mixed together, and an apple. Our beverage was water that we brought with us from the block.

One day the meat apparently wasn't up to inmate standards and a shouting match took place between the prisoners and the policemen, and the prisoners and the kitchen help. No one wanted the meat that had been doled out on the trays, so the line halted until more acceptable fare was provided. I would later realize that whenever mutton was served, the same riotous behavior occurred. Most of the complaining came from the UAE nationals and other Gulf Arabs. It seemed that, despite their incarceration, they maintained a sense of superiority that they freely demonstrated in the community.

I also learned that the Arabs held the police in very low regard and treated them, despite their authority, as being from a lesser class. That was easy for them because none of the police were Gulf Arabs themselves. Most were from countries such as Morocco, Mauritania, Sudan, Somalia, and Nepal and already they were treated like the hired help. Almost exclusively, ranking officers in the prison were UAE nationals and had the respect of the Arabs. When these officers were called to quell a disturbance, order was quickly restored.

On many occasions, even before the last person had been served his rations, the police would blow their whistles and order the prisoners to return to the block. Many men ignored these commands and wandered out into the courtyard to call to their friends who were in the upper blocks. At this point the police would come running and make the perpetrators move on. Defiance of the police was routine, and it seemed that the prisoners enjoyed seeing how far they could go in challenging the guards' authority. In some instances, however, the police took no nonsense at all and sent those who were repeat offenders to solitary confinement.

The prisoners in Block 3 included citizens of many countries including most of the Gulf States and Egypt, India, Pakistan, Bangladesh, Iran, Morocco, Sri Lanka, and the Philippines. Many were from the UAE itself. Charges against them included theft, writing bad checks, rape, murder, having sex with a woman who was not one's wife, drinking without a permit, dealing and using drugs, burglary, violation of immigration laws, and homosexuality. Ages ranged anywhere from twenty-five to sixty-five.

Because of the high respect Indians have for older people, and because I was an American, they were very kind, courteous, and helpful to me. Everyone in my room as well as most of the prison population, except for the Gulf Arabs, called me "Mr. Paul." Everything that happened on that first day in Al Wathba was new to me, but I learned very quickly that the routine would be drab and monotonous over the course of the next thirty-three months.

Around four o'clock the foreman of the block came to our room and said that the police wanted people to go downstairs to clean the eating area and the courtyard. Just as people from Asian countries routinely perform jobs requiring manual labor in the UAE, so too in the prison the same class structures seemed to be in place. Since it was beneath the dignity of the "locals" to be seen doing manual labor, those from the Asian countries were picked for the menial jobs that came along. Reluctantly, some of my roommates volunteered and soon were employed downstairs hosing down the common areas and mopping up with squeegee brushes.

While they were gone, another three persons were needed to go to the kitchen and bring back large urns full of hot tea. This was a ritual that would be practiced twice a day every day. Each morning hot tea came to the blocks around 6:00 o'clock and again around 4:30 in the afternoon. The morning tea came with milk, or a milk substitute, whereas the afternoon tea was black. It was always very heavily sweetened and there was an ongoing rumor that other ingredients had been added to reduce our sex drive. Although it didn't taste like tea that one would make using a tea bag, it was something besides plain water and it created social moments where people would sit and chat for a few minutes. Life in the block slowed down during those times.

At the entrance to each block there was an area enclosed in bars where police could enter without actually coming inside the block. From there they could see clearly down two of the aisles and assess what was taking place inside. It was to this area that the tea was delivered each day and distributed among the prisoners.

The chaos that surrounded picking up one's tray of food at lunch paled in comparison to the mayhem that I witnessed at tea time. There were no lines, just a mass of screaming, shouting, and pushing bodies as people tried to get their cup of tea. At first I thought this was just a lot of good-natured jostling, but I soon realized that this was a time when serious fights broke out over who was going to get their tea first. The mob mentality that prevailed seemed particularly bizarre because the distribution occurred twice a day every day and there was always enough tea for everyone. Organized lines were foreign to most prisoners, and I learned that this was because of the way they lived their lives on the outside. Due to the poverty in many Asian countries, people had to fight for every morsel of sustenance. That behavior was carried over into the prison situation.

Somewhere in my subconscious all this registered. It seemed so unnecessary and foreign to me, and I knew that, even if I were the last one served, I would still get my full cup of tea. I began to resolve that I would never let myself become like those desperate men and give in to their animalistic lifestyle of fighting and scavenging for food.

At dinnertime, as with lunch, a policeman would come to the front gate and blow a whistle to announce that it was mealtime. If you did not respond, there was no second chance, so it usually didn't take long for the block to empty out. Once congregated in the eating area, some groups, especially the Indians and Sri Lankans, stood in orderly lines while the rest pushed past them creating havoc at the front of the line. When I got to the point of picking up my food, I could not help but wonder what all the shouting and fighting was about. No one was going to get anything better or more substantial than anyone else for that night's dinner. That was it!

After we returned to our block, most people congregated in their rooms or in the corridor to enjoy a cigarette and some conversation. Often people formed into groups to play cards, chess, and other games. On my first night in Al Wathba, I took a walk through the corridors and was invited to join some of the locals who were sitting in the hallway joking and telling stories. As soon as I joined them, they stopped talking in Arabic and quickly turned to English. That didn't surprise me because many of the Arabs in the Middle East, especially the ones aged forty and younger, have a conversational command of the English language. It was a jovial group and we told jokes and talked a little about my case. After a while, someone made a comment about the good physical shape I was in and I explained that prior to my coming to Al Wathba, I had exercised in the gym on a regular basis. Soon casual comments turned to challenges from some of the men who wanted to see if they could do more pull-ups or push-ups than I. So, I began to accept their challenges even though some of the men looked to be in very good physical shape themselves.

At first, I usually won these contests, sometimes doing seventy-five or more push ups and eight to ten pull ups. When I beat one competitor, another would step forward to try his prowess. That would be okay for three or four rounds, but by the fifth competition in a row I was tired and unable to beat a fresh contender. When I lost, the new victor became the hero of the day for he had just beaten an American. I would congratulate the victor and we would all become friends again and celebrate the winner's "superior" strength. To this day, I really don't think the Arabs comprehended what was really happening there, and that's how it would be throughout the duration of my stay. For some of the men these feats of strength were for more than just fun. They were pitting themselves against America, and when they won it was the best thing that could have happened in their day.

By ten o'clock I was exhausted. I had survived my first full day at Al Wathba prison, so I took the time, as I try to do every night, to thank God for the day and for keeping me safe. Sleep came easily, for I was mentally and physically exhausted from taking in all the new sights and sounds of the day.

11

First Visit from the Embassy

I AWOKE ON THAT FIRST WEDNESDAY morning when the lights came on about 4:30 a.m. I didn't have my watch to ascertain the time, but I was curious as to why the lights came on so early. After asking some of those who were already up what the time was, I was told that the first prayers of the day would be about 5:00, and the lights were on so that the Muslims in my room could prepare for their religious duties. When I realized that the activity didn't involve me, I pulled the blankets over my head and went back to sleep.

    Later, I was again awakened by loud talking outside the room and some shouting by the front gate. I was told that the tea had arrived, and it seemed that even early in the morning people fought over who was going to get their tea first. When I finally received my share, it tasted more like caramel than tea, but it went down well on an empty stomach. Just as I finished it, police arrived at the gate and started blowing their whistles indicating it was time for our block to go for breakfast.

    Everyone put on his prison uniform and headed downstairs. Breakfast that Wednesday morning consisted of bread, as it did every morning, and two boiled eggs. I thought that the line would move easily since one egg looks like the next, and there would be nothing for people to complain about. But a few of the eggs had slightly cracked shells, and the men who got those created quite a stir by yelling at the police and the kitchen staff. It was difficult to understand the logic, since they would be cracking the shell anyway in order to get at the yolk. I realized later that prisoners would use any excuse to harass the police or vent their frustration at being confined. Receiving a cracked egg gave them such an excuse.

After returning from breakfast, I sat in the hallway talking. Sudi approached and offered me a book by James Clavell entitled *Gai Jin*, the story of the British colonization of Japan and the subsequent resentment of some Japanese toward the Imperialists. As I had no reading material with me, it was a welcome gift that provided a distraction from the routine of prison life.

That same day I noticed one young man from India who had lesions on his arms and legs that apparently had not healed properly. When he noticed I was looking at them, he volunteered that they were scars from blisters he had developed in the intense heat of the summer. Since the weather was so pleasant in early October, I hadn't given any thought to the fact that the block was not air conditioned. Indeed, the block was open to the outside through the horizontal holes in the wall abutting the courtyard area; the windows in the rooms had only bars. I was very familiar with the high temperatures that endure from June until September, and at that moment I realized what a devastating effect exposure to the unrelenting heat can have on one's body. I wouldn't have to worry about that for another eight months, especially since I thought that I would be gone from that place well before such an issue became a problem.

About 10:15 that morning a prisoner who had been sitting by the front gate came to tell me that I had a visit from the Embassy. I was excited, for finally I would have a chance to find out what was happening and see just how long I might have to stay at Al Wathba. I put on my uniform, grabbed my ID card, and headed to the front gate. There a policeman was waiting and he motioned for me to follow him. We went upstairs and turned down the long corridor toward the administrative area near the prison entrance. At the end of the hallway there was a police checkpoint, and after my escort explained to those stationed there who I was, my card was checked and I was frisked. Another prisoner was also at the checkpoint and it turned out that he was an Egyptian national with U.S. citizenship named Mohammed Shala. We were both accompanied further down the hallway to a section that divided into two narrower passageways. We took the route on the left which led to the visiting area for male prisoners. At the end of this corridor, we climbed to a landing, walked a little further, and descended several more steps. I later learned this strange configuration resulted because the floor levels for the administrative wing didn't line up with the floor levels where the prisoners were held.

We were led into the visitation room. It was a rectangular room about 6 feet by 20 feet. In the middle, spaced around the room, were stationary tile-covered concrete blocks for the prisoners to sit on. Each faced a metal screen through which one could see and talk to visitors. Wednesdays were visitation days for Embassies, and when we went in, Mohammed Shala and I were the only prisoners there.

I learned from Mohammed Shala that he had a five-year sentence and had about nine months left to serve out a conviction that involved writing a check with insufficient funds in his account and being caught in possession of alcohol. The latter was a serious offense because he was a Muslim.

A few minutes after we took our seats, I heard approaching footsteps and turned to see two people from the consular section enter on the other side of the screening. They introduced themselves to me: one was Jamal Bafagih and the other was Justine Sincavage. Then Jamal took a seat opposite Mohammed and Justine sat across from me.

The first thing she did was assure me that my family had been advised of my whereabouts and the reason for my being detained. She told me that the charges against me were very serious and that I would need to exercise a lot of patience, not only to deal with the situation in the prison, but with the slow moving legal and judicial systems. She indicated that with my visit to the Public Prosecutor, a file had been opened for my case, and that, now that the file was open, we would have to allow the judicial process to follow its course. Once a sentence was passed, the Embassy could make pleas for release on my and my family's behalf. If the Embassy had been able to get to see me earlier, then the trip to prison might have been averted.

When I asked how long it might take for a sentence to be rendered, I was stunned to learn it might take five to nine months. The thought of spending that long a time in Al Wathba made me nauseous. She told me that despite what I might know about the U.S. legal and judicial systems, I should not expect much of a similarity in the UAE. The U.S. could not interfere in the legal procedures of another country, regardless of how much we might disagree with them. I would have to go along with their method of handing out justice. She went on to fill me in on the efforts the Embassy had made in trying to locate me during the past several days. Indeed, they had contacted the Mina Police Station and the Drug Enforcement Agency where I had been held, and had been informed that I wasn't among the detainees in those locations.

By now Jamal had finished his conversation and he joined us. Justine told me that Jamal would fill me in on the remaining details and she went to talk with the other American. Jamal assured me that he had been in contact with my manager at ELS Language Centers. I explained to him that the family of Sheikhs Shaya and Khalid bin Hamid al Hamed, the owners of ELS in the Middle East, were close friends of the ruling royal family, and that, surely, they would put in a request for my release since I had been productive for them in their business. He told me he would check with them to see what they would do.

Because I had not previously registered my presence in the UAE with the American Embassy, Jamal had brought a form for that purpose. On it I was able to indicate those to whom the Embassy could divulge details of my arrest and incarceration should they be contacted. He gave the paper to the policeman who had escorted them in and who, in turn, left the room and arranged for it to be given to me for my signature.

He also advised me that I might want to have an attorney represent me. After telling him I knew none, he indicated that the Embassy had the names of some and he would give that list to me on the next visit. I also shared a comment made by the translator during my interrogation at the office of the Public Prosecutor. He had said that he would see to it that my trial got a lot of publicity in the newspapers and that my picture would be included. Jamal indicated that that would not happen, and because of the determined way in which he said it, I felt confident that my case would not be spread across the headlines for everyone to read.

When it finally dawned on me that my hopes for an early release had been dashed and that I was in a very serious situation from which the Embassy was not able to extricate me, I felt totally deflated and I began to cry. It was a low point in my life when I realized that I was a prisoner and I wasn't going anywhere soon.

By now our discussion was complete. Jamal indicated that he would contact my brother Richard to let him know that he and Justine had visited with me and that they would contact the State Department in Washington so my case could also be monitored from there. After I thanked them for coming to visit me, I dejectedly followed the policeman, who had been watching all these proceedings, back to the security desk where I was again frisked and then led to the block. Along the way the other American tried to reassure me that things would work out and that, if I ever needed anything, to let him know. I could always get a message to him through our foreman who could get the word passed to him.

I was let back into the block where the others crowded around wanting to know what the Embassy had said and when I would be going home. When I told them I had no real news and that I would be there for some time, they were both surprised and disappointed. I realized later that the reason for their reaction was that they had felt that, if an American were let go, then there might be some hope for them. Conversely, if an American couldn't get out of that place, then what chance did they have?

As I stood in line for lunch that afternoon, I mulled over what had transpired during my visit a short time earlier. I concluded that the Embassy had been very guarded in what they had said, and I could appreciate that they couldn't give me any hope for clemency without being certain that it would happen. But I held onto the belief that they were really working for my release behind the scenes and that I would surely be out soon. Again, that turned out to be wishful thinking on my part.

12

Settling In

IF YOU'VE EVER BEEN CONFINED TO one place such as a nursing home, hospital, or jail, you know the feeling of isolation and loneliness that comes over you when a visitor leaves. You feel abandoned and left to survive on your own. That's how I felt when I returned to my block after meeting with the Embassy staff.

I was in a place where I did not know anybody; where the culture and background of those surrounding me were so entirely different from mine that no one could possibly comprehend what my life was like at home; where I couldn't understand most of what was being said; where the comforts that I took for granted weren't available. I was just one of six non-Muslims, the only Westerner, and likely the most highly-educated person in the entire block.

In one day I had seen many shocking examples of animalistic behavior among the other prisoners. They fought over who would get tea first; they fought with the police at any opportunity; they yelled and laughed as though being in prison was playtime. Personal items were constantly being stolen, and less assertive persons were singled out and picked on. No consideration was given to people waiting in line for showers or the toilets, and prisoners would yell back and forth between blocks after the lights had gone out for the night. Those who smoked didn't consider the effects of the smoke on non-smokers around them, and there was constant harassment of the police and kitchen help when food was served. All of that was completely foreign to my sense of propriety.

For the first few days, I took it all in as I tried to figure out how I would survive in such dismal circumstances without letting all those annoyances upset me. It all came together for me one day when I finally decided that I simply had to accept people as they were. I may not like how they behaved, but that was just the way they were, either because of their culture or their pent-up energy. I recalled a prayer I had heard many times before: *Lord give me the strength to change those things that I can change, and give me the patience to accept those things I cannot.* There was that word "patience" again.

Thus, I decided that I could not judge the people around me by my own standards. That did not mean, however, that I would have to become like them. Indeed, I made a conscious decision to behave as normally as possible, and hopefully, I would be an example of a decent person and a good American. I had a choice in such matters. I could try to fit in and be like the rest, or I could adjust and do those things I needed to do for survival without losing my integrity and sense of propriety. It was the latter that I chose.

So, there I was in that dismal block with no inkling of what I would do with my time. As I walked around and observed all that was happening, I sensed that most inmates had no plan for using their time wisely. Many slept, some played cards or games, a handful read, a few were learning how to chant the words from the Koran. Others simply sat and stared into space. Most of that seemed like a waste of time to me, so I set out to find what other options were available.

That wasn't hard to do as most of the inmates were very glad when I, "The American," took the time to sit and talk with them. As much as America had been maligned in the press, I found that generally the people at Al Wathba looked on the United States as the land of opportunity and longed to learn more about the country and its people. They harbored a dream, albeit one they knew they would never realize, about one day living in the United States and having a lifestyle similar to what they had viewed on television.

While talking with people, I gradually ascertained more about what we could and couldn't have access to in prison, and what we could and couldn't do in our blocks. And just because we didn't have access to something or weren't permitted to do something didn't necessarily mean it wasn't going to happen.

Because one of the ongoing challenges for inmates was to find a way around any regulation that the prison officials imposed on them, we lived a constant game of cat and mouse.

I learned important things during those first few days and the list was long:

- No games or cards were allowed to be brought into the prison, and if the guards discovered any of these items, homemade or otherwise, they would be confiscated.
- All in-bound and outgoing mail was read by censors; incoming mail was delivered to the blocks on Thursday mornings, while outgoing mail was picked up on Saturday.
- Prisoners were responsible for keeping their own rooms and common areas of the blocks clean.
- Bar soap and laundry soap were delivered to the blocks for distribution about once each month.
- Disposable razors were given to each prisoner about once every three weeks for a period of two or three days.
- Radios and televisions were not allowed.
- Occasionally the police would deliver pails to the blocks so that the men could wash their clothes.
- Once a week one or two representatives from each block were allowed to go to the library to pick up Arabic and English-language books for men in their blocks.
- Outgoing telephone calls could only be made by inmates who had been arrested on money charges (forgery, writing checks with insufficient funds, theft, and embezzlement).
- Once or twice each day a nurse would come to distribute prescribed medicines and to give out simple things like aspirin to those with headaches or nausea.

Most often the rules were not followed and the prisoners did what they felt they had to do to get what they wanted.

If a prisoner needed to see the doctor or the dentist, he would theoretically have to give his name to the foreman who was supposed to prepare a daily list of those who wanted to receive medical attention. The foreman would then give those names to the nurse who came by the blocks around 7 a.m. and then returned to the clinic. There the names collected from all the blocks were scrutinized and persons who would be able to see the doctor that day were selected. A slip of paper was then distributed to each of the designated prisoners and that paper would serve as their pass for going to the clinic. It was the responsibility of the nurses to decide who would be chosen each day, and their choice, one would think, would depend on the severity of the symptoms displayed. What was really subjective about the whole process was trying to figure out who was faking and who actually needed medical help. Although each block might submit ten names or more, it was rare if more than three persons were picked from any single block.

Even the foremen took it upon themselves to screen the names that appeared on their lists. The fact that only a few men were selected led to the chaos that always ensued when the nurse came around to each block. Those whose names were on the list, those whose names didn't make the list, and an assortment of onlookers always gathered at the front gate waiting for the nurse to come each morning. And when he did show up, everyone had their sob story ready and waiting—everyone at the same time. The shouting and shoving and fighting were generally amusing to watch, and after a while, you got to know who really was sick and who wasn't. Even the police guards would get into the fray and start shouting at the prisoners, and sometimes, at the nurse when they disagreed with what he said. Most who were trying to see the doctor feigned illness so they would have a chance to get medicine or see their friends in other blocks along the way to the clinic. That often left seriously ill prisoners unattended.

Fortunately, I never had a problem in getting my name on the approved list to see the doctor. The nurses were for the most part Filipino and well educated, so they knew what was going on and tried to do their job as best they could under very trying circumstances. They respected me for not trying to abuse the system and knew that when I asked to see the doctor, there was good reason. There was never a time that I was refused a visit to the doctor on the day I requested.

Some of the prisoners had missed their calling as actors. One minute they might be roughhousing with us, and the next, when the nurse arrived, they displayed symptoms of illness close to the point of death. So, often I had to laugh with friends about the pathos of it all. One time later in my stay, a prisoner had tried for several days to see the doctor because he claimed he had chest pains and was having difficulty breathing. Each time the nurse came, he ignored his pleas to see the doctor. Unfortunately, he succumbed to a heart attack in the block after being ignored by the medical staff for five days. The man, an Indian, left behind a wife and several children. If only the family had known what had happened, they could have made a claim against the management of the prison and collected "blood money" from the government. In Arab countries it is common for the courts to award "blood money" as compensation to the victims' families in cases involving death, whether the death was intended or not. Compensation was usually paid in the amount of 150,000 Dirhams which was equivalent to approximately $41,000 in United States currency. For most people from the Indian subcontinent and Asian countries, that might have been more than they would earn in their lifetimes. If a prisoner was involved, even though he had served his sentence, he would not be released until the blood money was paid. As a result there were men lingering in prison for years with no hope of being released unless someone on the outside was able to come up with the money for them. Sometimes friends would pool their life savings to get those prisoners out of jail. Once in a while the victims' families would formally forgive the prisoners and waive the requirement to pay the blood money.

I noticed, too, that a few of the prisoners from my block left several mornings each week with notebooks and pencils in hand. When I checked, I learned that they were attending classes at the prison school. There were classes in English, Mathematics, Islam, and written Arabic. All classes were taught in Arabic, so that precluded my participation. The classes in English and Mathematics were very basic, so I would get nothing out of those anyway. But I had an interest in learning some Arabic and getting some information about Islam. It would be several months before I would get the chance to participate in those classes.

In talking with my roommates who attended the classes, I learned that the teachers were other prisoners. Most of those who attended were poorly educated and had one of three motives for attending. They either had a genuine interest in bettering themselves, they just wanted to go to the school and visit with friends from other blocks, or they wanted to escape the heat of the blocks for at least a portion of the day. Anyway, the issue of going to the school was a moot point in my estimation, since I believed I would be released in a very short period of time so there was no use in getting involved in something like that.

That first week was a fact-gathering opportunity, and I constantly planned how I would survive in a place like Al Wathba. Playing chess and exercising and talking to others were fine but not very productive.

My sense of easing into prison life was about to be jarred dramatically.

13

The First Few Weeks in Block 3

AFTER A FEW WEEKS, I SETTLED INTO a routine. I learned to cope with all the noises around me: the shouting between blocks, the fights, the guards blowing their whistles, and the bullying of prisoners. I learned to ignore the pandemonium over tea and food and the arguments over the outcome of card and chess games. I spent time reading novels, something I really hadn't done for several years. I was becoming used to sleeping on a few blankets over the concrete floor. And I was learning more about my fellow block-mates and why they had been put in prison.

It seemed that everyone had a story to tell and that each inmate was innocent of the crime for which he had been arrested. The number one question that would be asked of a new arrival, even before asking a person his name, was "What did you do?" or "Why are you here?"

Typical of the stories that didn't always stand up to the facts was one told by a Filipino fellow assigned to our block one day. He told us that he had been working as a retail sales clerk in a jewelry store along with several Filipino girls and that they had been unjustly accused of stealing.

The Filipino explained that it was standard operating procedure for retail clerks to record each transaction by providing a receipt to the customer for the purchase; the clerk would then sign the receipt. At the end of the day, the company accountant would collect the proceeds, post the transactions, and then deposit the money in the bank. After the books of the company were closed and audited at the end of each month, a check would be issued to the company's sponsor for his share of the profits.

To understand his story one must understand the logistics of how business was conducted in many Middle Eastern countries. In order to establish a business, one had to have a local sponsor. This sponsor owned at least 51% of the company and typically was a silent partner. Usually the running of the business was left up to the business owner who was responsible for keeping the 'local' up to date on the company's progress and who would pass on to him a share of the profits.

According to the Filipino, at the end of one rather good business month the accountant, an Indian, absconded with the month's proceeds. The sponsor was obviously upset with not receiving his income, and assuming that all the retail clerks were in on the plot, notified the police who subsequently arrested the clerks and had them thrown into prison despite their pleas of innocence.

That kind of story was not hard to believe, because it was something that happened on a regular basis. One does not cheat a 'local' when it comes to paying him his fair due since his accusations carry much weight in the eyes of the courts. But other people told me that his story just didn't hold up because it didn't match what had been written on his prison identification card, called a 'bataka' in Arabic. The cards were usually displayed in each room so any police officer who came by could scan them if he was looking for a particular person or wanted to verify some information. On the Filipino's card was written "having sex with a male." The Filipino would say only that the police had made a mistake in transcribing the information when his card was prepared. Later on, though, other inmates who were in court on the same day as he would tell me that his punishment was for male-male sex, and that he had been caught in bed with another man by the police. His sentence was eventually passed down as three years.

His initial story was typical of many who didn't want others to know their real crime. As so often happened, however, you would learn the real story later after making friends with other prisoners and gaining their confidence.

All of us both dreaded and looked forward to our appearances in court. You wanted your name to appear so you could get on with the trial process, but at the same time you were afraid of what the result might be. But going through the trial process was necessary in order to get out of prison whether or not you were convicted of an alleged crime. Stories were plentiful among the inmates regarding the fickleness of the system. If you believed them all, you would have a picture of a corrupt judicial system where sentences were passed down arbitrarily, the prisoners had no fair opportunity to defend themselves, and judgments were handed down in violation of the constitution.

It would not be long before I had a chance to experience the system first hand. Court days ranged from Saturday to Wednesday. Every afternoon prior to those days, the police would come to each block and give the foreman a list of prisoners who had to appear for court the next morning. When a prisoner knew his name was on the list, a visible change would come over him. There was a tightening of the body and the stress showed on his face as he began to prepare himself mentally for the strain of going before the judge. Some would go to court knowing this was only one of many appearances during the processing of their case; others knew that the next morning they would receive their sentence. Seldom could you rationally predict the verdict.

On the tenth day of my incarceration, my name again did not appear on the list and I went about my regular routine of reading and passing the time. That night at dinner, a policeman whom I had never met came over to me and told me that I had a court appearance the next morning. I was singled out and every one assumed that The American was being taken to court to be freed. I desperately wanted to believe that was true, and hoped that, indeed, the American Embassy staff had pulled strings that would set me free.

It was an anxious night for me. Sleep was difficult to come by as I worried what might be in store for me the next morning. I wanted to believe that the end of my incarceration was near. What else could this special summons mean? My spirits had been dampened, however, by the disconcerting attitude of the Embassy staff when they had come to visit me. Surely they wouldn't have been so pessimistic if they had felt that they could do something to get me out of prison.

Morning finally dawned, and the fellow responsible for making sure that those in the block going to court were up and ready came by to make sure I was awake. After a quick shower, I dressed in my prison clothes and went to the front gate to wait for the others to congregate. It was about 6:00 a.m. and all was very quiet since most prisoners were still sleeping.

Eventually, the prison guard came, opened our gate, and motioned for us to go downstairs to eat. About fifty prisoners were gathered for breakfast before heading off to the courthouse, but I didn't have much of an appetite and was very tense not knowing what the day would bring. Being fairly new in the prison, I attracted a great deal of attention as I entered the eating area. Everyone had heard about an American being in prison, and now they actually got to see him.

After we had eaten a quick breakfast, we were again herded upstairs and directed to the far end of the corridor near the library. There we were told to be seated and await further directions. For about forty-five minutes we sat while headcounts were conducted several times to make sure that the number of prisoners gathered was equal to the number assigned to put in a court appearance that day.

Smoking was prohibited, but as soon as the guards were out of the direct line of sight, cigarettes magically appeared. Our seating along the corridors was open to the outside air, so lit cigarettes were held at arm's length through the openings in the walls to minimize the smell of the smoke. Regardless, the guards soon became aware of the transgression and arguments ensued between them and the prisoners involved. After those confrontations settled down and the guards again retreated, the cigarettes came out again and the smoking resumed. What was happening was just one small example of the cat and mouse games that took place during my entire stay at Al Wathba prison.

Eventually, orders were given for us to form a line and proceed for further processing prior to boarding trucks for the ride to the courthouse. So we gathered in haphazard single-file and started our long walk down the corridor flanked on all sides by guards. One counted us as we left the waiting area. After a walk of about 300 meters we were stopped by more guards and ordered to form three single-file lines. One by one we were frisked and searched thoroughly as this would be our last physical check prior to arriving at the courthouse. If the uniform a prisoner was wearing wasn't clean or if his sandals had a metal buckle or a bright color, he was ordered to return to his cell and change. Those who passed through the search gathered at the far end of the hallway and waited for those prisoners who had been sent back to their blocks. Finally, when all was in order, we were told to follow a guard as we descended to the ground level.

All that was spoken was in Arabic, so I followed the crowd and hoped I was doing the right thing. A few who knew that I didn't understand translated for me and explained what was going on and what to expect next. At the bottom of the stairs was the cell that housed the gay male prisoners. It was apparent that many of those going to court knew many in the cell. They stopped to talk and slipped messages to them from prisoners in other blocks. Noticing this, the guards blew their whistles in an attempt to keep the lines moving. However, we were gathered now in a long narrow hallway, and when we lined up along both sides of it, the end of the line stretched all the way back to the cell where the guards were trying to control the prisoners.

At the head of the line were several guards who had a roster of those who were supposed to go to the courthouse. Eventually, the gate opened and one by one they called our names. All was in Arabic and I had to strain to listen for the names. When I heard mine, I approached the front of the line where they validated my identification card and checked my name off the list. Those whose names had been called assembled around the corner along another hallway parallel to the one in which we had just been waiting. This one led to the holding cell that had been my home for the first night I spent at Al Wathba. As we waited there, we could hear trucks being pulled up outside the building and the clanking of what seemed to be chains.

Finally, we were ordered to move along the corridor to the outside where we had to form a single line along the building. Three trucks, larger but similar to the one in which I had been hauled on the night of my arrest, were parked there, and it was obvious these were to be our transportation to the courthouse. The back of the truck was enclosed by wire mesh and along each side were two bench seats that appeared to be able to hold about ten persons each. Now, there were about five guards watching us and for the first time I saw guards with pistols at their sides.

The noise of chains that I had heard earlier had been made by shackles now heaped in three piles in front of us. Guards motioned us to come forward where we were shackled and returned to our spot in line along the wall. Once everyone was back in place, we were directed toward the trucks and one vehicle at a time was filled with prisoners. We were pushed in and squeezed together along the seats. In minutes all the prisoners were settled, headcounts were taken, and the doors at the back were padlocked shut.

After the guards were satisfied that we were all accounted for, the trucks moved out to the front gate where, one by one, another guard counted us again before the outside gate was raised to allow the trucks to leave the inner part of the prison. Each truck had a driver and a second armed guard riding in the front seat. There were no guards in the back enclosed area with the prisoners. Once the three trucks had moved past the gate, an SUV with four armed guards pulled up behind us and the convoy moved out of the prison.

As we drove out along the highway, it was refreshing to see the outside world again. There were very few vehicles because we were traveling back desert roads, but there were some camels and herders along the way. As we approached the main highway to Abu Dhabi, the guard vehicle went to the front of the convoy and stopped traffic along the highway so that the three truckloads of prisoners could stay together as they entered the traffic. Then for the next half hour we made our way to the courthouse.

During that time there was a good deal of talking among the prisoners, though for me and many others on this trip, the knot in the pit of our stomachs got tighter and tighter as we approached Abu Dhabi and our impending fate. It was apparent that some really didn't care or already knew what was in store for them. These men were very light-hearted about all that was happening, and many acted as if they were going to a picnic. Some broke off splinters of wood from inside the truck and were able to open the shackles and remove them during the ride. It seemed that the guards had not locked the chains and it was easy to trip the locking mechanism. Why they were not secured, I couldn't understand.

Eventually, we saw a sign that read Sharia Court and we could see the courthouse complex in the distance. I recognized it as the place where I had been brought for my interview with the Public Prosecutor. The three trucks pulled into the compound while bystanders stood and gawked at us. Some who had come there to attend court proceedings strained to find their friends or loved ones among us. The trucks moved into an area guarded by many policemen and backed up to the doors of one of the buildings. Shackled in single file and under heavy guard, we were marched into the courthouse and led to a holding cell which was a bare room approximately 15 feet square with walls about 15 feet high. There we found places to sit on the floor as a heavy steel door clanged shut behind us. Barred windows about three feet from the ceiling provided adequate sunlight and we were even able to see some sky.

Again, cigarettes appeared out of nowhere and one cigarette was shared by several prisoners. Most huddled in small groups at this point and talked quietly, concerned about what was going to transpire in just a few minutes. A few people whom I did not know came to ask my nationality and why I was there. My stomach tensed into knots and I was thankful that I had eaten and drunk little for breakfast and had used the bathroom facilities just before leaving the prison.

After about twenty minutes, the door was opened and a few men were taken either to the court or to see a judge in his chambers. The opportunity to ask to go to the bathroom or to use the telephone was not missed, and several prisoners rushed to the door and engaged in loud dialogue with the guards. A few were allowed to leave the room. The process was repeated several times in the next hour as more were summoned to the courtroom. Eventually, some of those called first were returned to the holding cell and it was obvious from their demeanor whether or not things had gone well. Some smiled while others were glum to the point of tears. No one that morning came back and said that they had been found innocent, but those who smiled indicated that their sentences were short enough that the time already served was equal to their sentence. Others had sentences ranging from a few months up to four years. My heart sank when I heard the duration of sentences that were handed out.

After waiting for close to two hours, the door opened and my name alone was called. I didn't know what to make of that, since many names at one time had been called previously. Perhaps it was a good sign and I was going to meet with a judge or the Embassy people and be released then and there.

But all hope faded immediately when I walked out the door and was greeted by one of the policemen I had met that first night at the Drug Enforcement office. He looked at me and asked, "Why did you leave the drugs in your refrigerator?"

14

Return to the
Public Prosecutor

Monday, November 2, 1998

I HAD REPLAYED OVER AND OVER in my mind all that happened during the night of my arrest and I had come to the conclusion that the police at the Drug Enforcement Center were trying to use the "good cop–bad cop" approach with me. This was the good cop and I knew instantly that he wanted to hear something like "Yeah, I shouldn't have put it there," but I was not about to placate him.

My reaction was quick and to the point: "What are you talking about?"

I was shackled. He led me slowly down corridors that looked familiar until finally we arrived at the office of the Public Prosecutor where I had been brought on the morning I was transferred to Al Wathba prison. In the hallway outside the office I recognized the two policemen who had driven me to the Public Prosecutor and eventually on to Al Wathba. My feelings of "good cop–bad cop" heightened as I realized now that that was exactly the kind of game they were trying to play with me.

My shackles were removed at the entrance to the office and I was ushered inside and seated by the desk along with the translator whom I had also met previously. The policeman left. I was not sure what to expect, but deep down I hoped that someone was going to tell me that, because of the small amount of cocaine that had been found in my bag, they were about to let me go. I had no idea what the policeman had been talking about.

It took only a few seconds for me to realize that things had just gotten a heck of a lot worse.

I was informed that my apartment had been searched. Apparently, it had also been sealed, for when ELS Language Centers wanted to use it again for someone else, the police insisted on another search prior to allowing them access. Through the translator I learned that the Public Prosecutor's office had found some incriminating things in my apartment. This information was disclosed as the officer placed a large brown envelope on the desk.

He opened the envelope and pulled out several items that I instantly recognized; some others I did not. There was another bottle of DHEA in the form of pills that still had the safety seal intact. Again, I explained the purpose of this life-enhancing hormone and indicated that it was freely available in stores throughout the area. I had bought mine in Jeddah, Saudi Arabia. Next was a candy dish that I had had on my living room coffee table. I admitted that I recognized it as mine, but, when he showed me the inside, my heart skipped a beat. There I saw a few butts from what looked like marijuana joints. I was numb. Where were the Hershey Kisses that I usually had in there? They asked me if the contents were mine and I said "No!" Then the Prosecutor produced a small bottle of what should have been hair shampoo that I had brought back with me from the Baron Hotel on one of my trips to Cairo. He took off the top and I looked in and saw what looked like a few twigs. I turned the little bottle upside down to try to get them out so I could see what they were and I was ordered to stop. When I said that I didn't know what the contents were, the Prosecutor claimed the bottle contained marijuana. I said, "I don't think so! I have no idea where that came from, but I do recognize the bottle as being similar to ones I brought back with me regularly from hotels where I have stayed." Then things got decidedly worse. The Prosecutor produced two small clumps of tin foil each about two inches long and about as thick as a regular pencil. He opened one and exposed a brown piece of what looked like a portion of a Kit Kat candy bar. He told me that it was hashish. At that I froze as if I had just been hit by a hammer. I denied any knowledge of what this was all about and had no idea where any of the alleged drugs had come from.

As the nightmare unfolded, my mind spun frantically trying to think how those objects could have been placed in my apartment. The only explanation that came to mind was that, prior to leaving for the vacation in Greece, I had arranged for my neighbors to take care of my plants while I was away. They were the only people except for my secretary who had access to my apartment. But were they responsible? Or was this just a ploy by the police to make things more serious for me by planting these items in my apartment?

At that moment, I thought the guilty parties had to be the two guys next door who were caring for my plants. But how could I be sure? So I didn't mention to the police that someone else had a key to my apartment. I just denied knowing about any drugs, though I did admit that the candy dish was mine and that the hair shampoo bottle was similar to those I often brought back from the Baron Hotel in Cairo.

I was told that the police had considered being easy on me after finding such a small amount of drugs in my bag at the airport. However, in light of what they found in my apartment, the charges became much more serious. I was informed that now the indictment would include dealing in drugs, importation, and possession of narcotics. Through the translator I said to the Public Prosecutor, "How can I be accused of dealing in drugs when I don't know anything about these things?" The translator quickly said "Touché!" *Was this all a test or what?*

I was numb and I was no doubt as pale as a ghost. Things had just gotten astronomically worse. I thought I was going to be sick right there in the office. The Prosecutor told me that this was all they wanted to talk about, and he called for the policeman to come in and take me out. Again I was shackled and led back to the holding cell. I didn't remember how much time had passed and was unaware of most of what was happening around me. All the confusion and shock of the night of my arrest had returned. My mind spun frantically as I tried to make sense of all that was happening.

When I was put back in the holding cell, the room was full again and it was apparent that everyone else had returned from their court hearings. Some prisoners asked me if I had been let go and all I could say was, "No, they just wanted to talk with me some more." I wasn't in much of a mood to communicate anything further since I still couldn't comprehend all that had just happened.

Soon we were herded out of the room and onto the trucks for the return trip to the prison. I didn't say a word the whole way back and I could tell from the expressions of others that their day hadn't been any better than mine. Some had obviously been crying, so I assumed that they had received their sentences that morning. All the conversation was in Arabic, and I didn't understand what the specific results of the court hearings had been.

The ride to Al Wathba was uneventful as I stared out through the mesh siding at the passing landscape. I couldn't help thinking that I wouldn't be out there walking free for a long while. I had lost track of time. I was in a state of shock and was totally overwhelmed by what was happening.

Once we arrived back at Al Wathba, we had to be searched again prior to being admitted inside the prison compound. As we pulled up to the main entrance, additional guards surrounded us. Still in shackles, we struggled out of the trucks. The gate was raised, and we passed into the area where we had stopped that morning for the final headcount. We formed lines facing that same gate which was made of a very thick iron mesh. Officers with keys to our shackles stood on the other side of the gate and one by one they put their hands through the mesh and unlocked our chains. As our shackles were removed, we were told to sit on the ground in three lines facing away from the interior of the prison.

Then three guards took their places at the back of the lines and began to search each prisoner in turn. We took off our shirts and sandals. They checked those and then thoroughly patted down the rest of our bodies looking for anything that might have been passed to us at the Courthouse. After each prisoner was cleared, he put his shirt back on and walked part-way across the prison grounds to the place where we had boarded the trucks that morning. There we sat on the curb, side by side and close to each other.

It was about 1:00 p.m. and it was very hot in the open. Across the yard I could see another guard approaching with a big dog. As he and the dog neared, I realized that the dog was going to sniff us for drugs. The dog made one pass along the front of us and then another behind. When that was completed we were told to stand and were led back inside the prison to our respective cell blocks.

As expected, everyone in the block wanted to know how the group of us had fared. All I said was, "They just wanted to talk some more." I walked to my room amid questions from all of my roommates. I was mentally and physically exhausted and told them I would talk with them later, but right now I needed to get some rest.

Sleep came quickly and I hoped I would wake up with the events of the morning having been just another bad dream.

15

Reality Sets In

EMOTIONAL EXHAUSTION BROUGHT ON a sound sleep that lasted until dinner time. My roommates had recognized the look on my face when I returned from court as one they had seen many times. They realized I just needed time to myself and graciously kept quiet all that afternoon so I could get a refreshing sleep.

Information spread quickly throughout the prison, but I decided that what had transpired was something I didn't want to share with anyone else for the moment. Many people asked what had happened and I shrugged it off with a comment that I had seen the Public Prosecutor and he had merely wanted a bit more information so they could complete their file. That seemed to satisfy most, but I realized that a few of the more savvy knew there was more to the explanation than what I was revealing. A smirk or a grin or just a short comment like "Yeah, okay. We'll talk some other time," was their response when they knew something more definitive had occurred in the Public Prosecutor's office earlier in the day.

Up until that day I had clung to the feeling that at any hour I would be called to the front gate and be told that I had been released. This was contrary to the pessimism that the Embassy people had conveyed in their last visit to me. But after a good sleep, the reality of my situation hit me and I knew that I'd better accept the fact that Block 3 was going to be my home for a while.

With that in mind, I decided that I had to become more a part of the Block 3 community and abandon any notion I'd had that I didn't need to mix with the other men because of my imminent release. So that evening I left my room and made a point of mingling with the others. On either side of my section were inmates from the Gulf States. Many were from the UAE itself, and being the better educated in the block, they knew English well. I joined one group of them who were gathered on the floor in the hallway. As I approached they were speaking Arabic, but as I paused and listened they asked me to join them and switched to English. Among this group was one named Said who was an airline maintenance mechanic and who had been arrested for possession and use of drugs. Another was an executive assistant in the office of one member of the Royal Family. There were four people who had been arrested in a hotel room because someone had informed on them while they were smoking hashish. All were employed in various government offices. Another had been arrested for fighting and indicated it wasn't his first time in the prison. His nickname was "Scarface," and it was obvious why he had been given that name. Another was the foreman of the block who had been arrested for having written a check on an account with insufficient funds. He was an attorney at the time of his arrest and had a good grasp of the legal system. Earlier I had seen him writing feverishly and later learned that he had been working on the preparation of his own defense.

Scarface was the clown of the group, and after initial introductions the rest encouraged him to show me one of his talents. He was able to imitate the sound of a mosquito perfectly. One person in the group was sleeping in spite of all the talk around him. So with his nimble fingers and vocal ability, Scarface set out to bother him by imitating the touch and sound of a mosquito. He got the usual reactions of a person trying to swat a fly in a state of deep sleep, and that caused ripples of laughter among the rest of us. That was the first time in weeks that I had laughed. It truly felt uplifting, and I realized that even in that awful place I could experience some light moments with friends. Because of that, I opened up and began to talk about a lot of things: the work I had been doing, where I lived, about life in the United States, and about the events surrounding my arrest.

They all concurred that, because I was an American, I would soon be released. For the first time I heard the story about an American woman who had been arrested along with her son for possessing a large quantity of marijuana. The judge in her case had eventually set her son free, but she was sentenced to ten years in prison. With the help of her lawyer and the American Embassy, I was told that an appeal had been launched and she was freed.

I was to hear that story many times during my stay at Al Wathba. I had already learned that rumors and gossip spread quickly, and that some stories gradually took on a life of their own and became believable just because of the number of persons who told the same tale. However, in talking with Embassy staff later, I learned the reason why this woman was freed. Even though she was one of a growing number of Americans who legally can use marijuana for medicinal purposes, her reason held little sway in the courts of the UAE. Drugs are drugs and the country has no law allowing the legal use of narcotics for medicinal purposes. She had been in a very serious automobile accident that left her face severely scarred. Many skin grafting operations had been necessary to improve her appearance and she had endured several years of pain and discomfort as a result. A portfolio of pictures had been put together showing her appearance immediately after the accident and each subsequent surgery, and they were presented by the Embassy staff and her family to members of the Royal Family. They took pity on her and she was granted a pardon. That hardly resembled my case, but until I learned the full details of why she had been released, I had held out hope that perhaps I, too, would not have to serve a long sentence.

In the same breath that people would tell me about the American lady who had been released, the Muslims would say, "If you convert to Islam, they will let you go and you'll be out of here in two weeks." This happened frequently in those first few days, but I realized that the claim was made by those less educated and less politically astute. Never once did any of the people from the Gulf States try to convert me because they understood the rules of the land and knew that one's conversion to Islam had nothing to do with granting an early release. I would learn later, however, that there was the tendency among some in the judicial system to act on such a conversion. Especially in high-profile cases like mine, they could garner publicity and use that person to propagate Islamic beliefs while putting down his former religion. But the possibility of a release being based on a conversion to Islam was only speculation, and I never saw any evidence of it during my time at Al Wathba.

All forms of games were forbidden by the prison administration at Al Wathba. But this only inspired the creativity of the inmates. Any games that we had were made by the prisoners and hidden from the police. Decks of playing cards were fashioned from the cardboard containers in which our laundry soap came; domino pieces were crafted from the tops and bottoms of cigarette packs; and game boards were made from white T-shirts or other white materials. Periodically, these would all be confiscated by the police during inspections, but within days new ones would appear.

Although games were forbidden, periodically someone would organize a chess competition involving eight to twelve persons. These would always include other Gulf Arabs and Egyptians and always exclude Asians and those from the Indian subcontinent. Within a few days I found I was repeatedly challenged by other inmates. I hadn't played chess since college almost thirty years earlier, and even then I had played very little. But it was a good way to pass the time and I eagerly accepted the opportunities offered.

I learned the "prison rules," and got down to playing some serious matches.

Usually a crowd would gather around to see how The American was faring in a contest where the pressure of the games turned into an Arab–American or Asian–American confrontation. Whenever I was beaten, my opponent became a minor hero. A win for the Arabs was a real morale booster because they had proved themselves to be better than an American. I encouraged their moments of jubilation, since I understood how important that success was for them considering what little else they had in life. Whenever one of them won, it gave others who had been watching on the sidelines more confidence.

These activities fostered great camaraderie among my block mates, and because of those games I was soon to be challenged in many other things throughout my stay at Al Wathba. It was important for my fellow prisoners to hold bragging rights that said they had beaten an American, whether in exercising or in playing a game. Very often I felt that I had to uphold the strength and honor of my country in whatever I was doing.

The chess pieces were something that I really admired, for they were all made by prisoners using bread smuggled back to the blocks from meals. Different colored inks from ballpoint pens were used for coloring highlights; jam and cigarette ashes provided coloring for the pieces themselves. They were marvelous works of art. Eventually I would find myself sharing a room with the person who crafted most of the pieces for the entire prison.

Most Asians and Indians played board games. One was a version of Parcheesi and others were variations of games I had played years earlier as a boy. The Arabs, however, aside from chess and card games, enjoyed more physical contests. In the evenings there would always be one room where some of those physical competitions were held. One was a contest involving four people where each person selected a piece of paper on which was written either "Police," "Juror," "Witness," or "Judge." By asking questions of each other, they had to guess who held the "Police" slip. If someone guessed incorrectly, then he would be subject to whatever retribution the wrongly accused person desired. Otherwise, if he guessed correctly, he could dole out the punishment to the person with the "Police" slip. The punishments took the form of vicious beatings on the soles of the feet, smearing toothpaste over one's face, or the like. The other favorite game was set up with one person standing with his back to several others. One of those positioned behind would then aggressively strike him hard on the side and the person hit would have to guess who had done it. They only had one guess per hit. If he guessed correctly, the person caught would then have to take his place. In both games the physical hitting or humiliation often got the better of the person on the receiving end and fights would break out. Then, once again, the police would come, separate the parties, and demand that the games stop. They would stop for a night or two and then resume.

The first-time penalty for being caught smuggling bread or any food back to the block was public humiliation. Prisoners were handcuffed to the bars near the dining area with their hands high above their heads, their feet barely able to touch the ground. There they were left on display during the entire lunch hour so that prisoners from all the blocks could see them. Second and ongoing offenses led to any of several punishments: time in solitary, loss of sports' privileges, cessation of visitation rights, or public flogging. In spite of all the possible consequences, apples, oranges, and lots of bread always ended up back in the blocks. Desperate people do desperate things.

Arabs and non-Arabs, especially those from the Gulf States and Egypt and those from Pakistan and India, were separated within our block. This was a reflection of life on the streets of Abu Dhabi where those from India, Pakistan, Bangladesh, and Sri Lanka were allowed to come to the country as the "hired help." They were the ones who toiled as truck drivers, maids, office boys, servants, nannies, gardeners, street cleaners, taxi cab drivers, domestic help in hotels, and waiters. They were paid menial salaries for their work and were looked down upon as unworthy of any respect—even from their Arab brothers.

I was housed in a room with prisoners primarily from India and Sri Lanka and I felt a real kinship with them throughout my entire stay at Al Wathba. For the most part they were kind, gentle, caring, and friendly people who respected *me* and those around them. The number of people in my room swelled to thirty-four at one point, and we were packed in like sardines without an empty space on the floor. But in spite of all the overcrowding, we generally got along without fights or harsh words being spoken. It was these people who invited me to join them at meals and who would share any food or material goods they had with me.

I never felt the kinship in those early days with the Gulf Arabs that I did with my non-Arab roommates. Perhaps this lack of connection was spawned by my dealings in the business world as I had worked side by side with them in my positions with the ELS Language Centers. My administrative staff at ELS in Kuwait was entirely non-Arab, as was the case at our Head Office in Abu Dhabi. Never once was there any conflict between them and me. They were hard working, honest people who had an excellent work ethic, and they went out of their way to make me feel welcome. I could always count on them to help out when I needed extra effort on a project.

My business dealings with Arab people were no less harmonious and I met almost daily with Arabs in important government and military positions. We generally got along splendidly, and in many instances they helped me get my governmental paperwork processed quickly. Friendly and cordial to me, some became my friends and invited me to their homes.

So, in my time in Block 3 I had several distinct groups of friends that never mingled with one another. When problems arose, it was generally among persons within the same group.

One of the reasons that the groups never mingled was that Block 3 was primarily a holding block for persons awaiting their sentences. Consequently, there was a lot of movement in and out as persons were either released or transferred to other longer-term blocks after sentencing. The only time that conflict seemed to arise among the different groups in the block was when it came time to select a foreman. Each group wanted someone from their own friends to be chosen. This way, they would get the best representation with the guards and be able to exert control, though minimal, over the day to day activities.

The block foreman was responsible for maintaining order within the block, ensuring that the common areas were kept clean, keeping accurate lists of the prisoners housed within the block, and assigning men to specific rooms. He circulated information from the police including changes in procedures and court assignments. He arranged lists of those who wanted to subscribe to newspapers, distributed the mail on Thursdays, and advised the police of general needs and complaints. There were no benefits to the job, but being foreman was a matter of pride and importance. Frequently competition for the position led to violence.

The foreman was usually chosen by the police, but occasionally was selected by the inmates themselves. When it came time for a new foreman to be elected, names would be submitted to the guards who would usually reduce the number to two or three. Once that happened, campaigning would begin in earnest for several days prior to the voting. During that time much discussion would take place, since each group felt that they would be discriminated against in the block if someone from another group became the foreman. Many instances arose where discussions turned into loud verbal accusations followed by physical confrontations. As soon as the first punch was thrown, chaos would erupt as others joined in the melee and brawls ensued. Quickly guards would rush into the block and if instigators were identified they were either ordered to stop the fighting or they were removed from the block to be questioned or put in solitary confinement. I always kept my distance from such brawls and never took sides in the altercations. It seemed to me that the foreman actually had little authority apart from the responsibility to keep accurate lists of persons in the block, to organize cleaning crews, and to deal with petty squabbles. Other than that, the foreman seemed to have no benefits thrown his way by the prison administration. It all seemed to come down to having authority and power over others..

One night an Egyptian named Mohammed sought me out and asked if I would help him with his English in return for his helping me with Arabic. My Arabic was pitiful and his spoken English was fair, so we could communicate. For many nights following, we met and coached each other in trying to learn the nuances of each other's native tongue. There were variations between the Arabic he was teaching me and the little Arabic I had learned during a few sessions at the British Council while in Kuwait. Also, when I practiced the Arabic he taught me on other prisoners, they would tell me that what he told me was wrong and that their way was better. I would learn that each country had its own version of Arabic, but, if you learned the Egyptian version, everyone seemed to be able to understand it. As my teacher in Kuwait had told me, "Egyptian Arabic is the classic Arabic." Now I believed him. Eventually, trying to learn Arabic became extremely frustrating because no one seemed to agree on a common version. This all tied in, however, with a realization that Arabs in one country think they are superior to Arabs in another country. Their language differences were one way they used to hold themselves apart from other Arabs.

During this time too, a couple of Moroccans were assigned to my block. One in particular became a good friend. His English was about as good as my French so we each developed a plan to meet every evening after dinner to talk in each other's first language for practice. I enjoyed that intellectual exchange, and since he had an interest in astrology, one of my tasks each night was to interpret in French his astrological sign of the day. My skills in Arabic never approached those I had in French.

Thus, a routine developed that consisted of going for meals, sleeping, reading, playing chess, and talking with my friends as I tried to improve my Arabic and French.

16

Word from Home

MY ONLY CONTACT WITH THE WORLD outside of Al Wathba had been limited to contacts with the American Embassy. And it was through them, during a visit to me on October 28, that I got the first direct word from my family and friends.

During that visit Charlie Glatz, the Consular Official at the Embassy, read a fax he had received a day earlier from my brother Richard in Toronto. Richard wrote:

> Sorry for the delay in sending a communication to you, but we have been trying to organize support for you and I have not had a chance to send you a message earlier. Needless to say we spent a number of stressful days when Dad phoned me in the middle of the night on 10 October, 1998 to say you were missing. Contacts with the ELS office, US Embassy, hotel in Greece, RCMP, and Canadian External Affairs were made and then we waited. It was a relief to hear that you were okay but I must say we were mad that you put us through this ordeal. However, rest assured that your family loves you and we are prepared to assist you in any way to get through this challenge. Dad is in good spirits but this is and will be an ordeal for him until the case is settled.

> Susanne has contacted some of your friends in Florida and they are totally committed to assist us in any way they can.
>
> Please give the U.S. Embassy staff in Abu Dhabi our thanks for their tremendous support and assistance since your incarceration. They have been extremely helpful to us and have kept us informed of your status and any issues concerning your case.
>
> Mr. Ibrahim Al Tamimi the lawyer you selected has apparently talked with the U.S. Embassy staff and hopefully by now has reviewed your case and possibly met with you. I attempted to talk to him once. I was informed he was your choice but due to language difficulties we were unable to talk very much. He attempted to get a lawyer friend involved who could speak English but after a number of conversations nothing seemed to happen. Finally the U.S. Embassy indicated that they had talked with Mr. Tamimi. We have sent a US $1,000.00 retainer to him via Western Union. Please confirm that he has received this amount and ask him to communicate with us what his fee will be to represent you. I have a colleague at work who speaks Arabic so if necessary I can communicate with him through a translator.

Richard then went on to tell me about the support expressed by friends and family. Jim Garrett, a close friend in Orlando, spoke for all when he said, "All your friends in Florida are thinking of you and still love you. We are prepared to assist you in any way." Belinda, my secretary at ELS expressed her support, and all of my friends at the ELS' head office in Abu Dhabi hoped that I would walk through the office door sometime in the near future.

I was deeply touched by what I had heard. It was like a door had been opened to my tomb and I was able to breathe fresh air for the first time in weeks. Now I knew that my family and friends were doing what they could to secure my release. Whether they were successful or not, I felt I was a very lucky person at that moment to have the backing of all those I loved.

Now I was anxious to get things moving and work on my defense so I could go home. I urged the Embassy staff to contact Mr. Tamimi and tell him I wanted him to visit me at the prison so we could plan our strategy. They assured me that they would and I felt a little relief.

I questioned them about any support that I could expect from Sheikhs Khalid and Shaya, the men for whom I worked. I was told that I should expect no help from them because the case was drug-related and they did not want to get involved. This was a disappointment. I had counted on some intervention from them because I had worked hard and we had made excellent progress in bringing more and more ELS schools to a point of profitability. We were also developing plans to expand the number of schools. To hear that they wouldn't help me was a blow, and I cried in disbelief at the news. The Embassy told me they would keep in contact with the Sheikhs and perhaps they would have a change of heart. I knew that they were close friends of the Royal Family and a recommendation seeking my release would most likely have had a positive response. So now it appeared that it was up to my family and friends to obtain my release. Otherwise, I could be spending a long time locked up in Al Wathba.

My meeting with the Embassy was bittersweet. On the one hand I was thrilled to get news from my brother Richard, but on the other I was deeply saddened by the lack of willingness on the part of the Sheikhs to help me.

I knew that my incarceration had created a stressful and uncertain time for all those who cared about me, but I felt it would take the biggest toll on my father. My father and I were the closest of friends and we had shared many an intimate discussion. When I had last seen him at my mother's funeral, he was a very young looking eighty-six-year-old man who swam several mornings each week, was active in church work, and loved to travel and visit with family and friends. My situation would place a heavy burden on him and I prayed that I would get to see him again.

Although my father relied on my brothers to lead the way in trying whatever they could to secure my release, he was not about to sit back and wait for things to happen. On November 7 he wrote a letter to the American Embassy in Abu Dhabi in which he laid out the things that he wanted answered. He made an emotional plea for them to help free me so that he could see me before his life ended. He wrote,

> *We want Paul to know that all the family members are praying for him and even if all charges prove to be correct we still love him and want to do everything we can to help restore him to a normal life. We will need your help in letting us know just what the best way there is to assist Paul in his hour of need.*
>
> *I am 86 years of age and would dearly love to see my son alive again.*

Without considering the consequences to his own health, he offered to come and stand with me at my trial if that would help. He wrote,

> *Would it help Paul's cause if an immediate member of his family were present—brother Richard, daughter Jennifer, or myself?*

On November 17 the Embassy staff visited me again. They confirmed that it was unlikely Sheiks Shaya and Khalid would help me and that we would have to rely on the skill of my attorney, Mr. Tamimi, to get me freed or at least minimize my sentence. They also cautioned me that I should not expect to be in front of a judge any time soon for it generally took from three to five months for drug cases to begin. I was adamant that Mr. Tamimi come to visit me and I urged them again to pass that message on to him.

Back at the Embassy on the afternoon of November 17 Charles Glatz responded to my father's letter. In part he wrote,

> *My colleague, Mr. Jamal A. Bafagih, and I visited with your son, Paul, this date at the Al Wathba Central Prison outside Abu Dhabi. Paul was in good health and spirits. He told us that he had two colds since we last visited him, but he appeared fit. Paul is adapting well to his incarceration and has developed a regular daily physical and intellectual program to cope. He told us that he exercises, reads, and teaches English to some of his fellow prisoners. Paul has not reported to us any mistreatment.*

> *Paul's case now lies with the Presidential Diwan and will soon be referred to the Islamic Sharia Court for trial. Paul's charges are three-fold: 1)Possession of narcotics, 2) Importation of narcotics, and 3) Use of narcotics. Paul might face a prison sentence of between 8 and 12 years and fines of up to $14,000.*
>
> *There is no extradition treaty between the United Sates and the UAE so Americans who committed crimes in the UAE have to serve their prison sentences here.*
>
> *This morning, we again raised with Paul the topic of a family member's travel to the UAE. We concur with Paul's decision that any travel to the UAE by a family member be postponed for now. Trials take months to conclude and it is Paul's wish that, if a family member travels to the UAE, it is best that he/she attends the final sessions where sentencing will occur.*

How distraught my eighty-six-year-old father must have been when he received that letter. A sentence of eight to twelve years! That was a lifetime for him!

But the Embassy was right in being honest about the possibilities.

17

Getting the Message Out

I KNEW THAT THERE WAS A LOT OF speculation among my family and friends about the circumstances surrounding my arrest, my treatment in the hands of the authorities, and what the future held for me. As in other instances where there are so many unknowns, a difficult situation can be more stressful for those removed from it than for those actually going through the ordeal. Thus, I felt I had to get a message to them.

One of the things I had asked my Embassy to bring was stamps. It was frustrating to have to rely on them for so many of the things I needed, and something as simple as getting a stamp could be stressful. I would have to ask for them on one Embassy visit and wait five to seven weeks for the next visit. Then, if they forgot, I would have to wait even longer. In the meantime some friends gave me stamps. Knowing that most were very poor and that postage to the U.S. was $1.50 in U.S. currency, it was a very generous gift that they offered me time and time again. Finally, rather than ask someone for a stamp to the U.S., I was able to obtain one for $.35 that would allow me to send a letter locally.

I had been warned by fellow prisoners that all outgoing and incoming mail was censored for content, so I had to be careful what I said in my letters. I would learn over the following months just how much one could actually get away with in talking about life in prison. Generally, if one didn't disparage the government, legal system, prison officials, living conditions, and the food, letters would find their way to their intended destination.

I chose to send my first letter to my colleague James Ward, the Director of Academic Affairs for ELS Language Centers in Abu Dhabi and ask him to e-mail it to someone who would then distribute my message widely among my family and friends.

James had the responsibility for developing curricula for our Centers and ensuring that the Centers conformed to the standards set by ELS International for the Centers worldwide. He had an office next to mine and we had developed a fine working relationship and a mutual respect for each other's talents. We often traveled to other Centers together, and without a doubt, we had been instrumental, along with our Managing Director, in strengthening our position in the Middle East as a premier organization for the teaching of English as a second language.

It was natural for me to turn to James in my difficulty and he didn't disappoint me. In addition to making sure my family and friends got my communiqués, he handled my financial affairs by making sure that my brother Richard received copies of my bank and credit card statements so my payments could be kept up to date and my funds transferred to Toronto.

So I wrote the following to James in mid November 1998:

> As you know, I came to the Middle East to experience a new culture, do some traveling, and live as an expatriate for a while. All of those I have done but now find myself experiencing life in prison, something that has never crossed my mind.
>
> Through a series of events, the start of which was not of my doing, I am awaiting a court hearing that will give me my freedom or otherwise keep me here for some time.
>
> The American Embassy has been my only personal contact with friends and family. They have been supportive and yet honest regarding the possibilities. Your messages of support relayed by them through my brother in Toronto have buoyed my spirits more than you can ever imagine.
>
> The days move fast as I try to keep busy:
> 1. *Catching up on lots of reading of novels*
> 2. *Studying Arabic—lots of help there*

3. *Teaching English*
4. *Organizing exercise classes and teaching them*
5. *Participating in sports events twice a week*
6. *Improving my chess game*
7. *Reading the daily English newspaper*
8. *Improving my French with the help of a group of prisoners from Morocco*

My massage skills have enhanced my status here. There are a lot of aches and pains to work on and stress to relieve. In payment for my services, my needs are provided: towels, toiletries, an extra apple or orange for lunch, paper, etc. Everyone is nice and I am not mistreated.

This is the challenge of my life and I need your continued support and prayers. I take care of myself mentally and physically and my faith in God makes everything OK. In many ways I know this ordeal is more traumatic for you than for me, but I pray that God will grant you the peace to accept what is. This is neither a country club nor the "hole" that you may have seen in the movies. I have all the comforts—access to daily showers, lots of fresh water and fresh air. Yesterday we were given shavers for the day and I had my first shave in three weeks—glorious!

In America I would be a free man but things are different here. Before you go to bed tonight, just say a prayer of thanks for the privilege of living in a country where you truly have the freedoms you do.

All that can be done is being done. A note to your congressman or mine (Bill McCollum in Orlando, I think) on my behalf can do no harm.

I wish all of you good health and happiness. My memories of our times together are like movies I play over and over again in my mind. God Bless!"

I sent a separate letter to my brother Richard. The letter was identical except for the last paragraph. In his letter I wrote:

Richard, I can't tell you how much your concern for me and efforts on my behalf have meant. I've always looked up to you and love you so much. I am really sorry for all the hurt I've caused everyone. Tell Dad not to worry—I know he must be having just a terrible time right now. I pray for him and all of you. Everything will work out OK. God Bless!

Actually, things weren't quite as rosy as I had let on, but I knew to detail the problems I was facing would complicate the frustration and stress felt by those trying to help me from so far away. The uncertainty of my future was nerve-racking. Not being able to communicate directly with friends and family created a loneliness I hadn't experienced in a long time. The spontaneous acts of cruelty perpetrated by police and the acts of violence exhibited by other prisoners left me feeling insecure and vulnerable. Often I felt as if I were drowning. Only when the embassy staff came to visit, was I able to come up for a gulp of air before again dipping down below the surface and into the hideous life of the prison.

18

Meeting with My Lawyer

ON TUESDAY DECEMBER 1, I WAS aroused from my reading by the foreman who had come to tell me that the police wanted to see me at the front gate. He told me that I should put on my prison uniform because they wanted me to go with them.

I found this rather strange because it was a Tuesday. I knew the Embassy staff wouldn't be there to see me, and Tuesday wasn't a visitation day for friends and family so I wondered what had come up. Again, the only rational explanation was that I was to be released. I was going to be taken to the administrative area and told that I was a free man.

As in so many other instances, I was to be proven wrong. I was led upstairs, and after being frisked, I was motioned toward the visitation area. Still wondering who was coming on a Tuesday to see me, I turned toward the area where I had previously met with the Embassy staff. Instantly, the guard behind me said something in Arabic that indicated I was going in the wrong direction. When I turned around, he motioned me to follow him into a small room that was about eight-foot square and had a small table and two chairs. He motioned for me to sit, which I did still wondering what this was all about.

The guard left and shortly I heard the sound of people talking. Two rather large men dressed in disdashas appeared. I rose to meet them but was told to sit by the guard who accompanied them. One sat directly across the small table from me and the other sat to the side. The gentleman at the side told me in rather poor English that the man across from me was my attorney, Mr.

Ibrahim Al Tamimi, and that he was a friend who had come along to help with the translation. He told me that the Embassy had relayed a message that I was upset that Mr. Al Tamimi had not come to see me, and that they wanted to meet with me to discuss the charges that would be brought against me.

Mr. Al Tamimi spoke hesitatingly in broken English and with the help of his friend, I was able to understand the reality of what he was trying to say. He told me that the charges being brought against me by the Public Prosecutor were several: possession of drugs, use of drugs, importation of drugs with the intent to distribute, and drug trafficking. He told me that these charges were based upon the evidence that they had collected: the police finding .0659 gm of cocaine in my bag at the airport, my urine test being positive for the use of cocaine, police finding 28 gm of hashish in my apartment along with a small amount of marijuana. He told me that the charges were very serious and went on to outline the possible sentences if I were convicted on each offense.

Basically, he told me that my sentence would likely be somewhere from seven to twenty years!

In that instant a million thoughts crowded my mind: it was the end of my life, I'm going to die in the prison; I'll never see my friends and family again. The nightmare that started in October just kept getting worse. Again, the feeling of total helplessness overwhelmed me.

Mr. Al Tamimi told me that he would review all the documentation available for the case, including my sworn statements to the police and Public Prosecutor, and decide on what strategy he would follow. He said that the search of my apartment was illegal, but he would have to convince the judge of that. If he were able to do so, then the main charge would be the use of drugs. He thought that the charge of importing for the purpose to distribute would not be considered because of the small amount of cocaine that was found in my luggage. Still, he told me, a sentence of seven to twenty years was probable and that I should be prepared for that inevitability.

That was the last thing that really sank into my mind, and from this point on I was only remotely aware of what transpired. Finally, Mr. Al Tamimi got up and he and his friend left the room. I was dumbstruck.

That was our meeting. All five minutes of it! Incredibly, Mr. Al Tamimi had never asked me about my version of the events, nor had he discussed any of the evidence gathered against me—then, or at any time during the trial period!

After my lawyer and his translator departed, the guard motioned for me to get up and follow him back to the block. I remember thinking during that long walk back that my situation was totally hopeless; they should just take me outside and shoot me right then and there. That was another of the low points of my stay at Al Wathba. Any thought of an early release had effectively been obliterated.

19

The First Holidays Behind Bars

Thanksgiving to Christmas 1998

MEETING WITH MY LAWYER AND getting his dismal news created a cloud of despair that hung over me for a few days. I focused as best as I could on getting through each day and coming out of the ordeal mentally and physically intact.

A few weeks earlier I had celebrated Thanksgiving behind bars without friends, family, and a hearty meal. What I didn't forget, however, was to thank God for all the blessings he had bestowed on me in the past and was continuing to shower on me each day. On that Thursday I was very aware of how I had been protected and blessed throughout all my years, and I prayed that the future would unfold in a good way for me and that I would soon be released. When I thought about Thanksgiving at home, I grew despondent, but I wouldn't let it drag me down and drown me in sorrow. Instead, I decided that I had a life here; that I had to continue to fight for my freedom and take care of myself mentally, spiritually, emotionally, and physically.

Our only real contact with the outside world on a daily basis was the newspaper. There were two English-language papers that were widely circulated in Abu Dhabi. One was the *Gulf News*, a paper published in Dubai, and the other, *The Khaleej Times* published in Sharjah. Both had their pros and cons, but the one I favored was the *Gulf News*. It had more American news and sports coverage and even had a column on the editorial page written by American journalists six days of the week. The syndicated column featured such well-known writers as Dan Rather and William

Safire. But my favorite over the years was Elizabeth Schuett. Unlike Rather and Safire who wrote mostly political and social commentary, Elizabeth wrote about the ordinary: her acquaintances, stories about life "the way it used to be," reminiscences about her own past, or discussions she had had with friends over coffee. She wrote about typical things that happened in all families with children and described unique places in the country like Cedar Key, Put-in-Bay, and Amelia Island. Whenever I saw her column, I would save it for a special moment when I could read it at leisure, take in all that she had to say, and let my mind wander to the places she would take the reader. Her columns were a delight to read and a nice diversion from life at Al Wathba.

The two things you could usually expect to see on the front page of the *Gulf News* were a story and picture about someone in the Royal Family and an article about the United States in relation to some happening in the Middle East. More often than not, the article featuring the United States spoke of its perceived, alleged, or actual support of Israeli actions against the Palestinians and by extension against the Arab world.

But in November, 1998 the articles about the United States were about the visits to the UAE of several political leaders from the United States. Former President George Bush visited the UAE for several days and had conferences with His Highness Sheikh Zayed bin Sultan Al Nahyan. One of those conferences was at Sheikh Zayed's Wathba palace less than two miles from the prison where I was incarcerated. Pictures on the front page of the *Gulf News* showed him riding a jet ski in the waters off the coast and meeting with Sheikh Zayed. When I first saw the pictures and read about his conferences, my heart raced with hope that he would have said a word on my behalf. That was all it would have taken for me to be released. Sheikh Zayed would have considered it a small gesture of friendship to honor a request from a man he revered to release one of his country's citizens from a UAE prison. I waited eagerly in anticipation of a call authorizing my release, but former President Bush left the country and I was left behind. Over the course of the following few weeks, the UAE was again visited by top U.S. dignitaries: former President Jimmy Carter and Defense Secretary William Cohen; there was also a lengthy telephone call between Secretary of State Madeline Albright and Sheikh Zayed. I read about each arrival hoping that just one of these United States' officials would say something to Sheikh Zayed about my imprisonment in Al Wathba, but nothing happened. My hopes would be buoyed only to sink into another temporary mood of depression and followed by anger against my government. Never again during my stay at Al Wathba would so many influential American leaders have the ear of the President as they did in November, 1998. I was frustrated that I could not contact the Embassy staff to have them relay my plight to those dignitaries, and I was angry at my country for not using the opportunities to have me released.

During this time I got my first letter from my friend Jim Garrett in the United States, and in reply to him I expressed my frustration and dissatisfaction with my government:

> *It was a real surprise to get your note. I didn't know if my notes to others to send e-mail had gotten through or not. My only contact with Americans is the staff at the American Embassy. They have not been to see me for over three weeks, so your letter helped bring me out of the doldrums. They are nice people but haven't taken any bold moves that would have minimized this whole affair. Their main task is processing visas so I get attention as time allows but they have done some great work for me for which I am truly grateful.*
>
> *Most of my news comes from the English language newspaper. It has been frustrating to see that over the last four weeks Madeline Albright had a lengthy telephone call to Sheikh Zayed (the ruler) and there were state visits by William Cohen, Jimmy Carter, and George Bush. And yet here I sit while, according to the Embassy, we are holding no Emiratees in U.S. jails, even though their presence there far outnumbers the number of Americans here. I have no idea how well briefed these people have been but I have to wonder why Bush wouldn't have welcomed the opportunity to get some good publicity for his son Jeb, governor-elect of Florida. I would gladly have done a press conference or held a photo-op with him and given him all the credit for getting me out of here. Just in case he isn't aware, could you contact his office for me so he knows for the future? On a similar note the two Sheikhs for whom I worked are best*

friends with Sheikh Zayed and a word from them would end this. But so much for loyalty. The prodding by me and the Embassy so far hasn't budged them.

I have a local lawyer whom I have met and I feel confident that he will be able to help me somewhat. Realistically though I am preparing myself mentally for a long stay but am cautiously optimistic as I listen between the words of both the Embassy staff and my lawyer that some things can be done only after the sentence is handed down. As well, we just got a new Ambassador who has not yet presented his credentials to Sheikh Zayed so there is another opportunity. I cling to these opportunities and look to the next as they pass by.

As I wait for my trial I try to remain positive and use my time productively. I have good camaraderie with the other inmates and ironically I have learned more about the peoples and their cultures in the past two months than I did in the previous sixteen. I know I have disappointed many, especially my family. Regardless, like you, they stand behind me and I thank God for that. There are mornings I awake thinking it has all been a bad dream—until I see the bars!

I knew that my predicament was difficult for those who knew and cared about me. Movies had been made about Americans being held in foreign prisons and the atrocities that they had witnessed and were subjected to. I was sure that my friends and family conjured up in their minds similar circumstances for me at Al Wathba and worried constantly about my wellbeing. I felt I had to allay their anxieties by being strong and letting them feel that I was coping with the situation and that all my needs were being taken care of. Especially, though, I worried about my father since he was dealing with my mother's recent death as well as my incarceration.

I had given my father a copy of Redfield's *The Celestine Prophecy* about three months earlier and we had since discussed parts of the book and debated how relevant or realistic the author's ideas were. One of those topics dealt with 'coincidences' and I alluded to that in my first letter to him:

Thanks for the nice note you sent to me via the Embassy. Let me just say your trust is not misplaced as we can discuss when this is over.

Ever since reading "The Celestine Prophecy" I've looked at coincidences in a new light. I often wonder about the coincidences that happened to land me here and the coincidence of it happening right after Mom's funeral. With regard to the latter, I wonder if this is God's way of helping us to handle the grief by giving us something else to occupy our minds and time. As to why me and why I'm in this place, I can tell you I've learned more about peoples and cultures in the past two months than I have in the previous eighteen. I've found recently that a lot of the things I wish for have come true—scary! Now if my wish to get out of here would just come true.

Thankfully, my days pass quickly—reading, sleeping, some exercise, discussion, thinking, eating, some massages, etc. Most days are okay but I get frustrated and somewhat depressed at times. In the past month alone I've read where Madeline Albright (Secretary of State) talked with Sheikh Zayed (ruler of the country) and then William Cohen (Secretary of Defense) was here as was Jimmy Carter and tomorrow George Bush meets with Sheikh Zayed. You would think that one of them would ask for help for me. I'm looking anxiously to my court appearance and sentencing as I understand that if any intervention will take place it will be after that.

Although I missed Thanksgiving it wasn't as hard as I expected. The others here are all quite friendly and we act as family for each other. As much as I enjoy Christmas and the holidays I don't let myself reflect too much on them and know there will be others we will share together.

Take comfort in the fact that I am treated well, sleep well and am taking care of myself. This will all pass and we'll have lots to talk about. I keep you all in my prayers as I know you do me. I hope to see you soon.

Have a nice Christmas and take care of yourself. I know you worry about me but God is watching that I come out of this okay.

In the letter to my father I had alluded to the fact that many of the things I had wished for had come true:
- I had wished that while living in the Middle East I would have time to go to Morocco and learn about life there and use the time to improve my French.
- I had wished that I had more time to read books.
- Because of all my travels I had not met many local residents. I had wished to learn more about their lives and country and to establish friendships.
- I had wished that I had more time to learn Arabic.
- I had wished that I would have the time to learn first hand about life in various African countries.

In a way, all of those wishes had come true for me in Al Wathba! I had the time to read and study Arabic. I had met people from Morocco and we had discussed at length the geography and culture of the country. I practiced French with them. I had met people from Africa and learned about their countries and culture from them. And there were lots of men from the Gulf States who had given me first-hand accounts of life in their countries, their feelings about their government and their aspirations for the future. Within the course of a few months I had discovered more about different peoples and cultures of the region than I had ever expected to. Perhaps I should have been a bit clearer when writing my wish list by stipulating that I didn't want an experience in prison to provide the backdrop for all those opportunities!

Because the other inmates had learned that I was a certified personal trainer in the United States, a few of them who had been working out by themselves asked me to help them develop an exercise regimen. That was an invitation I eagerly accepted! I believed that staying healthy was of paramount importance in keeping mentally fit and in surviving for a long period of time in a depressing and unhealthy atmosphere. We agreed to meet for two-hour sessions four times a week in one of the inmate's room. From the onset we had a group of curious onlookers that included his roommates and others who just wanted to check us out. Fortunately, one of us was able to commandeer from the prison guards empty five-liter containers that had once held antiseptics used to clean bathrooms, sinks, and floors in the block. When filled with water, each weighed about ten pounds and became make-shift weights for our purposes. The containers had handles that made them easy to pick up one at a time for exercises requiring lighter weights, and to allow us to lift several together, we found a broken broom handle and used that for our weight bar. We tore T-shirts into strips that we wove together to form the ropes we used to fasten the containers to the broom handle. And it all worked magnificently. I developed exercise routines that minimized the amount of tying and untying we had to do and we settled into a routine that none of us would miss. This was a good time for us because we knew we were doing something positive for ourselves and it helped pass the time. But there was also another element that intrigued us in a strange way. What we were doing was against prison policy, yet we learned that many of the guards knew what we were up to and let on it wasn't happening. If we had been caught, our equipment would have been confiscated and we would have been reprimanded. It was unlikely that anything more severe would have happened for the first offense.

Exercising helped boost my spirits. It helped me rationalize that perhaps I could hold my own as far as my health went. And it was just plain fun!

During this time I also gained some notoriety for being a healer through my massage work. The signs of police brutality were evident as I watched people walk with limps or wince in pain as they moved. In talking with those people, I learned about the torture that the police used to extract information during interrogations. Many had their hands tied behind their back and were subsequently lifted by ropes hung over door frames so the full weight of their bodies came to bear on their shoulder joints. Several had had their shoulders pop out of their sockets. Many were beaten by clubs causing broken bones as well as serious injury to knee and ankle joints. Some were subjected to having lighted cigarettes pressed against their bare flesh while others were just held in black holes with little food until they were willing to talk. Many implicated innocent people in order to stop the torture; then, when they tried to recant their stories in court, the judges dismissed their statements and relied solely on their initial testimonies under torture. As a result, many people who were totally innocent languished in jail because friends had named friends and sons had named fathers. And those who had been wrongly named often turned to plans for revenge once they were freed.

It was those people who had been physically abused who came to me for help to relieve their pain. Having been left to languish by the police, some were so desperate that they were using broom sticks to help them walk and get around. I gave them my full attention and soon many felt some relief while others were totally amazed that their pain entirely disappeared. My reward was two-fold. First, I was given cigarettes, the currency of the jail, that I could use to buy fruit that had been smuggled out of the eating area; and second, I had acquired a network of people who told me they would protect me in case anyone tried to harm me. The latter was reassuring, because I always harbored a fear that someone with extremist thoughts might take it upon himself to harm The American.

While reading the newspaper one November afternoon, I came upon an article that talked about a method that had been developed for coping with stressful times. I read it with interest and found that it reinforced my beliefs about remaining positive in adverse circumstances and taking responsibility for one's actions. The article addressed the theory of Adversity Quotient developed by Dr. Paul Stolt, CEO of Peak Learning. His hypothesis consisted of four main components:

1. *Control*: People who deal with adversity are able to gain some sense of control.
2. *Ownership of the Problem*: People who hold themselves accountable for dealing with situations, even if they didn't cause them, tend to do better in adversity.
3. *Reach*: A person who deals well with adversity doesn't let fallout from the adverse situation spill into other areas of his life.
4. *Endurance*: People with a high Adversity Quotient (AQ) can maintain their hope and optimism by seeing past even the most seemingly insurmountable difficulties.

When I thought about what I had read, I realized that I was already following most of the guidelines laid out by Dr. Stolt. But what was most comforting and reinforcing for me was that the article not only reinforced that I was on the right path, but it gave me confidence that I would make it through the ordeal. I had to wonder, though, about the timing of the article in the newspaper and the good fortune I had in seeing it as I glanced through the newspaper. Was this coincidence something that had a deeper meaning for me as discussed in the *Celestine Prophecy*? I felt it was, and felt immediately that this was a sign from God that I would be okay. This gave me renewed strength and hope during the many difficult days that followed.

Prison provided a lot of time to think. Daydreams were something I used to transpose myself from that prison environment to memories of better times. I had often thought as I grew older that many things in my life seemed to change little throughout the years. One of those things was how I perceived my life and reacted to people and circumstances around me. I remembered how I, as a young boy, would marvel at the wonders of nature; how I would take pleasure in the splendor of mountains or the seemingly endless expanse of the prairie wheat fields. And that feeling only intensified as I became older. As I traveled throughout the world, beauty and nature always inspired the same feeling of awe and reverence for Creation that I had had when I was much younger. How I reacted to events in my life, both good and evil, was basically the same, though tempered somewhat by experience. Again, one day while reading the newspaper, I was taken aback when I spotted a quote from Pavese, an Italian poet: "A man is never completely alone in the world. At the worst he has the company of a boy, a youth, and by and by a grown man—the one he used to be." That struck me right between the eyes. Now at age fifty-three I had had a lot of life to remember, and as my daydreams encompassed the years of my youth, my adolescence, and my adulthood, I realized that the sum of all of those experiences made me who I am. When I realized that no one could take that away from me, I did not feel alone. I had some friends there with me: Paul the child, Paul the youth, Paul the adolescent, and Paul the man. And I liked them all. At any one instant I could be with them and relive a happiness that seemed distant and far removed from Al Wathba.

On December 23 I was called by the police to get dressed and leave the block to go for a visit with the Embassy staff. I met Mohammed Shala, the other American, at the desk where prisoners are searched prior to being led to the visitation area and together we went with a policeman to see the representatives of the American Embassy. This was our Christmas visit from the Embassy and it was Charlie Glatz and Jamal Bafagih who wished us holiday greetings. I felt it was rather touching that Charles and Jamal found the time during a busy season in their lives to come visit with us and bring greetings from our families. As well as verbal greetings, they surprised us by bringing individual serving-size cartons of whole milk and fruit juice as well as some cookies and potato chips. Several years earlier, a policy had been implemented that forbade visitors to bring food or drink to prisoners from outside the prison. However, the American Embassy was given an exemption in our cases, though there were conditions attached to the privilege. We were not allowed to take the food into the blocks all at one time. Instead, it was placed in the cooler in the prison kitchen and we were permitted once a day to get a container of milk and juice and some cookies. We had to open the containers and pour the milk or juice into cups before taking our drinks back to the blocks.

Throughout this process we were watched closely by the police to ensure that no weapons of any kind were concealed in the food. The first night I came close to being struck by an overzealous guard, because, when I opened one of the milk containers, a few drops landed on his uniform as he stood directly in the way. When he saw the spots, he screamed and pulled his fist back to punch me. Just before he threw the punch, he realized who it was that he was about to strike and knew that he would have been in a lot of trouble if he had done so. He quickly calmed down and tried to laugh off the incident.

For the first few days I went to the kitchen as planned to get my milk or juice and a few cookies. Then I tried to nonchalantly walk them through the block to my room where I would eat them when no one else was around. But I'm sure everyone knew what I was up to, so I decided that on Christmas Eve I would share them with everyone. On that day I got two helpings of milk and juice, and had the police give me all the Pringles, and Potato Chips and the remainder of the cookies. Now it was really hard to disguise what I had, since I had to take all these items out of the containers and put them on plates to carry back into the block. Of course all eyes were on me as I paraded back to my room. I had no idea how many cookies and potato chips there were, but I decided we'd pass them around the block as far as they would go.

Later that Christmas Eve night my roommates helped me arrange the potato chips and cookies on a couple of make-shift trays and we then took them from room to room and let everyone take one cookie and one potato chip. As in the biblical account of the loaves and fishes, everyone was able to partake and there was even a little left over. That allowed me to give a few extra to the foreman, to the people in my room, and a few others who had become better friends. Keeping the foreman on your side was always a smart move and he appreciated the gesture. For most of us that was the first taste of snack foods in many months and it was a glorious taste treat.

Now that everyone in my room was in good spirits, we began talking about Christmas Eve and what it meant to Christians. I cut the discussion short because I knew that any such discussion could be misconstrued by some of the more extreme Muslims as an attempt on my part to try to convert some of their faith. So I steered the conversation to ways in which Christmas is celebrated in different locales and talked about some of the songs and events that add to the holiday spirit. We were all in good spirits so I taught them the words to "Rudolph the Red-Nosed Reindeer," and after a few minutes the group was singing along with me. For some unknown reason I glanced out of the window, and to my surprise the night had become very foggy, an occurrence that I remember happening only one or two times during my entire stay in the Middle East. But what a perfect time for that to happen!

The mood of light-heartedness and fun changed abruptly, however, when several police and a few officers appeared in our room. All discussion stopped and the mood became tense as the officers started to look around. Next to one of the Indian boys they spotted a deck of cards that the boy had made. One officer grabbed him by his shirt and pulled him to his feet, choking him by twisting his shirt tight around his neck. He then ordered the boy to go with the policemen, and as the boy turned to go, the officer kicked him hard with his heavy black shoes. It was obvious the boy was in great pain as he was lead away by the policemen. I looked at the officer and glared at him. Realizing I was The American, he looked rather embarrassed and led the other officers out of the room. That put an end to our Christmas Eve fun. What had been a happier time for us turned into just another quiet despondent night.

The young man returned a few days later after having been confined in solitary. He was unharmed and like everyone in the prison, he just took the incident in stride as it was not out of the ordinary for the police to act in such a harsh manner. After all, no one in Al Wathba was supposed to show any indication of sharing in a happy moment.

On Christmas Day friends wished me a Merry Christmas and I did likewise. There were a few hugs among the handful of Christians in the block and life in Al Wathba resumed for us. I found myself humming my favorite Christmas songs all day, thinking about what my family and friends were doing back home to celebrate, and reminiscing about what I had done on Christmases past. It would have been easy to become depressed about spending Christmas in prison, but life continued, and for the most part, the holiday was a non-event in a place where almost all were Muslims.

Several times a month prisoners gathered to sing their favorite songs. To my ear all Indian music sounds the same, and that seemed to be true of Arabic music also. Considering that music is not widely sung in Islamic countries because it is not accepted in Islam, tunes typically relate to tribal life. So prisoners would come together and sing songs that had been passed down from generation to generation. To accompany the music they would beat on the bottoms of pails much like Jamaican music uses steel drums as accompaniment. On some nights you could hear the beating of the pails from blocks some distance away, but, when it was in my block, the loud and repetitive beat droned hard and boring on my ears. Regardless, it was fun to listen and watch the revelry and camaraderie that it inspired.

In a move designed to eliminate celebrating the New Year on New Year's Eve and day, the guards entered all the blocks and took away pails and any other object that could be used as an accompaniment to the singing. It was just another way for the police to exert their power and minimize any fun that the prisoners might create for themselves. It was typical of the harsh reality of life at Al Wathba.

The events of the holiday season and my continuing attempts to pursue any path that might help lead to my freedom were summarized in a letter I sent to my friend Rick Crocker for distribution to my other friends via e-mail:

Three months have gone by and there is really nothing new to report in my case. I'm still awaiting a court date so we can get this matter resolved in the next few months. Thankfully the days are going by quickly.

Just before Christmas my friends at the Embassy got permission to get some cookies and juice to me—something you don't normally get. My roommates and some other friends joined me for a Christmas Eve gathering as we shared those gifts. It was a very foggy night so I had to sing "Rudolph the Red-Nosed Reindeer" to them and they joined in.

I want to thank all of you who have sent cards and notes to me. I have been really touched by your support. I have learned that the Embassy is not pro-active in that they primarily are here to help me communicate with the outside. Even visiting dignitaries (recent ones have been Madeline Albright, William Cohen, Jimmy Carter, and George Bush) are not briefed on my being here. Many of you have contacted your congressmen. Thanks. I have already asked several of you to contact Jeb Bush, the new governor of Florida to intervene using the excellent relationship his father has with the ruler of Abu Dhabi, President His Highness Sheikh Zayed bin Sultan Al Nahyan. If anyone else wants to drop Jeb a note that would be appreciated (Jeb Bush, Governor, State of Florida, The Capitol, Tallahassee).

The weather here is very Miami-ish for this time of year. Sounds like the U.S. and Canada are having one of their snowy bitterly cold ones we last saw about twenty years ago. Everyone here in the Gulf is sweating the over-supply of oil reserves and the near-record low prices.

When I'm out of here I'll have enough stories to write a book. Stay tuned.

Love to you all, and best wishes for a happy and fulfilling 1999.

20

Ramadan Prison Style

THERE ARE TWELVE MONTHS IN THE Islamic calendar and the start of each is based on the sighting of the new moon. As a result, the Islamic months are usually twenty-eight days in length but can be as many as thirty days. The twelve-month Islamic calendar has about ten fewer days than the 365 day calendar that we all know, so each Islamic month does not fall at the same time each year. If you track one month such as the Holy Month of Ramadan, you will see that its beginning is about ten days earlier each successive year.

Ramadan is a special month for Muslims, just as the Lenten season is for Christians. It is a time when Muslims are supposed to forsake all manner of drink and food and other habits such as smoking and sexual relations during the period from sunrise to sunset. With regard to food, though, there is a major difference between how Christians and Muslims set their goals. During Lent Christians usually give up certain foods or forsake certain habits that they enjoy. Whatever they chose to do is supposed to apply to the entire Lenten season both night and day. In Islam, however, followers forsake things only during the daytime from just before Morning Prayer to just after evening prayer and can indulge in other pleasurable pastimes during the evening and night.

So what happens is that Muslims change their day to accommodate all that they normally would do without really forsaking anything. Let's take eating as an example. During Ramadan Muslims do not eat during the day, but after sunset the fast is broken and feasts of food are served up throughout the night. My experience is that many eat more during the nights of the Ramadan season than they would normally eat during the daytime. So, where is the hardship of giving something up? I never saw it anywhere. Before going to prison I was invited to homes of Muslim families where every evening feasts were served up that rivaled the Western world's celebrations of Christmas and Thanksgiving. So from a Christian's point of view the whole idea of sacrificing during Ramadan was just a lot of talk. Nothing was sacrificed. In fact the people ate more during Ramadan and slept more during the day so they could stay up later in the night.

Because of the change of lifestyle during Ramadan, there was also a noticeable shift in the way business was conducted. Many businesses opened later in the mornings so people could sleep later, and many businesses closed earlier to accommodate people who were fatigued from not eating during the daytime. Conducting business during Ramadan was extremely difficult because many governmental offices were practically empty of staff. Those persons who were there weren't especially enthusiastic about working.

It was a criminal offense in most Muslim countries to be seen eating, drinking, or smoking during the daytime in Ramadan. Penalties could be severe and could even include serving jail time. Non-Muslims were not excused from the rules and many would eat, drink, and smoke but it had to be done very discreetly and out of sight of any Muslim. If anyone saw you, you could be reported to the authorities.

So in prison, life changed during the month of Ramadan just as it did outside the prison. No food was served during the daytime, school activities were reduced during Ramadan, and sports activities were relegated to the evening hours. Night activities became daytime activities and normal daytime activities became evening and night activities.

Our first meal of the day during Ramadan was right after sunset and the fifth and last prayer of the day. Unlike the rest of the year, the food was brought to the block and distributed among the prisoners. Although I preferred the orderliness of going to the eating area for the meals, we were provided with extra food for the first meal of the day. It was delivered about an hour or more before sunset and then people from one room at a time collected all the food for the people in the room and took it back to them. The food was the regular noonday fare of rice, a cabbage and carrot salad, either meat, chicken, or fish, usually a piece of unleavened bread, and either a piece of fruit or custard. But it was tradition among Muslims that to break the fast of the day, they began the meal with juice and dates. Once the food got to the room, we then subdivided it among the prisoners in the room. On the first day of Ramadan, plates were distributed to the blocks so that each of us had a plate to eat from. And then we waited. From one of our cell windows we could see the setting sun and could very well estimate when the time to eat would come.

Eventually one would hear the call to prayer echoing from each of the blocks and that was the signal that it was okay to begin eating. The Muslims who prayed regularly usually ate the dates and drank some juice and then went off to Evening Prayer while the rest of us ate our meal.

I had never liked dates, so I didn't think it was any great thing to have dates with the meal. But someone suggested I should try them since they were fresh from the Gulf. Reluctantly, I did so and was happily surprised at how tasty they were. They have become one of my favorite fruits since having had them every Ramadan in prison. I liked them best mixed with bananas and rolled in the unleavened bread. What a treat!

After dinner, life in the block returned to normal except that the lights didn't go off as normal around 10:30 because most people had slept all day and we had our only other meal of the day around 1:00 in the morning. That was served in the eating area and usually was rice and some meat or chicken or fish. By 2:00 the last of the blocks had eaten and slowly things calmed down as people drifted off to sleep between 2:30 and 5:30 in the morning.

Daytime was very quiet as many prisoners slept until 3:00 or 4:00 in the afternoon, so for those of us who liked to read or study, it was an ideal time. And there was no smoking during the daytime as most slept!

Smoking had been an annoyance to me since my first day at Al Wathba and I had complained bitterly about it. It reminded me of times I had spent in bars where there was a continuous haze of smoke in the air. Because I didn't smoke and avoided being around those who did, being confined in a smoke-filled block was very difficult. Everywhere I turned, there were cigarettes. Fortunately, there was good ventilation to the outside, but I still knew I breathed a lot of second-hand smoke. As a result, I developed colds about every four weeks, an aggravation that I would not be able to shake during my entire term at Al Wathba. This was extremely disconcerting to me, since I had always been watchful of my health prior to going to prison. Now, not only was I being confined, but I felt my health was being compromised every moment I was there.

So I liked Ramadan for two reasons primarily. There was a lot less smoke to have to contend with and I had fresh dates and fruit juice each day. Actually I felt healthier during that month than during the rest of the year.

With the advent of Ramadan came an increase in the number of rumors about prisoners being pardoned by Sheikh Zayed. It was customary in the Muslim world for rulers to release prisoners during the holy month of Ramadan and also at the two Eids. Speculation was rampant that because of his advanced years there would be a major release of prisoners this Ramadan and every day people would say that they heard from friends outside of prison or from the guards that we would all be released before Ramadan was over. It didn't matter how skeptical one was about such rumors; everyone began to believe that something monumental was about to happen just because of the frequency of the stories that were circulating. So every day we woke with a feeling of anticipation that today might be the day we would go home, and every night we went to bed with the anticipation that tomorrow might be the day we would go home.

The heightened anticipation was fueled also by what we read in the newspapers. Throughout the Arab world we read that rulers were releasing prisoners by the thousands in honor of Ramadan. Surely Sheikh Zayed would do the same. But in the end little happened. And what did happen was for publicity only, as were many of the releases that were scheduled to come in the months and years ahead.

In the course of events at Al Wathba, it was customary that when someone finished his sentence, he would be transferred to an "out" jail. This was a holding prison where people were sent, and they stayed there until the necessary paper work was prepared and processed allowing them to either leave the country or return to life inside of the UAE. It was rare that the paperwork was dealt with prior to someone's sentence being concluded. As a result most prisoners spent additional time beyond their court-mandated sentence in custody.

Thus, when news finally broke that two hundred people were being released in honor of Ramadan, it was from the ranks of those who had already finished their sentences and were awaiting proper documentation. To people reading the newspaper and listening to the radio, it appeared that Sheikh Zayed was making a noble gesture in freeing prisoners. In fact it was a lie. No one's sentence had been commuted. And this misconception would be played out over and over again.

The numbers of prisoners going to court during Ramadan was less than at other times due to the general slowdown in business activity. If people were looking for an excuse to work less hard than they had been, Ramadan provided it. The newspaper was replete with stories about increases in automobile accidents and pleas for people to be more careful during Ramadan. People were coddled because law enforcement officials considered the fasting to be responsible for people not paying attention to traffic laws and many were excused for their stupid behavior. There were stories about an increase in accidents near the end of the afternoon work day as people sped home to get some rest or prepare for the breaking of the day's fast. Numerous accidents were caused by the recklessness, but most got away with slaps on the wrist.

Ramadan was followed immediately by lesser Eid which is a time of celebration. People acknowledged it as Westerners would acknowledge the New Year. I was awakened on the first morning after Ramadan by sounds of revelry, and immediately noticed that most prisoners had dressed in their best attire. They moved from room to room greeting each other with shouts of "Eid Mubarek" (Happy Eid!), and shaking hands, and hugging. For a few moments all animosities were forgotten and everyone was on friendly terms. The daily fasts were gone, and that morning we had a special meal of cake and a sweet chicken dish for breakfast. That was a nice treat, but by noon the meals returned to normal and we again had to go to the eating area for all our meals.

21

The Year of Reckoning Begins

MY NAME APPEARED ON THE LIST OF prisoners who were summoned to the courts on January 3. I had heard nothing about this hearing from either my lawyer or the Embassy, so I was extremely apprehensive about what would happen.

My sleep the night before my court appearance was fitful at best. I lay awake most of the night trying to anticipate what the following morning might bring and wondering why no one had contacted me to discuss strategies for my case. More than once I asked God to be with me and give me the strength to face whatever happened with courage in the knowledge that my Maker was with me and I would be taken care of no matter what the verdict might be.

Morning finally came and I went through the routine of joining others going to Court that day for an early breakfast. Afterwards we waited in the hallway for an hour or more before we were finally ushered out for a body search and downstairs for roll call and the ride to the Court in Abu Dhabi. As before there were some on our truck who made light of the situation and joked about events in Arabic. Again, they broke off pieces of wood inside the truck to pry open the shackles around their legs. I tried to put all of that out of my mind as I stared at the passing countryside and reveled in the opportunity to be outside in the fresh air enjoying the open sky. I watched milling cars and bustling people with new-found appreciation, albeit from inside a wire cage.

Finally we arrived at the courthouse, and as before, the trucks were backed up to the receiving doors and we were ushered out under heavy guard into the holding room where we managed to squeeze in and find a place to sit on the floor. Many stared into space absorbed in their own thoughts or quietly closed their eyes waiting for whatever fate was in store. As usual, the few who faced light sentences or just didn't seem to care about what might befall them, joked and produced cigarettes for friends to share. My stomach was queasy and I was extremely tense and frightened. No one had talked with me about this visit to the courthouse, so I did not have any inkling about what to expect. *Was this to be my first day before the judge? Was I going to be confronted again by the Public Prosecutor? Or was I going to be freed?* I knew by now that the latter thought was probably absurd, but still I clung to that hope.

Before long the heavy steel door opened and a policeman called the first of the names of those who had to appear in one of the nearby courtrooms. Before the door could close, though, there was a rush of other prisoners clamoring to use the bathrooms or to make telephone calls. One or two at a time were accommodated and eventually they returned to take their places and await their turn to be called to the courts.

For a couple of hours this process continued, and whenever the door opened I listened intently for my name to be called. Nothing happened. That waiting had a cumulative effect on me. The pressure built as I knew that sooner or later my name had to be on the docket. Finally, my name alone was called and everyone made sure I understood that I was the one that they wanted. Fearful of what lay beyond, I hesitatingly moved to the door. A policeman told me to go with him and I followed him like a robot. We entered an elevator and rode upstairs to the area where the courtrooms and judges' chambers were located. On the way up the policeman asked me what my nationality was and once I told him I was an American, he smiled and told me I was going to see a court clerk. I was ushered into an office where a man wearing a white disdasha sat behind a desk that was cleared except for one file folder.

"Are you Paul Ciceri?" he asked.

I acknowledged that I was.

He told me that it was customary that all prisoners had to be called to the court at least once every thirty days whether they were to appear in court or not. He went on to say that I would not be in the courtroom that day, but that I would be called again in one month, and if the prosecution was ready to proceed, then I would make my first court appearance. That was it. Thirty seconds. I told him I understood and the policeman then ushered me out of the room and back to the elevator and downstairs to the holding room where everyone wanted to know what had happened. When I told them that nothing would happen that day, the word spread quickly. A few prisoners approached me and in excellent English told me about their cases. They tried to reassure me that everything would turn out okay and that I would be on my way home soon.

Knowing that nothing more would happen to me that day, I relaxed and said a prayer of thanks. Suddenly I was more receptive to talking with those around me. Eventually, the steel doors swung open and the word was given that we were to board the trucks for the ride back to Al Wathba. I took in much more of my surroundings on the return trip since my mind wasn't working overtime trying to anticipate what the day might bring.

As usual everyone in the block was curious about what had taken place. It wasn't a surprise that it was a non-eventful visit, but it was becoming apparent by their reaction that they felt that the American Embassy knew the inner workings of the UAE government and was passing along information to me about upcoming releases. As absurd as that was, I realized that these people with whom I was imprisoned looked upon the Americans as their salvation, and that I was the one who was supposed to give them the insight they sought. They wanted me to announce that, yes; indeed we were all to be freed on a specific date in the not-too-far future. In a way, I was disappointed that I didn't have wonderful news to share with them, and as time went on I think they came to realize that we were all victims of the same vicious regime.

I continued to read, play chess, exercise, and try to learn Arabic. I found myself spending more time with those roommates who seemed intent on proving to me that I ought to become a Muslim. Rather than say we held long discussions talking about our respective religions, I think it would be fairer to say that I spent a lot of time listening to my friends expound about the validity of Islam. They believed that Christians had been misled over the centuries about the true nature of Christ, and felt that all

Christians had been brainwashed about the concept of the triune God. I found it truly amusing one morning when, after listening about the great tolerance of the Islamic people, we moved to the room set aside in our block for personal prayer and religious reading. My friends and I were quickly expelled by other Muslims because I was a non-Muslim. It was an insight into the extremism of some Muslims and representative of how many Muslims are misinformed about their religion. Imams later would explain to me that non-Muslims are indeed welcome in the mosques and the people who told us to leave were ignorant about their religion. In some ways listening to various people talk about Islam was as confusing as learning Arabic from Arabs of different Middle Eastern countries. Each had his own viewpoint about what was the way of truth.

During the first week of January two flight attendants from Gulf Air were assigned to my block. They had been arrested at Abu Dhabi airport, and each had been found to have a small amount of marijuana hidden in one of his socks. Like me, one of their friends had forewarned the Customs' agents, alleging their possession of drugs. In their case, a fellow worker had notified the authorities because one of the two arrested had started dating his most recent girlfriend. Both were from Bahrain and they spoke excellent English as did the other Bahraini Saeed who had been in Block 3 for quite a time before I had arrived. I formed a quick friendship with these men, but more so with the one named Mohammed Jennai. He and I began to play some challenging chess games, and since he had lived in Daytona Beach not far from my home in Orlando, we both shared experiences to which we could easily relate. His friend Mohammed Ginger decided to copy the Quran in his own handwriting and thus earn favor with Allah for having done so. This, in my opinion, was another example of energy misdirected in the furtherance of one's religious beliefs. In Islam one thinks that a scorecard is kept of all the good one does and this was an activity that he felt would increase his favor on the day of reckoning.

Mornings became a favorite time of day for me because many people went back to sleep after breakfast and some went to classes so it was fairly quiet in the block. I took the time to read and study some Arabic. One day I mentioned to the inmates who went to the library to get books for the rest of us that I would like to go and have a look at the English language books. Shortly thereafter, I got my wish. There, among the few books, I found an excellent text that taught French for the English reader. Delighted, I spent many mornings pouring over the lessons trying to improve my French. I filled most of the pages in one notebook with new words and phrases and was happy because I felt I was doing something productive with my time. Two things, in particular, excited me: I discovered a French version of the Lord's Prayer and I also found the words to the French national anthem. *La Marseillaise,* in my opinion, is the most beautiful national anthem of all those I had heard. I committed both to memory. Reciting the words to the Lord's Prayer brought back comforting memories of an occasion years earlier when I had attended a Catholic Mass one Sunday in the quaint town of Jonquière, Quebec. The prayer came alive when I read it in French:

> *Notre Père qui êtes aux cieux,*
> *que Votre nom soit sanctifié,*
> *que Votre règne arrive,*
> *que Votre volonté soit faite sur la terre comme au ciel;*
> *donnez-nous aujourd´hui notre pain quotidien,*
> *pardonnez-nous nos offenses comme nous pardonnons*
>   *à ceux qui nous ont offensés;*
> *ne nous induisez pas dans la tentation et delivrez-nous*
>   *du mal;*
> *ainsi soit-il!*

On February 4, I sent letters to my friend James Ward at ELS Language Centers and asked him to forward them to my brother Richard and daughter Jennifer. In them I began to vent some of the frustration that I was experiencing because I saw the Embassy staff so infrequently. I had read stories in the newspaper that I felt I could have acted on to help my situation, but I had no way to get messages to the Embassy to ask them to forward them to my family. I knew that the wait for freedom would take some time, so I asked that some books be sent to me.

> *"Time marches on and I am still waiting for my case to come up in court but hopefully that will be soon. Recently there were two stories in the press relating to a Russian and a Brit whose cases of having been set up*

are identical to mine. They were both acquitted. Although I am hopeful of the same verdict, those two received their sentences in Dubai. Even though Dubai and Abu Dhabi are only 75 miles apart and in the same country, the courts don't see the law the same. For a crime of theft it's like having a court in Tampa giving the culprit a slap on the hand and a court in Orlando ordering the hand to be cut off.

I am doing fine but get very frustrated sometimes. This week I saw an article about Al Palladini, the Ontario Minister of Economic Development heading a trade delegation here. I haven't seen my Embassy for six weeks and I have no telephone access so I had no way of getting a message to Richard to put in a word for me. From the subtleness in conversation with the Embassy and my attorney I feel that the Embassy will make an effort to have my sentence commuted once the verdict is in. So I wait and remain optimistic. My health is good and my spirits are high. Your letters and notes of encouragement have been so important to me.

Jennifer's letter arrived without the pictures. For some reason prison officials kept them. I hope Dad had a great Caribbean cruise. Boy does that sound good in light of the miserable winter all the north has been having.

The only thing I could really use are some novels. Although the library is a decent size I am going through the books quickly and the most recent are from 1996–1997. Any one from the top ten list would be good but don't spend money on hard backs as all the books must stay here when I leave. I like John Grisham books and I haven't read The Chamber, A Time to Kill, or the Rainmaker yet. The new Op-Center books by Tom Clancey would be good but all mystery, adventure, action, and war books I would also enjoy. I did read the Secrets of the Ya-Ya Sisterhood already.

I have learned to watch what I wish for—last September I was telling my friends how it was difficult to meet local Abu Dhabi people to hang out with and how I missed the beautiful crisp autumn days back home.

> *Also I wanted to get to Morocco to meet people there and improve my French. Well I got to see those nice days back home under bad circumstances and as for those local guys and Moroccans—they're here! At least my French has improved as I get to use it every day. Now I'm just wishing to get out of here and see all of you soon.*
>
> *Thank you for doing all that you have—my friends have been very supportive too. Where do we go from here? I think we just have to wait for the sentence and then perhaps build some pressure in the press for the Embassy to act if they don't take the lead themselves. In addition to letters to Jeb Bush perhaps Peter could send a letter to his governor George Bush, Jr. asking his dad to help.*

And then I went on to mention two things that had a significant impact on me and provided some calming effects when anxiety about my situation arose:

> *I have been having some wonderful dreams involving Mother recently. Maybe she's putting in a good word for me. Religious books are not allowed but all the words I need and those of our church service are in my head.*

A few days later, I had another visit from Charlie Glatz and Jamal Bafagih of the United States Embassy. They informed me that my first day in court would be four days later on Sunday, February 14. As usual, I was apprehensive at the thought of going to court and had had no briefing from my attorney about what I should say or do during the procedure. They told me that there would be a representative from the Embassy there to monitor the trial and report back to the State Department and to my family what had taken place. They told me not to worry because the trial would take place in stages and I should expect to return to the courtroom several times before the verdict was handed down. Regardless, I became anxious. It was my life that was at stake in all this and the last word from my attorney was that I should expect a sentence of from seven to twenty years. Not a very happy thought! They told me that they expected my lawyer to try and get the evidence secured when my apartment was inspected by the police to be thrown out of court because the search was illegal. By law I, or a member of my family, was supposed to be present when the search was conducted. If that was true, then my case would all come down to the .065 gm. of cocaine that was found in my suitcase at the airport on that fateful night of October 7, 1998.

Again the Embassy staff put me in a bind. They hadn't brought me stamps and I had had to ask other inmates for stamps for all my letters. Now it appeared I would have to continue to do so. That was frustrating in that it limited the number of letters I could send to perhaps one or two every other week. Since that was the only communication I had with the outside world other than my minimum contact with the Embassy, I felt more cut off than ever from my family and friends.

Over the next few days I thought constantly about the trial process. I felt totally out of control and was certainly not at all confident in what might transpire in the courtroom the following Sunday morning. Those were an anxious three days of waiting. I had continued to say my prayers as I had always done, but in those three days they became more intense and pleading. The disposition of the rest of my life was at stake.

22

The Trial

FINALLY, SUNDAY MORNING, FEBRUARY 14 arrived and I was called by the foreman to meet at the front gate for the customary early breakfast and subsequent transport to the courthouse.

Breakfast was of no interest to me. My stomach was in knots, my heart was racing, and I knew my blood pressure had to be sky high. But I went through the motions of going to breakfast, waiting for the body search, and then being shackled and loaded onto the waiting trucks for the ride into Abu Dhabi. Though my mind was cluttered with all manner of thoughts about what the day might bring, I continued to pray in silence as I tried to remain calm and reassure myself that everything would work out. I remember little of the ride as I stared blankly into space without taking into account what was happening among the prisoners, or the countryside, or the traffic around us.

A half hour later I saw the sign for the Sharia Court that I had seen on my previous trips to the courthouse. This time, however, it took on a new significance because at last I would actually go inside the courtroom and be subjected to the Muslim version of justice. The trucks were backed up to the doorway where prisoners entered the court building. We were ushered under heavy guard to the now familiar holding room where we again sat, some lost in quiet reflection and others caught up in laughter and loud talk.

It wasn't long before the first group of names was called and mine was among them. My time of waiting was over and now the process of deciding my fate would begin.

Eight of us were escorted out of the room and down the hallway about twenty feet to a waiting elevator. Because the elevator was small, only four of us along with a police officer were able to get on. We rode up one level, exited, and stood in a hallway where we were surrounded by several policemen. The policeman who was with us in the elevator returned to the main floor and in a short time returned with the remainder of our group. Then we were all led a few feet to a door that opened to a courtroom. We were ushered into the room and then into a cage of steel bars approximately 4 feet by 8 feet that stood just inside the courtroom in the right front corner.

After being placed in the cell, I took a quick glance around the courtroom and noticed two of the Embassy staff sitting in the rows reserved for spectators. Jamal Bafagih and Justine Sincavage were there, but I noticed that they weren't sitting together. Jamal was sitting on the left side of the courtroom and Justine was on the right. I realized then that the protocol of separating unrelated men and women extended even to the courts. We had eye contact and with a nod I acknowledged their presence. But I didn't see my attorney.

Shortly, thereafter, some additional prisoners were brought to the courtroom and now there were about twelve of us crammed into that small cell with no seating.

The courtroom was approximately 50 feet square. The back half of the court contained seats for guests who wanted to view proceedings. There was a central aisle and an aisle down each side. At the back in the center was a double door where the guests could enter and leave. This area was separated from the front of the courtroom by a low railing. The left side of the room had many windows so the room was bright. Along the front wall there was a door through which we had entered which was about 6 feet from the right wall. Another door was also visible along that wall about six feet from the opposite wall. Between the doors was an elevated area with a long desk where I assumed the justices would be seated. Directly across the room from our cell was another desk for the prosecutor. In front of the platform where the judges would sit there were several tables. Two long tables I assumed were for the attorneys and there was one smaller desk. A few policemen milled about.

Soon more spectators arrived and many of them entered the courtroom through the same door through which we had been led. There were women, children, men, and what appeared to be a group of attorneys and legal staff. Many came over to our holding cell and talked with some of the prisoners. There were tears and hand shakes. Little children of some prisoners were there to see their fathers. Lawyers in their black robes talked with their clients. But mine still wasn't there! Policemen stood by to make sure that nothing got passed between the prisoners and those who had come to talk with them. I was surprised at the fact that prisoners were allowed to touch their guests. The policemen in this facility seemed to have a lot more empathy to the prisoners' plight than those back at Al Wathba prison.

After ten minutes the policemen apparently received a signal that the court was going to come to order for they made all the visitors move to seats in the gallery. The courtroom became quiet and something was said in Arabic. I assumed it was a call for order. The far door at the front of the courtroom opened and the policemen came to attention as five people entered. Three took their places along the front of the courtroom and the fourth took his place at the desk across the room from us. The three were dressed in black robes and the one in the middle wore a fez. I had been told about him. He was a short Egyptian man who prisoners had nicknamed "The Hanging Judge." I trembled with fear. The man across the room was dressed in a white disdasha and I knew that he must be the Public Prosecutor. The fifth man who appeared to be Indian took his place at the small desk between the judges and the other desks at which a few men where now seated. Just as they were being seated, my attorney, dressed in a black robe, appeared through the door and took a place at the two desks facing the judges. He joined a few others dressed in suits whom I also assumed were lawyers.

I learned later that all three gentlemen seated at the front were judges, but the one in the center was the one who made the decisions in the cases that came before them. The others were there for consultation. The judge in the middle had a stack of folders, one for each case to come before him that day.

He opened the first and called names in Arabic. The police guards opened the gate to our cell and three people stepped out to stand side-by-side in a line facing the judge in front and just to the right side of the judges' bench. Their lawyer rose from his seat and moved to a podium that was placed between the two tables reserved for lawyers directly in front of the judge. All the dialogue was in Arabic as the judge first addressed a few questions to each of the three inmates in turn. After that the judge turned to the lawyer and they had a brief dialogue. Then the judge dismissed them and they were escorted out to the hallway and back to the holding cell. Their friends and family followed right behind hoping for a chance to talk with them before they were put in the cell. I learned later that the three were accused of using drugs and each had denied the charges. The judge then set a date for their next hearing one month later.

    I was still trembling as another name was called and another prisoner faced a round of questioning. Then the judge began to read from prepared notes. When he was done, the prisoner began to cry and loud wails emanated from family members in the audience. A prisoner beside me whispered that the man had been given a fifteen-year sentence for trafficking in drugs. As family members burst to the front of the courtroom, the judge angrily ordered the jailers to have them removed and the inmate and his relatives were quickly escorted out of the courtroom. *"My God,"* I thought, *"I'm gonna get killed!"* The trembling increased.

    Then my name was called and miraculously the trembling stopped. I was alert, confident, and ready to show everyone in the court that I wasn't afraid of their justice system. I was escorted out of the cell and led to the place where I could face the judge and the Public Prosecutor on the other side of the room. I glanced briefly at the Embassy staff and felt that at least someone was there on my side. My lawyer stood up and the judge said a few words to the Public Prosecutor. Then for at least five minutes the Public Prosecutor read the case and charges that the government was bringing against me. I understood none of what he said and nothing was translated for me. All I could pick out were the words cocaine (he pronounced it co-ca-een) and hashish and marijuana. My mind was numb, but I looked directly at the Public Prosecutor without moving my head at all. Through my peripheral vision I could see my lawyer listening to the charges and glancing back and forth from the Public Prosecutor to the Judge.

    Eventually he finished his reading and sat down. The Judge gave my lawyer a furtive look and then said something to the translator. The translator rose and faced me and said he would translate a few questions that the Judge had for me.

The Judge said, "There were drugs found in your apartment."

Without hesitation I said the first thing that came to mind, "That's what they told me."

"Who told you that?"

"The Police," I replied.

"Weren't you with them?"

"No, I was not!"

With that response the judge looked menacingly at the Public Prosecutor and made a comment to the judge to his right.

Then the Judge said to me, "Hashish and marijuana were found in your apartment."

I gave the same reply, "That's what they told me."

The Judge looked at me and realized he wasn't getting anywhere with that line of questioning. I glanced quickly at my lawyer to see if he would give me any kind of signal. This was a nightmare. I was told earlier not to expect any questions from the judge, and my lawyer had not counseled me about what to expect in the courtroom. No one had given any indication as to how I should respond to the questions that might be directed at me. My lawyer gave me no sign to do anything different; nor did he acknowledge that I was doing okay. It looked as though he had been caught completely off guard.

Then the judge asked another question. "Have you ever smoked marijuana?"

"Yes," I replied.

"Where?"

"Amsterdam."

"And when was the last time you did that?"

"December of the year before last."

"1998?"

"No sir, it would have been December of 1997." And then I blurted out "But I've never smoked marijuana in this country!"

The translator gave me a hand signal out of view of the judge to stop and say no more. I guess he had seen too many people say too much hoping it would help their cause when in fact what they said was used against them. I didn't think I had said too much since what I had said was the truth.

But I had blundered. I would learn later that the government had successfully prosecuted people who were in the UAE and who had used drugs in other countries. Indeed, I would read later that the Consular Sheet that contained information about the United Arab Emirates stated "UAE authorities have been known to arrest travelers upon their arrival to the country, and based on recent prior drug use, to prosecute those travelers."

Then the judge paused, talked with the court clerk, and told me through the interpreter that my next appearance in court would be March 6. The policeman standing beside me indicated that I was to follow him and he led me out of the courtroom. Right behind me came my lawyer and the Embassy staff. We met outside in the hallway, and the lawyer told me through Jamal that I shouldn't have admitted using marijuana. I countered that he hadn't prepared me at all for any questions that might be directed at me. Justine was upset with him too, and said that I had simply stated the truth. With that, the lawyer excused himself and the policeman led me onto the elevator followed by Justine and Jamal. Jamal conferred with the policeman, and once we arrived downstairs the policeman approached and talked with the officers in charge.

He had arranged for me to have a few moments with the Embassy staff in the commander's office with several police looking on to make sure nothing was passed between us. Once we were seated, I told Jamal that I wanted him to get a message to my family. He gave me a pen and a yellow note pad and I scribbled a note as fast as I could. I knew we didn't have much time.

> *I'm writing this from the courthouse and hopefully the Embassy can get this to you.*
>
> *Thanks for your help so far. Now that Jeb Bush is the Governor of Florida he should be made aware of my status and be asked that he contact his father on my behalf. His father is well regarded here and spent 3 days here recently with President His Highness Sheikh Zayed bin Sultan Al Nahyan and they have a good relationship.*

> *I am doing okay and hope for a just resolution. Two similar cases in Dubai resulted in acquittals but the courts aren't the same here.*
>
> *After sentencing it may be helpful for Dad to come. Will play that by ear.*
>
> *Thanks for all your prayers. I love you.*

I gave the note back to Jamal and he said he would get it to my brother. With that we were told our time was up and Jamal said they would be out to see me when they could. We got up and I was escorted back to the holding cell.

Once again I was alone with my thoughts. I felt that I had done well in front of the judge. Now it was on the record in open court that I had not accompanied the police when they inspected my apartment and that was something my lawyer was going to challenge as being an unlawful search. Anyway, I felt a bit relieved that I had been in the courtroom in front of a judge and I had seen the process that was in place. In spite of the fact that the previous defendant had been sentenced to fifteen years in front of me, I took the time to enjoy the fresh air and the vast expanse of scenery during the ride back to Al Wathba.

In response to a query from a friend in Boston about what had transpired at the court hearing, Jamal Bafagih of the Embassy staff wrote on February 17, "Nothing much was said or done." Yet, it was a big deal to me.

23

Police on the Rampage

WE ARRIVED BACK AT THE PRISON and about 1:30 p.m. cleared through our security check. Because it was near the end of the time for lunch to be served, our group was immediately directed to the eating area for our noon meal. When we got there, my block was eating, so I joined my roommates and filled them in on what had transpired at the courthouse.

As people finished their meal, they got up and headed for the gate so they could go back to the block for the afternoon. But there was something different this time. The gate remained closed and the police told us we weren't allowed to return until further notice. Those who had been in prison for some time knew what that meant and passed the word that the police were doing a search of our block. This was rather chilling in that it was likely the police were going through each room and searching everything in our possession. We could expect a lot of destruction when we finally arrived back in our area. We mingled and talked for about an hour before we were allowed to head back to our block.

What I saw when I looked over our living area made me nauseous. The destruction was as if a tornado had torn through our block. Anything that had been glued to the walls as decoration had been torn off. Clotheslines that had been created by tearing up sheets and stringing pieces together had been cut and everything that had hung on them was scattered on the ground. Every bed had been searched and the blankets had been tossed helter-skelter. Clothes had been dumped out of shelves and other clothes that had been left by beds or elsewhere had been scattered. The little areas where we lived had been thoroughly ransacked.

An eerie silence enveloped us as we stared in disbelief trying to comprehend what sort of mind could do such a thing. There was clearly intent to inflict as much damage to our meager belongings as possible and to disrupt our already shallow lives. The bastards succeeded. A few cried openly and those of us who didn't cry aloud, wept on the inside. We felt mentally raped; helpless to respond, and very vulnerable.

We learned later from inmates in the block above us that about ten policemen under the direction of one of the officers had ransacked our quarters and had then enlisted other prisoners to come in and remove clothing and bedding that the police felt was excessive. Gone were the chess sets and other games that we had created. Even pictures of family members had been torn off the walls and ripped into pieces. Wanton destruction.

Slowly we began to pick up what lay scattered about and created piles of our own clothing and other personal belongings. Because the blankets all looked the same there was some bickering about which blankets belonged to whom. Eventually those disputes got resolved and items that were not salvageable were piled outside the rooms for later disposal. The prisoners in most rooms took the opportunity to do a thorough cleaning, so we piled all of our belongings on the beds or outside in the hallway until the floor was barren of possessions. Then we filled buckets with water and washed the floors using the water and soap that we had saved for doing our laundry. That process went on room by room most of the afternoon. When the floors were dry, we moved our belongings back in, made up our beds on the floor and on the few beds, refolded our clothes and put them away. After many hours we were organized again and ready to continue our drab life in the block. It was made even more dismal by the fact that all the games we had made were gone. Even some of our books had been removed as well.

Over the next few days each block was subjected to the same destruction as ours had been. When the block above us was being ransacked, we watched in silence as the police moved systematically room by room in a seemingly enjoyable rampage, spreading as much destruction as possible. We seethed with hatred as we watched our fellow inmates' possessions being wantonly destroyed.

Over the next several years I would relive such inspections many times as the police made it a habit of disrupting our lives in this manner every several months.

Bastards!

24

Politicians Feign Interest

FOLLOWING MY FIRST DAY IN FRONT of the judge, e-mails started to circulate in the United States detailing what had transpired that first day in court. Because the Embassy had previously sent a message stating that nothing had happened, word was spreading that Paul's attorney had merely asked for a postponement until a date in March. Little did they know that we had actually had a hearing and I had been questioned by the judge.

In response to my request that Governor Jeb Bush be contacted, both my father and daughter sent off letters to the governor's office. In my father's letter he asked for specific help from Jeb's father, the former President, George Bush, Sr.:

> We understand on good authority that your father, Mr. George Bush, is a personal friend of the President of the United Arab Emirates and recently spent some time in Abu Dhabi visiting the President of the UAE.
>
> I am writing to you for two reasons: the first is to let you know that one of your Florida citizens needs your help so that he can be returned to North America; secondly hopefully you might contact your father and use his influence to have a citizen of the United States of America returned to either Canada or the United States of America. If released into my custody Paul would be placed into a detox center where he would receive treatment for his alleged offense.

> *I am in my 87th year and would dearly love to see my son alive. Paul is fifty-three years old and would still have a lot to offer in any gainful employment.*

My daughter Jennifer wrote:

> *I am extremely afraid of what may happen to my father. There have been no pretrial discussions and I have heard the trial date is set to March 6th. I know if this happened in the United States my father would be a free man but I believe in my heart that something must happen so my father can return to the United States where he belongs. I am very afraid for my father's health (physical and emotional) overseas and what the end result will be without any assistance from the United States. I love my father very much and would do anything I could to help him. I miss my father very much and I am grateful to this day that he is still alive.*

Governor Jeb Bush's response arrived three months later on May 27, 1999, three weeks after I had received my sentence:

> *I received your letter regarding your father's imprisonment. I am very sorry to learn about his situation and apologize for the delay in responding.*
>
> *I certainly hope your father's situation has been resolved. If not, you may wish to contact United States Senator Connie Mack at 1342 Colonial Boulevard, Suite 27, Fort Myers, Florida 33907. His telephone number is (941) 275-6252. Because this is an international legal matter, my ability to intervene is limited. Your best source of assistance is Connie Mack.*
>
> *I hope this matter is soon resolved. If I can ever assist you with any state issues, I hope you will let me know.*

There was no mention of his father George Bush or of my family's request that he use his influence to secure my release.

At the same time that the letters were sent to Governor Bush, my friends and family had also written to Senators Bob Graham and Connie Mack of Florida, Senators Evan Bayh and Richard Lugar of Indiana, and Congressman Barney Frank of Massachusetts. They in turn sent letters to the Embassy in Abu Dhabi and were informed what had precipitated my arrest and what was happening to me. The politicians' response to family and friends was to pass the buck back to the Embassy. There was nothing they could do.

The letters from the Embassy in Abu Dhabi included the following:

> *Paul Brian Ciceri (DPOB: June 8, 1945, Canada) was arrested at Abu Dhabi International Airport, United Arab Emirates (UAE) on October 7, 1998 upon his return to the UAE from Canada. Mr. Ciceri was residing in the UAE as an English language teacher. When his brother, Richard, could not contact Paul to verify his safe arrival in Abu Dhabi, he asked the Embassy to make inquiries as to Paul's welfare and whereabouts. The Embassy subsequently learned that police at the airport had found 5 grams of cocaine in Mr. Ciceri's baggage. During a subsequent search of his residence, police discovered and seized a quantity of hashish. In addition, according to the police laboratory, a urine test Mr. Ciceri submitted to tested positive for narcotics use. The public prosecutor charged Mr. Ciceri with possession, use, and importation of an illegal narcotic, three separate and distinct charges under the UAE criminal code. These charges carry a possible combined penalty of 8–12 years imprisonment and up to a 50,000 UAE dirham (US $13,613) fine.*

The information given to the politicians by the Embassy was flawed on two points. First, 5 grams of cocaine was not found in my possession at the airport. It was 100 times less at .065 grams. Second, I was not employed as an English language teacher. In fact, I was the Director of Marketing for all English language schools throughout the Middle East and North Africa. This misinformation was a manifestation of the fact that no one, neither the Embassy nor my lawyer, ever asked me for specifics of what had happened. Nor did they inquire what I was doing in the Middle East. Had they just written me off? Or was it a matter that I had no hope of being judged innocent? Were they just going along with the system and then would deal with the problem after I was sentenced?

As politicians were being contacted, the trial moved forward. On March 6, I was again called to the courthouse for a second session in front of the judge. The Embassy had forewarned me that my lawyer would be asking me a few questions during this session.

Now that I knew the procedure, I was not nearly as frightened as I had been during my first visit to the courtroom. What occurred in the courtroom before my case was called, however, was very unnerving indeed. Six women prostitutes were given their sentences by the judge. All of them were given six-month prison sentences and four were also condemned to receive forty lashes by the cane. When that was announced, there was a rash of screaming and wailing from the four as well as from their supporters seated in the courtroom. After this outbreak, six other people from my block were questioned by the judge. He became outraged when all six, under direct questioning by the judge, indicated they had not smoked hashish, nor could they explain how the police had found hashish and hashish residue in their room the night police had broken into their hotel room. After their lawyer spoke to the judge, their case was remanded to a further date. Immediately after this decision, one prisoner was given a sentence of nineteen years for dealing in drugs. As soon as the judge issued his sentence, the mother of the prisoner burst into the courtroom area directly in front of us, and began weeping and pleading for leniency. "Please do not put my son behind bars for such a long time," she wailed. The judge merely summoned the police and had her escorted from the courtroom. All of those proceedings were numbing as I realized the reality of what could happen to me.

My name was finally called and I was led to my place in front of the judge. He spoke briefly with my lawyer and then my lawyer addressed a few questions to me through the interpreter.

"Mr. Ciceri, did you know that there was cocaine in your suitcase the night of October 7, 1998 when you arrived in Abu Dhabi from Athens?"

"No sir," was my reply.

> "Was that the first time you saw the drugs in your suitcase?"
>
> "Yes."

And then my lawyer talked with the judge and through the interpreter the judge told me that my next hearing would be on April 12.

I was then escorted out of the courtroom and Jamal, the Embassy representative who was present during the session, got permission from the police to talk with me for a few minutes. We were escorted into a small office where Jamal asked me about the statement I had made to the Public Prosecutor after the police had confronted me with the evidence gathered during the search of my apartment. He said that in the statement I had acknowledged that the marijuana found there was mine. I told him that that was not what I had said. Rather, I had told the Public Prosecutor that the container was like one I had brought back from the hotel in Cairo but, because I wasn't allowed to look at it, I couldn't have known if the contents he had shown me were marijuana. Jamal told me there was a discrepancy in my statement then, and it posed a problem since they had written that I had admitted to owning the marijuana. Our conversation lasted only a few minutes before the police indicated I had to return to the holding cell. Quickly I asked Jamal to pass on my regards to my family and tell them I was doing as well as expected.

I didn't know at that time that my family and the attorney had not yet agreed on the terms of his representing me. The attorney had been acting in good faith during the first two sessions before coming to an agreement with my family. Eventually, a fee was negotiated that would be determined by the leniency or severity of the sentence I would receive. I had not heard of such a fee plan before, but I felt that the incentive of a higher payout would make Mr. Al-Tamimi work harder to have me found innocent.

Going to the courthouse and being in front of the judge who would determine where I lived for the upcoming years was a stressful and uncertain time. Some of my thoughts were detailed in a letter I wrote on March 26 to my friend Dean:

> *I am keeping positive but the time to get through the legal process is slow and frustrating. Remember*

> *that lawyers put the worst spin on everything so when things turn out well they can take all the credit. I don't take anything here lightly but I just must look for the best, within reason.*
>
> *I've heard survivors of serious car crashes say that when they realized what was going to happen their body entered a bizarre state where everything seemed to move in slow motion and nothing at first hurt them. It was as though they were watching a movie. That is how things have been for me. It seems that I have not really been here—I know my body is, but my mind is so detached that time has sped by so that the day I came here is vivid but the rest is a blur. I guess I'm lucky because others agonize over the long days they endure. Don't get me wrong; it is not fun here—quite the contrary!*
>
> *We're getting closer to a resolution. I pray that this nightmare ends soon.*

My sights were now set on my next appearance in front of the judge which was scheduled for April 12, 1999.

Back home in Orlando my friend Jim Garrett was doing something of which I was totally unaware until I got back to the United States and was able to review all that had transpired while I was in prison. To this day I am appreciative of and humbled by his efforts to raise funds for my defense. On March 28, 1999, he wrote the following to my friends and family on the e-mail that spread the news of my incarceration:

```
     I am addressing this note to Paul
Ciceri's e-mail list. Some of you I recog-
nize, others I don't, so I will introduce
myself as a longtime friend of Paul's in
Orlando.
     As you know from prior e-mails, Paul
is in prison in the United Arab Emirates.
All the facts are not clear, but it seems
that Paul was caught bringing drugs into
the country. In all the 20 years or so I
```

have known Paul, I never knew him to use drugs. Some of you may have.

What is now important is that Paul's trial, after several delays, is going to be held on April 12th. Paul has retained a UAE lawyer who has a very good reputation. As you all know, good attorneys are expensive. Already, the costs are approaching ten thousand dollars.

In the past, when I have asked him for help, Paul has always been there, even when it was not convenient. Many of you probably say the same thing. With this in mind, if you can and feel the cause is worthy, I am asking you to help a friend in need. Any amount will help.

Paul's ex-wife, Susanne, has offered to collect any moneys and will combine and forward them to Paul's brother to send to his attorney. Checks are fine and should be payable to her at_____.

Paul has been in prison since October. Things must move slowly over there. Whatever you think about Paul's status, let's try to reserve judgment until all the facts come out. I am.

Keep Paul in your prayers and let's hope for a good outcome on April 16th. Hopefully we'll be able to hug him soon.

Every time I read this letter tears come to my eyes. I just thank God for friends like Jim and all those who felt as he did, whether they were able to respond monetarily or not.

25

The Defense

THE FOUR WEEKS BETWEEN VISITS TO THE courthouse moved quickly. I had been alerted by the Embassy staff that all that would happen at the next appearance was that my attorney would present my defense in the case.

It seemed bizarre to me that I was paying a good amount of money to an attorney whom I had met in private only once before my trial began, and who had not yet asked me for my version of the events leading up to my arrest. Nor did he ask about the narcotics that the police supposedly found in my apartment. I was told that this was the way things happened in the UAE judicial system and that my attorney would work from the statements that I had signed. Since these were entirely in Arabic, I had no assurance that what was recorded was representative of what I had said. The situation was frightening.

In a letter in mid March to my friend James Ward, I described the anxiety I experienced as I spent my time waiting for the resolution of my court case:

> *My third visit to court comes up on April 12th. My first two were positive, and if we meet our objective for the next, I will be elated. Proceedings are moving slowly but I'm hoping for a positive resolution by the end of May.*
>
> *People keep moving in and out—some move to other blocks when they are sentenced and others gain their freedom. My closest friends these days are a Russian, two Bahrainis (flight attendants) and a Filipino.*

My French lessons paid off in that I can now converse with some of the guards (from Africa). I'm brushing up on my Russian in exchange for some English tutoring.

I go to Islamic classes four times a week where we compare Islam to Christianity. I've learned that a lot of my perceptions of Islam were wrong and I've found a strengthening of my own faith in the process.

I remain positive in spite of the absurdity of it all. At the outset I adopted a formula for dealing with adversity. The process was formalized by a management consultant firm: 1. Control—taking charge; 2. Ownership—holding oneself responsible even if he wasn't the cause; 3. Reach—not letting the problem pervade the psyche; and 4. Endurance—retaining optimism as you work through the situation.

From a south-facing window I look onto an expanse of dirt about two football fields wide with some trees in one area. There, birds gather and I watch some cats vainly attempt to catch them. The cats have free roam of the prison as they enter/leave through barred doors—some even end up sleeping with us on the colder nights.

Three Canadians just successfully crossed, on foot and camel, the Empty Quarter—one of the harshest terrains on the planet—ending up in Abu Dhabi. It was written up in today's magazine section of the local paper (on the internet at www.gulf-news.co.uae. The pictures with the article made me realize I will really miss this place—in a few respects.

I've got some novels and technical manuals on the way to me, so for now I have all I need—thanks for offering to send me things.

I hope you all had a wonderful Easter and I hope that God blesses you as much as he has me.

Amazingly I was quite calm in the days leading up to my hearing in front of the judge. I guess that was because I was told that I would not be asked any questions and that my attorney would do all the talking.

On that day, April 12, I was ushered into the cage in the courtroom shackled at the ankles along with about twelve other prisoners. When the judges finally entered the courtroom, my attorney was nowhere to be seen, although Justine and Jamal were present from the American Embassy. I could tell that Jamal looked concerned about his absence and actually left the courtroom to find him while other cases were being heard.

For an hour I waited as other trials droned on and slowly the cage emptied out along with the crowd of spectators in the courtroom. Finally I was the only one left in the cage and there were only a few spectators left. My name was called and I took my place in front of the judge as usual. There was a dialogue between the judge and my lawyer and then my lawyer began to speak, reading from his printed notes on the podium.

I knew that he had faxed a thirty-three-page document in Arabic to my brother specifying the details of the defense he was putting forth. It appeared that he was reading verbatim from those pages. I understood nothing, but I tried to watch the expression on the judges' faces as they listened. After about fifteen minutes I sensed that the judges were getting bored, and at one point, the main judge seemed agitated. He asked my attorney to speed things up. He questioned him, I was sure, and admonished him for taking so long. It was almost as though his mind had already been made up about the disposition of my case, and he just wanted to put his day in court behind him.

Finally, my lawyer finished presenting his case and sat down. The judge asked no more questions and had a brief discussion with the court clerk. Then the translator turned to me and said, "Your next session will be May 1. You will get your sentence then."

May 1! That was to be the date I would learn my fate. Freedom or more years in confinement would be the verdict. And as I was escorted out of the courtroom I was numb at that reality. I neither had a chance to speak to my attorney or to the Embassy staff before I was hustled away to board the truck back to prison.

26

Waiting for the Verdict

I KNEW THAT THE NEXT THREE WEEKS would be filled with anxiety if I allowed myself to be consumed with the possibilities. So I decided to keep myself busy. In a strange way, I continued to feel the great calm that I had felt throughout most of my time at Al Wathba. I experienced an inner peace that was a result of my knowing that I was not alone; God was with me. He had shown me His presence and would continue to do so in the many months ahead. Whatever the outcome on May 1, it would be the right verdict for me in my life at this time. I would survive whatever lay ahead. Over many months of my going to court, I had come to realize that the truth had little place in the courtroom; no one seemed to want to know the facts and the verdicts were apparently directed by the President's office. The judges were merely the mouthpieces of the President's inner circle. I knew I would not be set free, but I also believed that I would not get the maximum sentence.

As I stood before the Court and listened to the judge and my lawyer speaking in a language I did not understand, I had a chance to scrutinize their faces and actions. Gradually, I began to realize that the two of them were working in harmony. My sentence had been decided from the outset and I knew it would be at least four years. All the rest was just a waste of time, a matter of going through the motions pretending that justice was being served. They thought theirs was the best justice system in the world, yet in reality what a sham it was!

During this time I learned that my father had sent a Bible to me at the prison. A letter in Arabic came with it written by an Imam that my father had sought out in Canada. The letter, written to the Manager of the Prison, beseeched him to let me have the Bible. The writer told how people of all faiths were allowed to practice their religion freely in Canada and that the Manager should extend that right to me by allowing me to have the Bible. Despite his plea, the Manager decided that I could not have the Bible in the block, but instead placed it with the librarian and said I could go to the library to read it any morning during the week if I wanted to.

At first I was upset, but I realized later that his decision was a blessing in disguise. Although I would not have the Bible to read whenever I wanted, its placement out of the block was my ticket to spend time in the library and meet other prisoners who had been given library privileges.

My weekday mornings were now occupied with my Islamic classes and going to the library, the afternoons with sleep and exercise, and the evenings with reading, playing games, and socializing with the other prisoners. We talked about everything from life in each person's individual country to the repression in countries like the UAE to our hopes for the future.

Meanwhile, the dynamics of the people in my room had changed dramatically because of releases, transfers, and the addition of new prisoners. Many of the quiet, friendly Indians had moved on and in their place we had a couple of Arabs, one of whom snored loudly each night. Other occupants included an Indian who was rowdy and disrespectful of other peoples' right to privacy and quiet; a Russian who helped me with my Russian language studies; and my Filipino friend who had decided to move from his spot in the corridor.

The room was filled beyond capacity and with such crowded conditions nerves sometimes became frayed. The man who snored kept most people from getting a decent night's sleep, and all night long people kept nudging him so he would roll over. Arguments erupted every night as he stubbornly refused to move his bed outside to the corridor so he wouldn't bother anyone. The police declined to move him because no other room wanted him and he had a right to be in a room. The welfare of the rest of us didn't matter. On top of that, the Indian who showed little respect for others invited several of his friends into our room every afternoon to play card games. Those of us who tried to get some sleep at that time to make up for a poor night's sleep were kept awake by this group of card sharks. As a result, heated arguments broke out over the use of our room as a place to congregate for card games. My Filipino friend and the Russian were the most vocal in expressing disdain for this lack of consideration. A few of us approached the foreman to have him intervene, but he didn't want to get involved. The Filipino's aggravation intensified when he was groped one night by one of the Indian prisoners who had been trying to convince us that Islam was the ultimate way to salvation.

Soon the inevitable happened. A fight broke out between the Russian and the Indian one afternoon and the entire block population descended on our room to see what was happening. The foreman appeared and angry discussions took place. I used the opportunity to tell the foreman that his inaction had led to the major problem we now faced. So that the police would not come in and put some of us in solitary, he finally decided he had better take action.

A shuffling of prisoners followed and I ended up in a smaller room with the Filipino, the Russian and three of his countrymen, a Brit, and a couple of Indians. The area was much quieter and we all got along well. One of the Russians was a talented artist and he sketched scenes of life within our block as well as pictures of the prison itself. Of course, all his pictures had to be hidden in notebooks so the police would not confiscate them. The other Russians, whom I mentally compared to the bumbling thieves in the "Home Alone" movies, had been arrested for transporting alcohol for the purpose of distribution. They had been caught when they had stopped at the scene of an accident to gawk at what had happened. Of them all, the British inmate, James, however, became my confidant.

James had been working for a local company in Abu Dhabi. During the course of his employment he had taken a loan out with his company's help to pay tuition for the college education of one of his sons. Subsequently, he had arranged with the controller, an Egyptian, to pay the money back with a set of postdated checks. Unfortunately he had given the Egyptian a set of signed *blank* checks with the agreement that the Egyptian would spread out the payments and fill in the amounts. Subsequently, James learned the lesson that many of us already knew: you couldn't trust Arabs, including Egyptians, in business dealings. The Egyptian took the first check, filled in the total amount of the loan, and sent it to the bank for processing. Of course, when there were insufficient funds in James' account to cover the check, the Egyptian had him arrested and put in prison.

James, who never hid his distaste for all the Arabs, the jailors, and the politicians, had a great sense of humor and we became good friends. One of the "Home Alone" Russians also took a liking to James and followed him wherever he went. Often if James and I would try to find a quiet place to talk, the Russian would come by and nudge James over so the three of us were squeezed into one tight space. Sometimes James would find that his towel was wet when he went to use it, so the two of us kept an eye out until one day we saw the same Russian use it to dry himself after a shower. At least twice a day he would bum a cigarette off James until James periodically gave him a pack of cigarettes just to get rid of him. Eventually he gave him the towel to use. It became an amusing pastime to watch James' 'pet Russian' follow him around. Since he understood no English, we could talk about his antics right in front of him and roar with laughter. I'm sure he must have wondered what was so amusing.

All the Russians were good chess players so the four of us would hold chess tournaments. It was intriguing to see the way they played because each had an individual strategy that he followed game after game. After I figured out what their characteristic strategies were, it was easy to develop one of my own to counter them. Winning became routine for me. Even though their 'code' had been broken and they started losing every game, they kept to their same game plan. I had to wonder about the mentality of such an approach, and James and I had a few laughs while comparing their tactics to the overall policy of the Russian government in staying with Communist-held theories even though these had proved an abysmal failure over time.

The Russians also provided a bit of humor to our Islamic classes. As with the rest of us, their primary motive in attending these classes was to escape the block several times a week; they also went to meet Russians from other blocks who attended the classes. Because most of them did not understand English well, they spent their time talking among themselves in Russian. I knew enough Russian to know that their discussions were all social in nature, but when confronted by the teacher, they explained that they were merely translating and discussing what he had just talked about. The teacher would look at me and with a bit of a grin, acknowledging that he knew what was really going on.

The Russians were all Russian Orthodox Christians and we got into some very interesting discussions with them over basic Christian doctrine. The Russians claimed that Jesus and the Jesus Christ in the Bible were two different persons. They did not believe in the concept of the Trinity and insisted that God the Father, Son, and Holy Spirit were three separate beings. This supported one of the main criticisms that Muslims had concerning Christianity: that we Christians had three Gods while they believed in only one. So, there we were—Christians in an Islamic class, debating among ourselves about the true nature and belief of Christianity, and lending support to the Islamic theories that the Christian community can't even agree over the basic tenets of their religion. Of course, the same could have been said of Islam.

Jim Oakes added another dimension to our discussion since he considered himself an atheist and thought that we, Christians and Muslims alike, were on the wrong path. He had a way of using humor to prove his point and I came to admire the man for his honesty and the steadfastness of his beliefs.

I felt sorry for the Russians since they had no books in Russian to which they could refer and had to rely on their very limited English in discussing their views with us. No Russian books were allowed in the prison and no letters in Russian could pass in or out of the confine because there were no Russian translators on the administrative staff. Not even the Russian translation of a book like *Robinson Crusoe* was allowed. That seemed absurd to us because it was obvious that the censors never even read allowable English books. There were many sections in those novels that would have been banned had the translators had a better grasp of the English language. Eventually the lieutenant who oversaw the "school" obtained a Russian language edition of the Koran for the Russians to read.

Sam, the British prisoner who taught our class, told me that I should ask to be transferred to Block 8 once I received my sentence.

Because we were in the Islamic class and the lieutenant in charge there had some pull with the administration, he could do things for us that could never otherwise be done. Apparently, the police in the administrative area could determine our block assignments. The Islamic class was the pride of the Manager of the Prison since he could show his superiors, and especially Sheik Saif, one of the President's sons and Deputy Minister of the Ministry of the Interior responsible for prison systems, how he was promoting Islam within the prison. Whenever visiting dignitaries came to the prison, they were routinely escorted to our classroom. There they could see that an American and some British citizens were learning about Islam and they could hope that perhaps we would one day convert. Little did they realize the real reasons why we attended the class! Regardless, to keep us happy and coming to the class, the lieutenant treated us well. His prestige was on the line too.

So I was hopeful that I might be transferred to Block 8 once I got my sentence. I still held on to the hope that I'd be set free without further complications, but I had come to realize that there was a possibility that this was not likely to happen now. I had been in prison over six months and there was no way the government could acquit me. After all, how would it look if they had held an American in their most secure prison for all that time and in the end he was innocent?

So the days passed quickly as May 1 approached, and I became more and more confident that all would work out well. I knew that the Embassy could make no entreaties to have me released until after my sentence had been handed down. Thus, the sentencing was actually something I wanted to face head on and put behind me. Then I could concentrate fully on getting out of Al Wathba.

27

The Verdict Is In

MAY 1 FINALLY DAWNED, AND AS ON previous Court days, I was up early, ate little, and said a few extra prayers before heading out to join the others for the tedious trek into Abu Dhabi.

At breakfast that morning the policeman named Mohammed from Mauritania, who had been on duty at Al Wathba when I had been confined to the holding cell, was on duty watching over us. He greeted me, and when I told him that I was going to court that day to be set free, he smiled and wished me well. Just having him there gave me confidence because I liked him as a person and he had been respectful of me as a prisoner.

We were searched, loaded on the trucks, and sent on our way. During the ride some of the younger prisoners began picking on one of the Iranian boys by taking his sandals. I wasn't in the mood for such tomfoolery because in a short time I faced some very serious life-altering decisions. The fellow beside me was the instigator of the whole affair, and at one point when he raised his hand to hit the boy again with his own sandals, I grabbed his wrist firmly and said, "No!" He stopped and looked at me in disbelief. How dare I interfere with his fun? I simply repeated "No." He looked at the others trying to figure how he could get out of this situation gracefully without getting into a fight with The American. Another Arab fellow whom we both knew looked at him and nodded that he should stop. He backed off and gave the Iranian his sandals back and then started joking with his friends. I am sure he was talking about the interfering American, but at least the strain of that situation was diffused and I could continue staring at the countryside as we rode into town.

At the courthouse we were ushered into the now familiar holding cell. Once the door was closed, cigarettes again magically appeared, and those who were concerned about what lay ahead of them that morning sat quietly. But those who had been picking on the Iranian in the truck resumed their attack, this time joined by some of their friends who had been transported in the other trucks. I kept from getting involved further, because my intrusion would have led to a fight and I didn't want anything to interfere with my appearance before the judge. I wanted only to end this phase of my imprisonment.

Eventually my name was called and I joined others in the courtroom cell where I had been three times before. Now that I was used to the routine, I wasn't nearly so nervous, a response which actually surprised me. Somehow, as I faced my sentencing, I felt a pervasive calm knowing that my God was with me and that whatever happened I would survive.

For what seemed a long time we waited in that cell wondering where the judges for that day's cases were. Eventually, my lawyer entered the room and gave me a quick glance as he walked past. Immediately after he took his place, the policeman in charge gave the call for order and the judges entered the courtroom. The thought immediately flashed through my mind: *What deal did my lawyer cook up with the judges?* I had no doubt that this was all a show and that my lawyer had talked with the judges outside of the courtroom. Everything had been prearranged.

A few cases were called ahead of mine. In one, five persons on a drug charge were questioned for a few minutes by the judge and then dismissed; in another, the defendant was sentenced to fifteen years for drug dealing. Then my name was called. This was it! In a matter of minutes my fate would be known. Whatever the decision, I was ready to get on with my life and have the cloud of uncertainty lifted.

I took my place in front of the judge. I wasn't nervous. He picked up a document, flipped several pages, and then began to read in Arabic. The courtroom was quiet. An American was getting sentenced in a UAE courtroom. Everyone was focused on the moment. The judge read for about one minute. He stopped. He put the paper down. My lawyer showed no expression. I know he knew the result already!

The translator turned to me and said, "Your sentence is four years. Your drugs will be confiscated and you will be deported at the end of your sentence." That was it. Finished. Done. Over. **Four Years!** I repeated calmly to myself. In those flashing seconds a sense of relief passed over me. **Only Four Years! I Got the Minimum Sentence!**

The policemen flanking me motioned for me to follow them out of the courtroom. One led me to the elevator and back to the holding cell. No sooner had the door closed behind me, than it was opened again and my name was called. But in those few brief moments inside, everyone in the holding cell knew my verdict and they were predicting that the Embassy would get me out. I would be going home. I wanted so much to believe them; just having it reinforced by so many gave me some confidence that it just might be true.

I was ushered into the Captain's office where Jamal and my lawyer were sitting on one of the couches. I took my place beside them and Jamal began to talk.

"Paul, Mr. Al-Tamimi thinks that this is a very good verdict. Obviously it is much better than the seven to twenty years that could have been imposed upon you by the judge. But it is also, in a way, better than being acquitted."

Okay, I thought to myself. *A sentence of four is better than being acquitted? Boy, math and logic must have changed in the seven months since I was arrested.*

"Mr. Al-Tamimi thinks that a strong appeal would have been launched by the Public Prosecutor if you had been acquitted, and in the Appeals Court a much harsher sentence could be rendered against you. Even so, there is a good possibility that the Public Prosecutor might still launch an appeal against this lighter verdict, but the odds are much lower than if you had been acquitted."

I thought: *What he's saying is that I'm lucky to get four. If I had been acquitted, I could possibly be sentenced to more by a different set of judges. Okay, I got four years and at least now the Embassy can work to get me out. I just want to get the fuck out of here!*

"Okay," I said. "What do we do now then? Do we appeal the verdict?"

Jamal put the question in Arabic to Mr. Al-Tamimi and his answer was that we would wait. Both parties had fifteen days in which to make an appeal against the verdict. We would wait until the fifteenth day and if the Public Prosecutor hadn't appealed by that date then we would place ours.

I didn't really want to appeal. I just wanted to go home.

So, that was our plan. There would be an appeal. If not by the Public Prosecutor, then by my lawyer and me. I could think only that following such a course of action would merely delay any involvement by the Embassy in working for my release. I had to trust the lawyer. Maybe a sentence had to be given to justify the UAE keeping me in prison for seven months, and now maybe the appeal process would be their way to gracefully back off and let me go.

Our discussion came to an abrupt end when the police indicated that I had to return to the holding cell. I shook hands with Jamal and Mr. Al-Tamimi, and as I turned to leave, Jamal assured me that the Embassy would be contacting the State Department

Sentencing

to inform people there of the decision. My family would also be notified. I was grateful for that and went back to the cell.

Back at Al Wathba my block had already had their lunch, so I joined another block for mine. The eating area that day was below my block so I could look up and see my roommates as they peered down trying to see what had happened to those of us who had gone to the courthouse. I saw my friend Jim Oakes watching me and wondering what had happened. I signaled him with my hands that I had gotten a four year sentence. Others noticed our silent dialogue, and I knew that the information would be passed throughout the prison in a matter of minutes.

When I got back to the block, I had a brief discussion about that morning's proceedings and then lay down for a nap. I was mentally exhausted but at the same time very relieved. When I awoke, I felt refreshed and the evening passed as all the others had passed: in discussion and games and reading.

That night, just before going to sleep, I lay flat on my back looking up at the barred window and through the small opening formed by the crossing of the vertical metal bars with the horizontal concrete posts on the outer wall of the walkway. The little stretch of sky was black and starless. I closed my eyes and said a prayer of thanks. I thanked God for having been with me and for my having received the minimum sentence allowed by the Presidency. Regardless of my feelings about what should have been, I was grateful.

As I lay there, I opened my eyes again and focused on the little black patch of sky I had looked at earlier. There framed by the bars was a beautiful full moon. Surprised, I had to blink several times. *Where had that come from?* But I knew. This was just another of the many signs that I had received in my seven months at Al Wathba. All was well. That image of the full moon still haunts me to this day. It was placed there as a sign from my God that he was there with me and that I would be okay. I audibly whispered, "Thank you, God."

I closed my eyes and slept a peaceful sleep.

28

The Aftermath

THE WORD ABOUT THE VERDICT handed down was relayed rapidly to my friends and family. On May 6 an e-mail circulated back in the United States. Jim Garrett wrote:

> Well, the verdict is in. Paul was sentenced to four years with time already served deducted. In the UAE they do have sentence reduction for good behavior also. It is expected this will lop about a year off the sentence. In October, Paul will have been in prison for one year. Therefore, it is probable he will be released in October of 2001. His attorney evidently got one charge dropped or it would have been worse.
>
> All of this cannot be pleasant for Paul, but he has overcome other problems and he has been remarkably agile in his ability to adapt. This may be the greatest test of this ability. I'm sure he will want to know that, regardless of his current situation, he can count on his friends to still be there.
>
> At least the waiting is over and time will heal all this!

Things were starting to happen back in Al Wathba too. Once a prisoner receives his sentence, he is transferred from transit blocks, such as Block 3, into another block where prisoners who are serving their longer sentences reside. Sam, the teacher of our Islamic class, asked the lieutenant in charge of the schools if he would intercede to have me transferred to Block 8 where he lived. Fortunately, he obliged and I was reassigned to Block 8 and into Sam's room.

The process of relocation was fairly routine. We had to take all our possessions to the area where I had first been checked into Al Wathba. There we were re-fingerprinted, photographed, given gray uniforms in exchange for our blue ones, asked a few questions about the information in our file, and issued a new bataka (ID card). Then we were distributed among the blocks set aside for those prisoners who had received their sentences.

There were eight of us in the room where I was assigned and the men had done a splendid job of decorating their area. Using writing paper that had a background of clouds over blue sky, they papered all the walls and ceiling. It was a stunning effect that obviously had taken many man hours to accomplish. But more importantly, Block 8 was on the upper level and the window in our room looked over the prison walls enabling us to see the surrounding countryside.

What a splendid gift it was to see the world whenever I wanted! Just over the walls we could glimpse farms where the camels used for races were housed; beyond that was a highway where one could watch vehicles passing now and then. Off in the distance were the lights of a small town, and occasionally you could glimpse a passing plane. What a lift it was to my spirits to see signs of life outside the prison. Once in a while a camel caravan of traders would pass just beyond the prison walls. We would yell to them and some would converse with them. They usually consisted of anywhere from four to six traders with fifteen to twenty-five camels. I often wondered where they were headed and what goods they were transporting. Watching the riders bob up and down with every step of the camel, one knew beyond a doubt that this was anything but a smooth ride.

Block 8 was definitely a step up from being in Block 3 and my spirits soared beyond the confines of the prison walls. Sam was very kind and took me around and introduced me to several of the other inmates. Because Block 8 was a block for prisoners who had been sentenced, there were people who had been there a long time. Some young men had been incarcerated for eleven years and had spent their entire twenties behind the walls of Al Wathba. What astonished me the most, however, was that, for the most part, they were still positive people who had accepted their fate as simply part of their life. I didn't feel that I could complain about getting a sentence of four years. Even if I served the full term of my sentence, I would still be released before many of those who had been there ten years or more. The reality of Al Wathba was beginning to settle in fully.

I met and befriended several interesting people during this time:

- Uti (pronounced "you-tee") was an Indian who was gifted with many creative talents. He crafted most of the chess pieces for the inmates; he honed knives from pieces of metal torn off the bathroom doors; using plastic stripped from pails, he made combs; from bristles of the floor brushes, he crafted hair brushes. From these same brush bristles he could also make rivets to hold things together, and he replaced a lost screw to my eyeglasses with a 'rivet' that lasted for over one year. Physically, Uti resembled a Buddha and this quickly earned him the nickname "Little Buddha."
- Mohammad Al Jenaibi was a native of the UAE and was a pilot in the Air Force. He was about fifty-five and had flown to many foreign countries until he had been arrested for drug use. This was his second time in a UAE prison, though he had also spent time in a Pakistani prison for smuggling cocaine inside the legs of a table he had purchased. During my stay at Al Wathba, one of Mohammad's brothers, his son, and a nephew also were incarcerated for drug use. He had a penchant for young Filipino women and talked at length about his romantic exploits and his current marriage to a Filipino beauty. Indeed, when I knew him, he had two wives but clearly doted on the Filipino because of the attentions she bestowed on him.
- Saad, a Pakistani, had spent nine years in Al Wathba when I first met him. He was a big imposing man who basically was a gentle giant, though you always had the feeling that you wanted to keep on his good side. The scars of stab wounds he had received a few years earlier in a fight with another inmate had earned him a healthy respect among his block mates. He

and I spent many evenings talking about his life back home in Pakistan near the border with Afghanistan. He had been in the drug smuggling business for many years prior to his arrest, and he elaborated on the many ways that drug smugglers operated throughout Europe, Asia, and the Middle East. That was information I later offered to the State Department through the U.S. Embassy in Abu Dhabi, but they declined to talk with me about what I had learned. Saad's revelations were chilling and he detailed operations in which he had personally been involved in Europe and in the Khyber Pass area of Pakistan. He was also a fount of information about the different types of drugs that were being moved out of those countries into the United States.

- Mohammed was a Bangladeshi. He was a quiet young man who had been arrested for theft and was sentenced to three years in prison. He and I talked a lot about his home and the poverty that pervaded the population of his country. He desperately wanted to be my friend because it made him very popular back home when he told his friends that he had an American buddy.

- Majdi was a Syrian who spent much of his time teaching other Arabs English grammar and oral English. He would spend every evening talking one-on-one with other prisoners and encouraging them to learn English so they would have a chance at a better life outside of prison. Eventually, he and I would help each other by his teaching me Arabic and my coaching him in French.

- Khalid was a charming man of about thirty-five who had been sentenced to fifteen years for drug smuggling. He had owned a popular restaurant in Oman prior to his arrest. A quiet unassuming person, Khalid helped everyone that he could by having friends bring toiletries and clothes for him that he in turn would give to other inmates for their use. His one passion was to become fluent in English and he attended English and mathematics classes to better himself.

- Freddie was a Filipino who was nearing the end of a seven year sentence for drug use. To make money for his needs he cleaned the bathroom areas every morning and in return he would receive cigarettes from the other prisoners. These he would then trade off for the things he needed. He had converted to Islam in the hope that his sentence would be reduced, but he had never told his family about his conversion. We had interesting

discussions about how he would conceal that from them, especially when it came to praying five times every day.
- Jassem was an Iranian who had been in prison for seven of a fifteen-year sentence for drug smuggling. Somehow he managed to keep himself in fabulous physical shape without doing any exercising. He had a nice smile, played extremely hard at soccer, was a good artist, and was an organizer of evenings where Arab songs were sung while he kept beat on the bottom of a laundry pail.
- Mohamed Jen was a young twenty-one year old Egyptian boy who had been caught at the Abu Dhabi airport with one marijuana cigarette in his pocket and had been sentenced to four years. He had received his sentence not long before I did, and was currently going through the appeal process.

Every few days prisoners from other blocks were given the duty of cleaning the walkways on the outside perimeter of our block. Some of these persons routinely stopped to say hello when they were out of sight of the police guards. One that would eventually become a good friend in the months ahead was an Indian named Horace. He was as white as most of the British and one would never have taken him to be from India.

Generally he stopped by about the time that Sam, Mohamed Jen, and I exercised each afternoon. We had developed a good routine and Horace had a knack for appearing just when it seemed we most needed a rest in our program. As the summer wore on, I noticed that we were sweating a bit more each day as the temperature climbed steadily toward the highs of the torrid desert summers.

At this time the lieutenant in charge of the school had asked me to teach English to the younger male prisoners. They met in the classroom next to the one where I attended Islamic studies and their housing was separate from the other male housing to protect them from sexual abuse by the older prisoners. They ranged in age from sixteen to twenty, represented many of the Arab and African countries, and were incarcerated for a variety of crimes including theft, vandalism, and fighting.

I was surprised by the level of fluency in English demonstrated by most of them, especially the Africans. Generally, with the exception of young men from Yemen, the level of English of their peers from the Middle East Gulf countries was poor. This wasn't a surprise to me, since I had learned that the young men in the Gulf countries were so spoiled by wealth and indifference to their long-term future that they took school studies as an aggravation rather than as an opportunity. This was actually an embarrassment to the prison officials who encouraged the "locals" to attend classes, but who were mostly disappointed when these "locals" were upstaged in interest and performance by the Africans upon whom they looked with disdain. I was able to teach two different levels of study at the same time, and often combined the teachings when there was a chance to present new information to each group or to get them to interact with one another. This was a good experience in that I had a great deal of rapport with my students and they responded with enthusiasm to what I did for them. In addition, preparation for the classes filled some of my idle time back in the block, while equally important was the fact that I gained the respect of the prison administration for what I was doing.

29

The Appeal

AFTER THE PUBLIC PROSECUTOR HAD not appealed my four-year sentence, I learned from the Embassy staff that my lawyer had filed an appeal on my behalf on the fifteenth and last day he could do so. That meant that my case would come up before a different panel of three judges with a need to present the specifics of my arrest and detainment all over again.

I was dubious about filing an appeal and expressed my concerns to the Embassy staff. I had gotten the lowest sentence allowed by Sheikh Zayed (the lowest sentence allowed *by law* was one month), so I wondered if I weren't putting myself in jeopardy by proceeding with an appeal. The Embassy staff said they would pass on my concerns to Mr. Al-Tamimi, my lawyer. At the same time they delivered a letter that Mr. Al-Tamimi wanted me to give to the judge at my first hearing. He would not be able to attend the first session and this note of apology to the court asked for a postponement of the proceedings.

Subsequently, I was told to expect to be called to the Appeals Court within one month as the case load was lighter than at the original court. Sure enough, my name appeared on the court list for June 14 and on that day I joined the others who queued up for their hearings.

When my name was finally called, I was ushered up to a third floor hearing room that was far different from the room where I had gone before the court the last four times. Here there was a bench for the three judges to sit, but facing them were rows of chairs in which the prisoners were allowed to sit along with any family or friends who had come to encourage them. There were four other prisoners present and each had anywhere from four to eight supporters with them. I was alone. No lawyer. No Embassy staff.

As the prisoners were called, they stood in front of the judges, some with lawyers and some without. I didn't know what was happening since everything was in Arabic and I had no one to translate for me. Mohammed Jen, the young Egyptian from my block, was called right before me. He, along with his parents and some other relatives, was there to receive the decision of the judges regarding his appeal. I heard the judges pronounce the sentence. Mohammed said something to them and just shook his head. The lead judge responded to him in what appeared to be a sympathetic way, and afterwards he was led away while his mother sobbed. It didn't take a genius to realize that he had gotten no reprieve from his four-year sentence.

Then it was my turn. I stood up, walked over to the judge, and handed him the note from my attorney. He read it and said something scornfully to the other judges. Then he turned to me and asked me in English, "Do you have anything you want to say?" My mind froze. *Yes*, I wanted to tell him. *I've been set up and feel this sentence is unfair!"* Then I remembered how I had been chastised earlier by my attorney for saying what he thought was too much to the first judge. "No sir," I answered. *Did I miss a golden opportunity to state my case or did I prevent myself from making my situation worse?*

When we got back to the block, I asked Mohammed Jen what had been decided in his case. He told me that the judges had upheld his four-year sentence. When asked about what he had said to the judges he said, "Four years is too long a sentence for one marijuana cigarette." The lead judge had replied, "Son, Sheikh Zayed says it's four years, so it's four years. What can I do?"

This was amazing! To admit that his hands were tied took courage on the judge's part, for he was saying that, regardless of the law, he was not able to render a more just verdict. Mohammed Jen's situation helped to crystallize in my mind what I had to do. Cancel the appeal! Why risk receiving a longer sentence? I just wanted to get over this phase of dealing with the courts. I had my sentence, and now I wanted the Embassy to work to get me diplomatically released. A court appeal that led nowhere would just delay that process.

When the Embassy came to visit, I informed them of my decision and I asked them to instruct Mr. Al-Tamimi to cancel my appeal.

I was called again to the court on July 5 and was ushered to the same court room as before. As on the first time occasion, each prisoner was shackled about the ankles and handcuffed by one hand to another prisoner. It reminded me of the three-legged races at a summer picnic. When we arrived in the courtroom, the fellow to whom I was handcuffed was met by ten or more of his relatives. Each one had to take his turn in hugging and kissing him and saying some words of encouragement. That suddenly became ridiculously funny, as I had to stand next to him and reach with him as he hugged his family members. The policeman who was watching over us thought the whole thing rather ridiculous too, and to his credit, decided to release my handcuff. I guess he thought The American could be trusted not to run.

Eventually we were called into the courtroom and I took a seat while I waited for the hearings to begin. There was no sign of my lawyer or the Embassy staff, and I began to panic as I wondered what I was going to say to the judges. After a few minutes, however, Mr. Al-Tamimi appeared in the doorway and a policeman motioned for me to come into the hallway.

When we met, Mr. Al-Tamimi told me that he had just gotten word from Jamal at the Embassy that I wanted to cancel my appeal. He advised me that he thought this was a good idea. After assuring him that this was what I wanted to do, he led me to the office closest to the courtroom. There behind the desk sat the lead judge flanked by the other two judges. No one was yet dressed in his judge's gown. They had obviously been prepped by Mr. Al-Tamimi and as I stood in front of the desk, the judge asked me if it was correct that I wanted to cancel my appeal. When I assured him that this was my decision, he motioned for me to sit.

The flurry of discussion and page turning that ensued as they sought the procedure for dealing with such a request, made it quite obvious that this was not something that happened every day. Eventually, however, they all agreed on the steps to take; notes were written down, and my lawyer told me to sign the document to honor my request. After that was completed, my lawyer and I went out into the hallway where he told me that his job was finished and that now it was up to my Embassy to work for my release. I was led back to the holding cell and that was the last time I saw Mr. Al-Tamimi.

I enjoyed the ride back to Al Wathba that day for I knew that my court appearances were over, and that hopefully, I would be released when the American Embassy worked through the necessary diplomatic channels. As I breathed deeply of the desert air, little did I realize that that day would be my last out in the open for two years!

30

The First Long Hot Summer

THE MEN'S BLOCKS AT AL WATHBA were generally filthy. Walls were covered with graffiti, pictures and sayings were pasted throughout, and there were scars where supports for clothes lines and other things like shelving had been hammered into the concrete eventually falling off and taking paint and plaster with them. Twelve years of neglect had left most blocks looking bleak and ghetto-like.

Prison management had slowly begun to address the problem of improving the appearance of the facility by patching up holes, repainting the walls, and in some cases replacing the plumbing for sinks, showers, and toilets. In addition, they had begun a program of retrofitting air conditioning to the blocks. In the summer of 1999 only three blocks, other than the wing that housed the classrooms and the library, had air conditioning. For the rest of the inmates, life without air conditioning during the Middle East summers was brutal.

Renovation work on our block was scheduled to begin, so one morning after breakfast the guards came by and told us we would be moving to another area in one hour. Our new block was on the same level, but it was situated on the other side of the main corridor. The only view we would have would be of the prison yard. Over the walls there was nothing but endless miles of bleak, sandy desert. Reluctantly, we gathered our belongings and moved them to the front of the block. Several guards, led by the one in charge of prison security who searched us whenever we returned from court, arrived. One by one, he and the other guards meticulously scrutinized our belongings for any sort of contraband before we were allowed to pass from our old block to the new one. Fortunately, some of my cellmates were the first to be checked through and they secured a room for us so we could all stay together. We left behind our brightly decorated space for a freshly-painted bland and boring area that had no view of life outside.

In early July I wrote to Rick Crocker:

> *I am still a guest of the UAE government—free room and board and a man of leisure. Life is routine and any change is welcomed.*
>
> *Recently those in my block were moved to one that had been freshly painted. Although it is still called Block 8, the view has changed. We're still on the upper level, but from my window I now see flat barren land to the prison walls and beyond is all empty desert. Summer set in a month ago with temperatures well over 100 degrees.*
>
> *The months are slipping by and in 10 days I will have completed 25% of my sentence. As bad as that sounds, I am still one of the lucky ones.*

By mid June, daytime temperatures had soared to 120 degrees and were rising as July and August approached. The prison walls were concrete over steel, so the heat of the day was quickly absorbed and continued to radiate through most of the night making sleep close to impossible. When the prison was built, two large halls had been constructed with the hope that there inmates would learn trades such as woodworking and auto mechanics. But those areas had mostly remained empty. Since these rooms had air conditioning, prison management offered to allow those who wanted to escape the heat of the summer to move into them temporarily. By late June, as the temperature sapped my energy and made me physically sick, I decided that the air conditioning was worth any price.

Thus, a few nights later, several from each block were gathered together and moved into those large halls. When we arrived, blankets and the living necessities slung over our shoulders, we found ourselves situated in a filthy pit. The halls had not been prepared for us and a half-inch layer of sand and dirt covered the entire area. The air conditioning had not been turned on and tested. The guards threw brooms, squeegee brushes, and a hose at us and told us to clean it up. Amazingly, everyone cooperated and we placed all our belongings in one area while another was cleaned. After a few hours of bickering and complaining, the place was clean enough for us to arrange our bedding on the floor and to claim our space. Thankfully, that night we all slept well in our newly-acquired air-conditioned space.

Our new environment was a drastic change from being on the upper level of Al Wathba where one could look over the walls to the outside world. We were now situated on the ground floor in a big hall with no windows. It was like being in a hurricane shelter, except that we knew our stay would last for several months. We had only each other's company to keep us from going mad! Because prisoners from many different blocks had moved to our new area, I did not get a chance to say good-bye to some of those I had left behind in Block 8. I soon got to meet others, however, and make new acquaintances.

Sam and I and several others who had previously exercised together were joined by a few from other blocks as we continued our workout program. We became a distraction for the rest of the prisoners who quieted down to watch us go through our routines. Once in a while some brave inmate would step forward and join us to the cheers of his friends.

Unfortunately, after three days the air conditioning system faltered and the temperature started to rise. Years of neglect had left the system unprepared to deal with the demands of a twenty-four-hour-a-day operation. Mechanics were sent in to look at the problem, but after many attempts they decided that repair was futile and the system would have to be shut off until funds could be allotted for its replacement. It did not take long before we were all marched back to our original blocks to be reunited with our fellow block mates in the heat of the Arab summer.

Activity throughout the prison slowed as the relentless heat sapped our strength and left us irritable. Everyone tried to conserve energy, and for my part I was happier than ever that I was going to the air conditioned school where I was able to feel comfortable for a few hours.

Some of the men had begun to show the effects of the heat. Heat exhaustion had caused several to faint and they had to be taken to the doctor. Many had developed red sores identified as prickly heat rash on their body, and for that the doctor gave them powder to reduce the impulse to scratch the sores. One morning while showering I noticed that I was developing sores on my abdominal area and on my upper legs. That didn't alarm me nearly so much as the circumstance a few days later when, coming back from lunch, I was not able to climb the three staircases to the block without sitting down to rest. The heat had become so intense that it was difficult to catch my breath. A subsequent visit to the infirmary verified that I had a heat rash, and fortunately, a check of my heart showed no damage. Still the doctor recommended that I be transferred to an air-conditioned block as soon as possible. In the meantime, he gave me a powder to stave off the urge to scratch and told me that, if I scratched the rash, the sores could become infected and leave scars on my body.

Usually one would be transferred on a doctor's recommendation within a few days, but no one ever came to move me. So I endured the heat that was becoming more and more unbearable as the summer moved on. The rash gradually spread over my body to the point where I was covered from my neck to my ankles. I was truly concerned now for my health and sent a message to Sam's mother who worked at the American consular office in Dubai to contact the Embassy and have someone come out to visit me right away.

Within two days I had a visit from Jamal. It was not one of our planned visiting days, and he was concerned because he had been told that this was an emergency. With my prison clothes on, he couldn't tell that I had a rash, but when he asked what was wrong, I pulled off my shirt. The look on his face registered shock and concern. He promised that he would go immediately to see the prison manager and tell him to move me to an air-conditioned area. Despite his assurance that he would return to the visiting area within the hour, a guard ordered me to go back to the block as soon as Jamal left. "He is coming back!" I argued and subsequently was ushered to the security desk where I was again ordered back to the block. I refused. I sat down resolutely and informed the officers that I would not budge until something was done to help me solve my problem.

The clinic was located next to the security desk, so I demanded that I be taken to the doctor. Grudgingly, the policemen agreed after I showed them the extent of my rash. When the doctor saw how the rash had progressed since I had last seen him, he was horrified. "That can kill you!" he exclaimed.

Naturally, I didn't find that reassuring at the moment, but at least I felt vindicated in standing by my demands to seek medical treatment. The doctor promised that he would request to have me transferred to the clinic immediately.

After getting the doctor's pledge that something would be done, I agreed to go back to my block. A few hours later Sam revealed that he had spoken to the guards, and they had told him that orders had come for his immediate transfer to the prison clinic along with Daniel, another British subject, and me. Sure enough, the guards called us and we collected our belongings. Sam and Daniel were a bit surprised that their names had been announced along with mine because they each had only a few signs of prickly heat. We concluded that the prison manager must have become so frightened over the American Embassy's claims of prisoner mistreatment that they had decided to take no chances. They moved me and the British men who weren't in air-conditioned blocks to the clinic.

The part of the clinic that housed prisoners was one floor directly below the medical and dental unit. There were five rooms with beds for eighteen and when we arrived there were sixteen prisoners staying there. No one had any serious disease, but for the most part they had trouble walking either because of hip problems, broken legs, or old age. This meant they were not able to negotiate the walks that most often involved stairs leading from the blocks to the eating areas. Several inmates had convincingly acted out all manner of illnesses, thus ensuring that this would be their permanent locale. One older man, an imam, was in prison for sodomizing his children. He was so afraid of what might happen to him in the blocks that he feigned mental illness and the inability to walk even a short distance without collapsing. Another much younger man feigned back problems that required him to use crutches. When guards weren't around, he walked effortlessly and even climbed on furniture so that he could hide contraband razors and a radio behind a wall air vent. One man, a pleasant seventy-year old German citizen, had been in prison for several years. He had never had anyone contact the German Embassy for him because he didn't want government officials to know he was in prison. This way, he wouldn't end up with a criminal record once he was sent home. That may have seemed odd, but it was not out of the ordinary when you consider that it was against the law of the UAE for anyone over seventy to be held in a prison. In addition, the government was supposed to contact the respective embassy of any prisoner from a foreign country.

It seemed that there were only a few in the medical unit who were there legitimately. One was a severely depressed young Iranian who came to the clinic just a few days after we arrived. He slept on the floor on a few scattered blankets and rarely moved from his bed. I took an interest in him and began chatting with him whenever I had a chance. Slowly he began to open up to me. He had been arrested for theft, but had become so distraught over being in prison that he had tried to kill himself. Rather than get him sound psychological counseling, the police merely relegated him to the clinic so he could deal with his problems himself. All he was given were a few prescription medicines. Over the next few weeks as we talked and became friends, I watched him shake off his depression. Shortly, thereafter, I learned that he was sent back to his block and would be released soon. Several months later, I met him in the hallway on my way to the school and he told me he was being released that afternoon. He thanked me for helping him through a most difficult time, gave me his number, and told me to call his home in Iran once I was released.

The only other prisoner who seemed sincerely ill was one who, to an untrained eye, had a severe bronchial problem that resembled tuberculosis. His constant cough weakened him so much that he was barely able to get out of bed to go to the bathroom.

While I was in the clinic, there was a spare mattress that I was able to use. After lying on hard concrete for the previous nine months, it was heavenly to sleep on a mattress. I think on that first night in the clinic I had my best night's rest since arriving at Al Wathba.

Collectively, Sam, Daniel, and I were dismayed at the unsanitary conditions of the clinic. The bathrooms were filthy and the walls of the showers were caked in slime and scum. Even worse, the area where the food was disposed of was black and roach infested. The prison supplied no one to maintain the living areas and expected the prisoners to take care of their quarters themselves. It was appalling that this was where chronically ill prisoners were housed! The root of the problem, however, lay in the fact that, though many were capable of keeping the room clean, no one wanted to do it for fear that they might then be considered well enough to return to the blocks with the general prison population.

So, the three of us divided up the cleaning tasks. Together we washed down the hallways with antiseptic until the floors were shining. Then we split up the job of cleaning the bathrooms and the food disposal area. It took a lot of scrubbing, but we finally got the place looking and smelling clean and won the grateful admiration of the other prisoners.

A police guard was usually posted outside the clinic door, but because there was no air conditioning there, he often moved inside the clinic where it was more comfortable. The guards assigned to this duty generally remained the same, so we got to know them a bit. A few were very friendly and would spend time in our rooms talking about all matter of things. Fortunately, since a few spoke some English or French, I was able to converse with them.

During my second day in the clinic I wrote a letter to Dean Bauer, a friend in Boston, in which I expressed my frustration with the slow pace at which things seemed to be moving with regard to my release from Al Wathba:

> *I dream of Cape Cod, New England, the water, and the natural beauty of the outdoors. It all seems so far away right now but it keeps my spirits up. Usually I have a good attitude but I've had those really rough days, very infrequently though, where I've thought as I lay down to sleep that it would just be better not to wake up. But my friends help me through it and I see hope again.*
>
> *I know that you've had a lot of heat this summer already. I guess the summer here is quite typical with lots of heat and humidity. We've been running about 115 degrees here in the desert with about 95% humidity. I developed a heat rash covering 80% of my body and had*

a slight respiratory problem because of it but with the help of USE (the United States Embassy) I have been in the clinic for two days. The a/c is so welcome and for the first time in almost 10 months I'm sleeping on a mattress —well sort of!

I have been disappointed in progress here—especially by USE. Like corporate America its staff seems so overworked and short on bodies. With most Gulf residents fleeing the summer heat not many are around. The visit Wednesday July 21st was the first in seven weeks and only happened because a roommate's mom called them to say I needed help. Things I thought were done weeks ago haven't been—like shipping my clothes to the U.S. They still haven't given me copies of documents showing what I was charged with or the judge's decision. And I've been asking for stamps since December! But you know I have no one else so I can't get upset or angry—it is frustrating. Time goes on! They have been ambivalent whether my father should come to visit—it appears now it would be beneficial if he does.

I sent a letter via them to my friends Billy [President Clinton] in D.C. and Jeb in FL and George in TX giving them an update on things. I don't know if they are "working" during the summer, but not knowing how long it would be before I see USE again I didn't want to miss the opportunity.

Three times a day our food was delivered in bulk to the main entrance of the clinic. On those occasions those who couldn't walk when doctors were present were amazingly able to stand in line and bicker over the quality or quantity of the food. In general, though, I liked the arrangement we had because we could ask for as much as our plates could hold and request small portions of one item like rice and get a larger one of meat or salad. Another benefit of being in the clinic was that we could hoard our food for a later time, if we wished. That practice was not really permitted, but the guards generally allowed us to do so as long as the food from one meal was eaten before the next arrived. It was nice to be able to save fruit as a mid-afternoon or late evening snack, and it wasn't unusual to see oranges, bananas, or apples lying around the block.

This windfall came to an eventual end one night when the clinic was raided by a unit of policemen. I was awakened by the sound of someone rummaging through my belongings. As I opened my eyes, a policeman was reaching for an orange I had saved that evening. "I'm sorry to wake you," he said as he turned and saw me watching. Then he smiled, put my orange back, and covered it with one of my shirts. With a wink he indicated that this was our secret and he moved on to the next bed. The search went on for a half an hour. About all that they found was a razor that had been stashed in one of the bathrooms and a radio that had been hidden in the area where we cleaned our dishes. Ironically, the razor was mine, one that I had been able to hang on to when the rest had been collected a few days earlier. One treasure that they didn't find was a chess board and pieces that I had hidden under my mattress. A few days earlier I had found an out-of-date calendar that displayed a picture of Sheikh Zayed on the top half of one side. It was backed by cardboard about one foot square, and on this I drew a chess board. Using a bit of the remaining cardboard, I created one-inch square chess pieces. Since it was basically flat, the game was easy to slip under my bed whenever we heard the clinic door open and someone come in. To use a calendar with Sheikh Zayed's picture on it in such a way was definitely taboo. Fortunately, I was never caught with the chess board and pieces for being found with something like that would have earned me additional time in prison or a few days in solitary.

Twice a day the clinic was visited by one of the nurses who came to dispense medications that had been prescribed for each person. Those nurses were quite friendly and would do as much as they could for the prisoners that they liked. Whenever I needed additional prickly heat salve or antihistamines, they obliged me. Once a week the doctor came to check us out and would spend most of his time with those who had had operations or were more seriously ill. He always made a point, though, of talking with Sam and Daniel and me, and it was apparent that the manager of the prison was concerned that we receive proper care. Even though Sam's and Daniel's conditions had cleared up, we had all been assigned to the clinic for six weeks. The doctor allowed us to stay without question since he had received orders from the manager to that effect. Regardless, he liked us and knew that the conditions in the block in the middle of summer were intolerable. He wasn't about to send us back there.

After three weeks of being in the air conditioning, my condition cleared up remarkably well. I had resisted the urge to scratch my sores, but the few that remained on my body persisted in annoying me. The days passed quickly in the clinic and they were good days because they were quiet and all of us got along quite well. We had free movement between the rooms, the three of us and Mohammed, a Somalian, were allowed to continue going to our classes in the school, and Daniel and I passed many hours playing chess. I gave massages to several of the patients and received a great deal of satisfaction in knowing that I was able to relieve some of their discomfort. In return I earned a lot of respect and was given some extra food.

There was one thing, however, that was particularly difficult for me during this time. Our room overlooked the prison courtyard where twice a week prisoners received their canings as prescribed by the courts or by the Presidential Diwan. Every Wednesday and Sunday selected prisoners would be lined up outside our area as representatives from the court arrived to oversee that the punishment was being meted out. One by one the prisoners would be placed on a wooden bed and be caned ruthlessly by the police. The guards were supposed to hold a Koran in their armpit while they were caning the prisoners. Doing so would limit the range of motion of their arms and thus reduce the impact of the cane on the prisoners' bodies. Never once, however, did I see a guard use a Koran. As a result, the cane was raised high over the guards' heads as they beat the prisoners mercilessly, striking anywhere from the neck down to the ankles. No protection was placed over the kidneys or the back of the knees, both very vulnerable areas to damage.

It was sickening to watch this go on as prisoners screamed for mercy and writhed in agony. Even very young boys would be caned and once I saw a woman caned. She had to kneel in front of the guard while he beat her as brutally as he beat the men. This particular woman passed out during the caning, but women guards revived her with water to the face and immediately placed her back in position for the remainder of her beating. Once, an elderly man who could barely walk with the aid of a cane was brought forward for his beating. Since he could not lie down, he had to stand and hold on to a table. The guards were again relentless, showing no mercy as they thrashed him about the legs and backs of the knees. With each strike he would scream out in pain and try to stand upright with his cane swinging in the air. I could watch just enough to be able to document what was going on. The way the guards relished these opportunities to torture prisoners was atrocious, as was the fact that they did not follow the rule that required them to hold a Koran under their arms. The pure savagery outraged me, and to this day I am thankful beyond words that I was spared that indignity and torture.

Very quickly our six-week stay in the clinic drew to an end. We were upset, since it was only mid-August and the temperatures

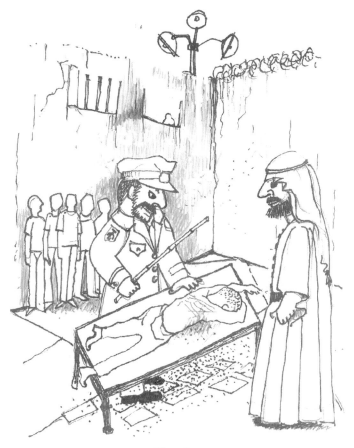

Flogging

were still extremely high. Fortunately, Sam talked with the doctor on one of his rounds and asked him to authorize our continued stay in the clinic. He agreed and told us that we had six more weeks to stay there. That was wonderful news.

However the clinic had filled up and the number of prisoners assigned to the area was well above capacity. Floor space in the rooms was crowded with bodies, most suffering from the effects of the heat. The overcrowding led to increased impatience among some "veterans" of the clinic and eventually fights broke out. As much as the guards tried to keep things under control, word of the problems reached the prison manager. He directed the head doctor to personally visit with every patient in the clinic and to send those of us who were not in distress back to the blocks. Half of the infirm, including the three of us, were ordered back to the blocks. Because temperatures were still very high, I was assigned to an air-conditioned block until later in September when things cooled down.

I was sent to Block 10, a dismal space on the ground level. To my dismay, I was told by the foreman of the block that all the rooms were full and that I would have to sleep in the non-air-conditioned hallway. I protested to the policeman guarding the block, but he said there was nothing he could do to help me. The foreman, however, was very accommodating and told me that he would find a place for me as soon as possible. About a week later, I was given space in his room. It was such a relief to be in a cooler area that I didn't even care that the room was windowless and small. I was told that I could return to Block 8 anytime I wanted to, and just had to notify the guard of my wish. I decided to stay there until the latter part of September when the temperatures would start to decline from near 140 degrees to the low 100s.

Block 10 was depressing and dark and one could barely see any sky, but I was thankful that I didn't have to live there on a long-term basis. Little did I know then that that dismal block would be my home for the last two years of my stay at Al Wathba.

In late September I notified the guards that I wanted to return to Block 8, and within a day I was granted my wish. It was nice to return to my old roommates and be in a place where we could see through the bars over the prison walls. And, thank God, the daily maximum temperatures were beginning to fall!

31

A Visit from my Brother

OTHER PEOPLE FROM BLOCK 8 WHO had been moved to air conditioned areas for the summer returned about the same time that I did. I was told that one third of the prisoners in Block 8 had been reassigned for the summer, so there had been less congestion for the remaining prisoners during this time. It was obvious to me that living in a non air-conditioned block during the relentless summer heat had taken its toll on many of those who had chosen not to relocate or who had not been fortunate enough to be moved. Many inmates had lost weight, some were still showing the prickly heat sores that had ravaged their bodies at the beginning of the summer, and lethargy was evident everywhere. Men were just plain worn out from the suffering involved in living in an oven for several months.

During recent visits with the Embassy staff, I had learned that Mohammed Shalah had finally been released from Al Wathba and that I was the only American left. We discussed the possibility that we should seek a pardon for me through diplomatic channels. It was agreed that my brother would come to visit either in October or November and that the Embassy staff would seek to arrange a meeting with some influential personage in the Royal Family. My hopes were high that I would be back in the United States for Christmas.

In spite of the usual problems that prisoners face after a release from prison, immediate financial security being one, James Oakes did follow through on his promise to contact my family once he was released. He e-mailed a copy of his letter to Richard

Branson to Jennifer, my daughter, and told my family that I was doing fine. He advised them that I was reluctant to have family come to the UAE with high expectations of securing an immediate release for me. However, he did offer to help in any way he could in lining up interviews with high ranking members of the Royal Family or providing telephone numbers of wives of the sheikhs. Sometimes wives could be very influential in the decision-making process of the country's leaders.

Traditionally in the Arab culture, much respect is paid to elders and their opinions, and their requests are seriously considered. It was felt that my father could have an impact on my release by meeting face to face with some of the Royal Family since my father was eighty-seven years old, an age comparable to that of Sheikh Zayed himself. Unfortunately, though, my father's health had not been good after the discovery of severe blockages in some of his major arteries and his doctor strongly discouraged a trip of such duration and stress. That came as a hard blow for my father had worked so diligently in all the years since his retirement to remain fit. He swam and exercised regularly and put many younger men to shame with what he could physically accomplish. I had never known my father to be sick with anything serious, and now I was confronted with a real sense of his mortality. I had to get out of prison to see him!

Having my brother come alone was what I counted on now. He had supported me from the first word of my arrest, and I knew that if any one person could get me out, it would be Richard. So I agreed with the Embassy staff that we should arrange for his visit sometime close and prior to the upcoming Ramadan. It is traditional that some prisoners be freed as an act of kindness in honor of the Holy Month of Ramadan, and we all felt that a one-on-one appeal would be most effective when consideration was being given to those who should be freed at this time.

What had concerned me most about my having canceled the appeal process was that the Diwan (the Presidential Court) would add some strokes with the cane to my sentence of four years. That specification usually came about one month after the last court appearance, so the thought of getting caned weighed heavily on my mind. When I had a visit from the Embassy, I used the opportunity to dictate a letter to Charles Glatz, the consular official, to

President Clinton asking for his intervention in the legal process within the UAE. In part I wrote:

> I am a 54 year old Orlando businessman and I've been in prison since October 1998 at Al Wathba prison in the UAE. I am seeking your assistance in securing my release from this prison where human rights and dignities are routinely ignored. Some examples are:
>
> 1. My block is set up to accommodate 72 persons and currently there are over twice that many.
> 2. Medical doctors have recommended that my diet be supplemented with vegetables and milk but the police have refused to comply.
> 3. My block is not air conditioned. Temperatures last week exceeded 115 degrees and our water supply was cut for three days, and because I've developed a body rash from neck to toe and I've had respiratory problems, the doctors have recommended that I be moved to an air-conditioned block but the police have not complied.
> 4. Most of my letters to family and friends have not been delivered.
> 5. All my family are residents in North America and because visitors are restricted to family, I have no visitors other than Embassy staff.
> 6. Books from my daughter delivered by my Embassy eleven weeks ago have not been given to me.
> 7. We are not allowed to walk outside.
> 8. I am not allowed any telephone calls.
> 9. A request from my family to have local clergy visit me was denied.
>
> Even though my court sentence did not specify it, I'm expecting the Diwan (an executive body that routinely overrules court decisions and delays release dates with impunity) will be issuing an order within two weeks for me to be lashed with a cane 80–150 times. Mr. President, you intervened on behalf of an American citizen in Singapore who was scheduled to receive 24

> lashes. Here no protection is given for the kidneys or the back side of the knees.
>
> I thank you in advance for your attention to this matter.

The Embassy staff never did send the letter to President Clinton, but it was forwarded to my brother for his information.

In the local newspaper there was mention of the fact that the UAE and Canada were discussing the idea of allowing prisoners from each other's country to return to their homeland and complete the remainder of their sentence in a home prison. I had my family research this, but they found that discussions had merely been preliminary and any agreement would be far into the future. Another dead end!

With the onset of the summer heat, many residents, including members of the Royal Family, left the country and headed to cooler climates. This was the time when Sheikh Zayed and his entourage normally left the country, and in recent years due to his health problems, was the time that he now visited the Western medical clinics. Whenever he did so, rumors were rampant that he was dying or that he was suffering from some major life-threatening condition. That kind of talk heightened the hopes of many that he would die and his death would trigger a general amnesty for prisoners. In August, we learned that Sheikh Zayed had left for England and possibly would seek medical treatment at the Mayo Clinic in the United States. Shortly thereafter, the rumors began to spread.

In a place where there is little hope of a fair trial or a commuted sentence, rumors take on a life of their own. One that spread like wildfire actually promised amnesty for all drug-related cases. Every few days the rumors made the prison rounds, and when you heard them again, they had been enhanced. I wrote to my father on August 21:

> *Prisons are rife with rumors and I've learned that, if you believe them, life becomes an emotional roller coaster as, one after another, they prove to be unfounded.*

Much as I believed that, I still held on to the rumors hoping that maybe one of them would prove to be true. They were all we had to hope for.

By now I had read many books and one that especially intrigued me was Scott Thurow's *One-L*, the story of students going through Harvard law school. In summarizing the end of the first year of law school, Thurow unknowingly drew a parallel to my first year at Al Wathba when he wrote: *In order to reach the 2nd and 3rd years, students must pass through the first year, and by then many have already had the stuffing kicked out of them. They have been treated as incompetent, terrorized daily, excluded from privilege, had their valued beliefs ridiculed, and in general felt their sense of self-worth thoroughly demeaned.*

In preparation for my brother's visit and the subsequent contact with one of the members of the Royal Family, the Embassy felt that it would be helpful to have a collection of letters from friends, business colleagues, and family who supported the request for my release. My father and brother made the Embassy's request known to our friends and encouraged them to drop me a note wishing me well. This was unknown to me and one Thursday, when letters were distributed, I was amazed (as was everyone else) when I received eight letters. I was ecstatic. Not only did I receive many letters from relatives, but I also had received word from a few friends of the family with whom I had not been in contact for many years. I read and re-read each one slowly, savoring the experience of hearing from so many persons wrapped up in my past.

If it was their intent to raise my spirits, then they succeeded. In a letter to Susanne, my former wife, dated July 10, 1999, I wrote:

> *I am very humbled by all the support you, Jennifer, the rest of the family, and friends have shown for my cause. It is only with constant pressure from all of you on the United States Embassy here that anything will get done. . . . What happened to me may seem totally absurd but compared to most others I am lucky. I count all my blessings. In spite of all that has happened I am still glad I came here—the experiences were invaluable and the overseas experience will look good on my resume.*

About the same time a cousin, retired from the Royal Canadian Mounted Police in the Canadian Security and Intelligence

Service, sent a letter to Sheikh Zayed in which he requested clemency for me based on the fact that he knew I was not a drug addict, and that I had learned my lesson concerning the kind of people I should associate with. No response was ever received from Sheikh Zayed.

In late July my lawyer sent my brother a letter:

> *We want to inform you that we appealed the issued verdict against Mr. Paul Ciceri and that was a precaution from our side in order not to miss the last date for the appeal and in case the prosecution might appeal the verdict from their side. We consulted Mr. Paul Ciceri about the possibility of ending his imprisonment with the competent authority and as Mr. Paul Ciceri asked and wished we waived the appeal and thus the verdict became final.*

Based on that letter, one would expect that my lawyer would visit me and we would discuss all the options available to us regarding the appeal process and the possibilities that could arise from an appealed verdict. Well, that didn't happen. The lawyer never visited me and he didn't even show up for my first appearance in front of the Appeals judges.

My brother kept in contact with Jim Oakes in preparation for his visit. That way Jim could communicate plans to me via phone calls to others within the prison who had telephone privileges. Conversely, Jim could relay information from me with regard to items that I wanted my brother to bring. On September 5 my brother reported the following information to Jim:

- George Bush Jr. and Sr. will not give any support to me as they consider my imprisonment a political issue and would not intervene.
- There is no prisoner exchange between the UAE and the United States.
- Canada is negotiating with the UAE for a prisoner exchange but it is unclear whether current prisoners would be included in any agreement.
- The Embassy in Abu Dhabi expressed confidence that at least one visit could be arranged with one of Sheikh Zayed's sons.

Jim was very helpful in arranging hotel accommodations for my brother and even offered to lend him his cellular phone so that he would be able to respond immediately to any summons from a member of the Royal Family if a meeting could be arranged.

My daughter continued her efforts to help me through her political contacts, and in early September both Florida senators Bob Graham and Connie Mack indicated that they had contacted the UAE American Embassy for more information on my case. Letters to both from Ambassador Kattouf and Consul Charles Glatz outlined my case as previous letters to other politicians had. That would be as far as the efforts to get them to intervene would go. All they did was send a copy of the letter to my family, as others had done. Connie Mack wrote on October 7:

> *After contacting all parties involved in the matter and carefully analyzing the information provided, the U.S. Embassy in Abu Dhabi generated a detailed response and forwarded a copy of the written reply to my office. I have taken the liberty of enclosing a copy of that reply for your records. Thank you for taking the time to contact me. It is always a pleasure to offer assistance to individuals that I proudly represent in the United States Senate.*

What a nice form letter! There would be no help from my Senators.

A letter from my father in mid September confirmed my fears that he would not be in good enough health to make the trip to personally plea for my clemency. He had encountered breathing problems, and after consultations with doctors, he was advised that his health had deteriorated to the point where his life expectancy was no more than two years. That left me in a state of extreme depression for I knew that, if my incarceration extended to my expected release date, I would never see my father again. With that apprehension on his mind, and still hoping to make the trip, my father assured me that:

> *We shall continue to pursue every avenue in order to obtain an early release, and hopefully the visit of your brother and father will have a positive influence. In the meantime keep praying and hoping knowing*

that the good Lord is in charge and things will happen according to His plan. God be with you.

He still was convinced that he would be able to come to visit me, but I knew this was not feasible because of his health. A few weeks later his cardiologist would ultimately tell him that he was not to travel such a distance. The stress of the long trip and seeing me would cause more harm than good. So, the stage was set for my brother to come alone and visit me. But prior to that time, my father remarried. As much as he would have liked for me to be present, fate would not allow it. I had sent a toast to the bride and groom that was read by Susanne, my former wife, and it apparently was well received. Not being at my father's wedding was another major disappointment along the road of my incarceration.

Richard, my brother, did come to Abu Dhabi and arrived on Friday evening, October 28. A lady from the hotel at which he would be staying helped clear him through customs and immigration in a timely fashion, so they were soon on their way to downtown Abu Dhabi. Richard's first impression of Abu Dhabi at night was 'a modern city with many tall buildings.'

His first full day in the Middle East was spent meeting Jamal Bafagih and Charles Glatz from the Embassy and then visiting ELS Language Centers where he identified my belongings. He wrote:

> *The Embassy had taken the initiative to prepare a document which contained all the letters sent to Abu Dhabi on Paul's behalf. I reviewed the documentation to be submitted to one of the President's sons and added an additional letter I had prepared on behalf of the family and some pictures of Paul.*
>
> *On Sunday morning Charles Glatz, Jamal, and I journeyed to Al Wathba prison to visit Paul. The U.S. Embassy was able to arrange for Paul and I to meet in the Major's (second in command) office and I was able to give Paul a big hug and kiss. A few tears were shed. My first impression of Paul was shock as Paul has lost weight and his complexion looked a little gray. Paul has definitely changed but his caring and positive attitude still remains. We had an opportunity to spend about*

> *1½ hours together and I brought him up to date on all the family members and the recent weddings, etc. I brought magazines, novels, a writing pad, soap, and stamps with me to the prison and the U.S. Embassy was able to get the Major to allow Paul to take all those items back to the cell. Paul was in good spirits and indicated that if need be he is prepared to serve out his time. Paul talked about his teaching English to prisoners five days a week and his taking Islamic religion courses and finishing first in the class. This impressed the course teacher so much that he asked Paul to give the course to new inmates. Paul is well liked by many of the senior prison officials.*

I knew the visit would take place that morning and I was thrilled, yet apprehensive, about seeing my brother. I figured our reunion would be an emotional time. Finally, I was called for the visit and led up to the administrative wing by a guard who told me to wait outside the Major's office. I could hear Jamal, Charles, and Richard talking as I became more excited by the minute. At last I was led into the visiting room where my big brother stood larger than life. Suddenly, I felt as if someone had thrown me a life preserver to pull me out of the ocean where I was sinking. It was a wonderful visit, despite the fact that we were watched closely to make sure that nobody passed anything to me. At one point Charles and Jamal excused themselves and told us that if I wanted to talk to Richard about the Embassy and their handling of my case, that now would be an appropriate time to do so. I assured them I had nothing negative to say as this was such a wonderful moment.

Richard brought with him a gift of my favorite magazines which included a *Men's Health*, *GQ*, and *Men's Journal*. After not having seen a magazine for a year, it was as though he had given me gold. What I received, however, was shy several pages after the Major went through each publication and tore out the pages that he felt didn't comply with the country's strict adherence to Islamic teachings. As he ripped out the censored pages that usually displayed pictures of lightly clad women, he placed them in his desk drawer rather than put them in the garbage can.

We expected that Monday would be the day that my brother would meet with a member of the Royal Family; I then hoped that he and the Embassy staff would come back on Tuesday to tell me what had happened. As is the case in most countries, the rulers' schedules can change at a moment's notice depending on the various circumstances that demand their attention. The visit on Monday did not come off as scheduled. The Sheikh with whom they had an appointment had to go to the airport, according to protocol, to be present when one of his brothers left the country on a diplomatic mission. Richard took advantage of the time to go back to ELS Language Centers to repack my belongings and arrange with a shipping company to have them sent back to the United States. My former secretary, Belinda Campos, invited him to her family's apartment for lunch and then drove him back to his hotel once everything had been organized. I was on edge that entire day wondering what had transpired with regard to their engagement to see the Sheikh.

On Tuesday I did not go to the school to teach, but decided to remain in the block so there would be no problem in locating me when the Embassy staff and my brother returned. I was anxious to hear the results of the previous day's meeting and as the time passed, I sensed that something must have happened. Absurdly, I even fantasized that perhaps the Sheikh had ordered my release right there and then, and that the Embassy was securing airline tickets and getting things prepared for my discharge from Al Wathba. That may seem like an unrealistic assumption, but when you are locked up as we were, you hold on to any thought of something good happening in your case. What actually did take place was described by my brother in a letter that he wrote later:

> *This was to be the day for the second visit to Paul. Jamal and I left the Embassy at about 9:00 a.m. and on the way out Jamal was constantly on the phone attempting to arrange for a meeting with Sheikh Diyab. In the event we could not see Sheikh Diyab, Jamal was to arrange a meeting with another influential sheikh in the administration. Just as we arrived at the prison, and in fact we had already cleared the front gate and were driving into the compound to park our car, Jamal received word that Sheikh Diyab had agreed to see us at 11:00. It was now about 9:45 and we quickly turned around and drove back to Abu Dhabi where we encountered a traffic jam and arrived at my hotel at 10:25 so*

that I could change into a dress shirt and jacket. We then had to drive to the Embassy to pick up Charles Glatz. Since no one at the Embassy knew the location of the building where we were to meet the Sheikh, Jamal arranged for the Sheik's personal secretary Gerald Nahed (a friend of Jamal's) to meet us at the Embassy and lead us to the building. We arrived at the location of the meeting at about 11:00 and five minutes later were ushered in to meet His Highness Sheikh Diyab bin Zayed Al Nahyan. Sheikh Diyab I think is about 35 years of age and is head of the Diva Court, the second highest court in the land. In power he is second to his brother who heads the President's court, the highest in the land. The first fifteen minutes were spent in casual conversation about U.S. politics and then Charles Glatz gave a brief introduction about Paul's case. I followed with an appeal for clemency on behalf of the family. I covered such items as Paul's role in the family, Dad's health, a brief explanation about the incident, etc. This presentation I thought took about ½ hour but the time just seemed to stand still during my presentation. At the end I presented the Sheikh with a binder containing letters sent to the Embassy on Paul's behalf. The Sheikh listened to our appeal, asked a few questions and indicated at the end that he would review Paul's case and was positive that something could be done. Charles Glatz ended the session by presenting the Sheikh with a book on Washington D.C. Both Charles and Jamal were pleased with our meeting and expressed their belief that they believed the Sheikh would act favorably. We pray this is the case.

The following morning Jamal and Richard came to the prison to meet with me. They briefed me on the meeting with Sheikh Diyab, and I was pleased that they were able to meet with someone so well placed within the Royal Family. When they described Sheikh Diyab's reply to their pleas, I was encouraged, but, because life in Al Wathba had so far been an emotional roller coaster with rumors of release, I was very guarded. I told my brother that I appreciated all that he had done and that if my release wasn't forthcoming, then I was prepared to wait out the remainder of my sentence. Jamal told me that it is rare that any sheikh would directly say what he would do; we would have to wait for a response—if, indeed, there would be one. He expected that if something positive were forthcoming, we would know within two to three weeks or certainly by the latter part of Ramadan. It was now November 2, so I figured that if we had no reply by the end of November, then I would be in Al Wathba prison for another Christmas.

My brother had brought clothes that I had requested in case I was released. We were able to go to the luggage storage area and leave them there, and I also deposited some money that my brother had given me into my prison account. Then it was time for him and Jamal to go and we embraced amid tears. Richard and I had always had strong family ties, but at that moment I was filled with pride and gratitude for what my brother had done for me.

Back in my cell I was bombarded with questions from my block mates. I told them nothing other than the fact that my brother had made a petition to the Royal Family for my release. I tried to be upbeat but was brought down to earth again that afternoon when another article appeared in the newspaper describing the visit of the British prisoner Ian Bamling's mother to Abu Dhabi and her comments about the shortcomings of the UAE legal system. I knew that article was going to upset members of the Royal Family and could, likely, have a detrimental effect on their consideration of clemency for me.

Now the waiting really became intense as my world revolved around the world of the prison. Seeing my brother was, in a way, a strange experience. I wrote to him after our visit:

> *I think I was in a 'faraway' state when you were here—it was really weird. My thoughts have been so totally focused on survival and coping that the world back home becomes like a dream. Things have been reversed. I got a card from one of my friends who got released recently and he was saying that once he got to London the outside world became real again and in an instant his life here became a dream.*
>
> *Rumors increase as we approach National Day and the holy month of Ramadan. Hopefully, just 10%*

are true and my name will show up on one of those 'good' lists.

A week later I wrote to my daughter about her uncle's visit:

It was nice to see Richard and have direct contact with family again. It's amazing all that happens in one year—deaths, marriages, jobs, new homes, etc. Surprisingly this first year has gone by fast and it's both a blur and one long bad dream. Here, the important things like pens, paper, and stamps would, in anyone else's case, seem rather trivial.

But fate would intervene and put more obstacles in the way of my release. After my brother left Abu Dhabi, the courts handed down a sentence to Ian Bamling who had been arrested along with a woman at the airport for possession of marijuana and alcohol. The American Embassy had convinced me and my family that a quiet diplomatic approach was the appropriate method to secure my release. However, the British fellow and his family, in spite of advice against it by the British Embassy, had decided to take the public route in securing his freedom.

In mid-October, at the encouragement of his family, the first of many articles appeared in the local English-language newspaper, *The Gulf News*, and simultaneously in the *Evening Standard* in London. Part of the article reads as follows:

Uk Tourists Jailed for Drug Possession . . . by Stuart Laundy

Abu Dhabi—Two British travelers who were arrested in Abu Dhabi International airport more than a year ago were sentenced to four years in prison for possession of drugs. Ian Bamling, 29, and 44-year-old Lynn Majakas were sentenced at Abu Dhabi Sharia Court yesterday.

The couple, who live next door to each other in south-west London, were found in possession of three grams of cannabis when their hand luggage was searched. In addition, both were sentenced to six months for possession of alcohol and fined Dh1,000. Neither Bamling nor Majakas are residents of the UAE. It is believed they were planning to spend a week here as part of a tour holiday. They will serve their sentences in separate sections of Al Wathba prison in Abu Dhabi.

> The pair were accompanied in court by their locally-appointed lawyers and officials from the British Embassy. Neither of the couple's families was present at the hearing, but members of Bamling's family are expected to come to Abu Dhabi to file an appeal against the sentence.

That article caused quite a stir among the prisoners because for the first time someone had dared to print information about a citizen from a prominent Western country who had been arrested by UAE officials. Things got even more interesting when another article appeared a few days later. After hearing her son's verdict, Ian Bamling's mother was quoted as saying that she would come to Abu Dhabi and not leave until she had secured her son's release. I did not think that this was a good thing to have happened when my brother had come to personally seek my release. Such public outcries against a verdict of the local court were appreciated neither by the local rulers nor by the Embassy staff. The Royal Family might just refuse to see anyone because of the bitterness that such articles created. And, since the article also included a comment by Bamling's family that the British Embassy was not doing enough to help Ian and Lynn, it angered them, too.

When Jim Oakes picked up on the story, he e-mailed my brother:

> *I hate to be negative but I thought that I should let you know that the British couple who were caught with drugs was given a 4½ year jail sentence. It is very much a live issue in the press here as the mother and brother have turned up from the UK and they have brought with them a national newspaper reporter too. They are here to appeal for clemency. The problem is that these people have caused trouble here before and are likely to again now. They have had articles printed in the UK over the past six months which do nothing but damage their cause. Anyway Richard I don't think this will do Paul's case much good at all. I hope I am wrong but I think you know what I mean.*

The outlook for my release was looking bleak.

32

Coal in My Christmas Stocking

THE RHETORIC IN THE BRITISH MEDIA regarding conditions at Al Wathba had increased once Ian Bamling's mother and brother had arrived home. They appeared on numerous radio and television talk programs in a relentless public effort to have Ian and Lynn released. They hoped that by disclosing the negative conditions that existed in the UAE prisons, Britain and the world would put pressure to bear on the Arab officials responsible for the inequities. On Sunday, December 5 an article appeared in the *Sunday Observer* in London:

> **"Al Wathba prison is a hell hole. I know that even when he gets home my son will never be the same again,"** said Ian Bamling's mother.
>
> The lush desert oasis should have been a perfect holiday destination. Instead, it had become a prison for two Britons arrested on drug and alcohol charges, and say their relatives, abandoned to their fate by uncaring British authorities. Lynn Majarkas, 44, head teacher of a special needs school, had not had a holiday in ten years, so she jumped at the chance to take a last-minute bargain break in Dubai in the United Arab Emirates with boyfriend Ian Bamling, 30, the school's welfare official. They flew off in October 1998 but have yet to return.
>
> The couple is now incarcerated in a stinking, overcrowded prison where the toilet is an open sewer, the food is more often than not infested by maggots, and floggings are common.
>
> The families of the pair returned to the UK from the UAE in despair last week, after a fruitless attempt to plead for clemency.

The families' options seem to have run out. The Foreign Office will not intervene in another nation's legal system, even though the prison conditions have been condemned by Amnesty International as 'inhumane and degrading'. The British Embassy in Abu Dhabi is equally powerless to help. Both families, and the parents of Majarkas's former pupils, appealed last month to Prince Charles, who was on a tour of the UAE. His advisers said it was a matter for the British Government.

But Bamling's family fear there is a lack of political will because of the UK's lucrative business relationship with the UAE. In 1998 Britain exported 1.56 billion (Sterling) of goods and services there, and trade is at record levels.

Capitalizing on all the talk in the British press about conditions at Al Wathba, Ian Bamling's mother organized a picket line in front of the UAE Embassy in London. I guess I was beginning to feel that, since our diplomatic approach to things didn't seem to be working, maybe we should go public also. I wrote to Richard:

> There was quite a crowd, including former prisoners and students from the school at which he [Ian Bamling] worked. I'm wondering if all the negative publicity had an effect on the Sheihk's decision in my case. Perhaps, though, it may be helpful for you to talk to the Brit's mom in the event you decide to pursue my case publicly in the press. Regardless I am awaiting the next visit from the Embassy to discuss what we do from here on—perhaps a visit to the UAE Embassies in Ottawa/Washington?, going to the Orlando/Toronto papers?, a visit from the American Ambassador here to the Sheikh?, a call from Madeline Albright? This situation is becoming more and more like what I've seen in the movie Midnight Express.

The Bamling family's feelings about the lack of intervention on the part of government departments and U.S. officials mirrored those I felt about the United States. The difference was that they aired their view publicly in the court of public opinion, while I kept my thoughts to myself or shared them privately. The rising outcries would do one of two things: cause the UAE government to spite the British families for going public by granting me clemency, or, fearing that there would be an even louder public outcry from those released, cause them simply to decide that no one would get released. I would have to wait and see what effect the latest developments would have on my situation.

One morning in mid December we were advised that there would be no school classes that day. That kind of news meant that there were going to be block searches, or that some very high-ranking personages were coming to visit the prison and the officials didn't want any prisoners in the hallways. This time, however, we were advised that there was to be a major relocating of inmates among the blocks. We were aware that the prison administration was biased against people who had been convicted of drug-related activity, and that morning we found out how right we were. Without a doubt, times were going to get tougher for those of us who fit into that category. We were told that all those convicted of drugs offenses were being moved to "drugs blocks."

We were ordered to move in together in one of two blocks: Block 9 was set aside for all those who were UAE citizens and Block 10 was set aside for the rest of us. Both were the same size, but Block 9 ended up with sixty prisoners while our quarters housed over one hundred and eighty-five. That was typical of the skewed thinking and lack of planning on the part of the prison administration. Many things were done without proper foresight, but it was customary for them to treat 'locals' with more respect and consideration than the rest of us. After all, they had to answer to the local families who sought clemency for their relatives just as much as mine sought justice for me.

That morning I learned that many people I had come to know through the course of my year in Al Wathba had suddenly become my block mates. As much as I had despised being in Block 10 after my release from the prison clinic, I now found myself relegated to spending the rest of my time there. I told Jamal at the Embassy about the dismal conditions when he next visited me.

"The block is situated in a dark and dank place with standing water and virtually no view to the outside. There is only a little patch of sky visible over the top of the upper floors of the prison," I complained.

There were no shelves or beds, no night lights as in other blocks; and here there was a concentration of dangerous drug dealers mixed in with the rest of us who had simply been convicted of using drugs. To add injury to insult, the toilets were broken.

Now I was in the same block as Ian Bamling. Joining us was Horace, a friendly Indian fellow whom I had met while upstairs when he came by our window on cleaning duty. He had been sentenced to five years, four for drug possession and one for having a *Playboy* magazine in his luggage when he had been searched at the airport. Horace had worked for several years on the offshore oil rigs. For the first time I met Rigo, a young Sri Lankan who was to become a good friend and exercise partner. He was a specialist in servicing jet engines and had been sentenced to four years for possessing a marijuana cigarette. Overall there was quite an assortment of nationalities represented in our group including Indian, Iranian, Pakistani, Arab, Egyptian, Filipino, Afghani, Russian and those from other Middle Eastern countries. There were also many from various African countries.

    I found a place in Room 4 along with ten others. Our area was about 12 feet by 15 feet, a stark section with four walls, only one of which had any windows to the outside. The windows were small and high, so you couldn't easily see out. All of them were covered with a wire mesh, and an air conditioning unit fitted into one opening blocked our view even further. Somehow we all managed to carve out a 3 foot by 6 foot space on the concrete floor and put down a blanket for a bed. There was a little room left over here and there to place our belongings. That I now found myself in the worst block in the whole prison added to my feeling that I wasn't going home any time soon. I was living in a dungeon and each day I became more and more depressed.

It was the middle of Ramadan, and as before, food was brought to our blocks for our main meal of the day. Though little order had existed in my previous blocks, here in Block 10, I faced chaos on a regular basis. People constantly fought over food. On my first night at distribution, I was standing in line when two huge Pakistanis got into an argument in front of me. One raised his plate high in the air and brought it down, edge first, on the head of the other. Needless to say, blood spurted everywhere and the fellow fell to the ground. Immediately guards came and took the two away; one to the clinic and the other to solitary. What a great beginning to life in our new block! I soon realized that, as a whole, this group was more hostile than any I had been locked up with before. I would have to be more cautious than ever to ensure that I stayed out of harm's way.

Once I met most of my block mates, I realized that there were about seven of us who were Christian. With Christmas only a few days away, I felt that we should do something to fittingly celebrate the occasion and lift our spirits. I talked with the other six and they agreed that we should have a service of our own. After getting clearance from the block foreman along with his assurance that no one would tell the prison officials of our plan, we set about to create our Christmas Eve service.

As a collaborative effort we came up with most of the words to our favorite carols and I copied several of the Christmas scriptures from my Bible in the library so that we could read them. People were assigned to read lessons and I was chosen to conduct the service.

Now and then I would calculate the number of days I had been held in prison, and on Christmas Eve I reached a milestone. I wrote: *It is Christmas Eve and also day number 444—ironically the number of days that the American Embassy staff were held hostage in Tehran years ago.* I still clung to hope that maybe day 444 would be my last day too.

On Christmas Eve night about 11:30 we gathered in my room. It was a very risky thing because, if word had gotten out, we would all have ended up in solitary confinement. Surprisingly, several of our Muslim friends, including the foreman, wanted to sit in the room with us to listen and watch as we held our service. We used some bread smuggled from the cafeteria and some fruit juice saved from a meal as the 'bread and wine' for our communion. We sang carols as best as we could, had scripture readings, and in place of a homily we shared our thoughts about what Christmas was like in each of our own countries. It was a very emotional time and many of us ended up in tears.

After the service, our Muslim friends surprised us by bringing out plates of fruit that they had saved from their meals and wanted to share with us. What a wonderful thing to do and it was something that brought all of us closer together. In a letter to my brother I wrote: *It was a nice time for all realizing that in the midst of where we are there is some good. I've only got one more Christmas to go in here and then I'll be able to join the rest of you again.*

By Christmas I knew that I wasn't going to be released as part of the Ramadan celebration. I had a visit with Jamal and Nicholas Papp, the Vice-Consul of the Embassy. Jamal told me that they had had no word from Sheikh Diyab, and that meant he would not grant me clemency. I wrote:

> *When Jamal gave me the news it was obvious that he was shocked and distressed at the outcome. Needless to say I was very disappointed but in the scheme of things here I am not surprised. One does not expect much in the way of mercy. By contrast we read in the papers here of prisoners being released in many other countries close by and today about the 139 murderers released for the holidays in Ireland.*

It was sad and depressing for me to hear that, and as the two men were leaving, Nicholas looked at me and sincerely wished me a Merry Christmas. I acknowledged his greeting, but I choked up as the tears came. My nightmare was to continue.

My Room

The news was passed on to my brother in an e-mail from Charles Glatz, the American Consul on December 26. He wrote:

> *I am sorry to report that it appears that the clemency request for Paul will not be approved at this time. Our contact at the Presidential Diwan has told us that the request did not get the Sheikh's approval. Our contact attributed the negative response to an increase in similar requests from different nationalities via other sources in the country. It may be that we will never get a definitive reply because to refuse such an appeal would be embarrassing for Sheikh Diyab. Thus they will probably just leave it pending with definitive action. During our last visit with Paul, Jamal Bafagih broke this news to him because he inquired. Naturally, he was very disappointed and distressed. At this time this is all I can report. We will continue to inquire with the Diwan and perhaps something will develop down the road. I am sincerely sorry to bring you this news during the holiday season but I know you would want to know ASAP.*

Not only were my hopes for a Christmas back home dashed, but I had so wanted to share in the New Year's millennium celebrations. What a special treat that would have been!

But as it was, Christmas came and went as a non-event for everyone but us Christians. The news that I would not be released was like getting coal in my stocking.

33

Next Year

FOR WEEKS THE NEWSPAPERS HAD BEEN filled with stories of celebrations planned to welcome in the new millennium. From the reports just before year's end, however, it appeared that many of the more elaborate plans had been canceled. People simply had refused to pay the inflated prices and decided to stay close to home. Still, it would have been nice to participate in any New Year's Eve celebration anywhere outside of prison.

As expected, the guards came through the blocks early on New Year's Eve and collected all the plastic pails so that we couldn't use them as drums to make noise as part of our celebration. Most of us stayed up late and talked and listened to some of the Arabs sing a few of their traditional songs. In a letter to my friend Dean in Boston I wrote later, "The best we could muster was a bit of yelling and hand shaking at midnight." Eventually, we all went our separate ways, and as I drifted off to sleep, I thanked God for having delivered me safely to the year 2000. My final thought that early morning was that I would be going home next year. Not two years from now but *next year*!

Now that Ramadan, Christmas, and New Year's had passed and a token number of prisoners had been released, it was time to focus on the present and get back into our routine. As it turned out, the announced prisoner release was just another publicity event for the UAE government and mostly reflected the prisoners in the 'out prison' as in the previous Ramadan. Smoke and mirrors! For those of us who really knew what was going on, it was maddening that the outside world was being hoodwinked by this government into believing that they were doing something generous and compassionate for the prisoners.

Because I always looked for the next opportunity to secure my release, I spent a lot of time wondering if maybe we had made a mistake by choosing the more diplomatic approach to my early release. I had to keep reminding myself that, although Ian Bamling's family had taken the public approach, they hadn't been successful either. It appeared that neither of us was going to get out early, so I figured that maybe we should just spend the time trying to garner public support against the repressive UAE regime. In a visit from the Embassy on January 26, I asked Jamal to pass on the following message to my brother:

> I do not hold any illusions at this point of an early release. As I have come to expect, blatant religious hypocrisy and inhumanity is the norm for this regime in dealing with those they find to be undesirables. I would like to devote some of my efforts in my remaining time to highlighting those above aspects in the civilized world. A British roommate, Ian Bamling, came here two weeks after me in a similar case. Whereas we have pursued a quiet, diplomatic approach to clemency, his mother has been very vocal in the local press and also in the newspapers, radio, and TV in England. Both efforts have ended in the same 'no response' result.
>
> I would like you to consider lending our support to her efforts by going public in the media in the U.S. and Canada. Alternatively, I have no qualms in your pursuing a financial deal quietly with any media organization, including tabloids, for an exclusive on my release.
>
> Also you should visit Amnesty International's website for information regarding Al Wathba prison. The things to be highlighted include both the operations of their legal system and the treatment of prisoners. I respect your decision whether or not to pursue these avenues.

My brother responded to Charles Glatz, the U.S. Consul:

> I received your communiqué and will be discussing Paul's comments with the family. At this point in time we do not want to do anything that will jeopardize

> *Paul's early release from prison (i.e. serve only 36 months instead of the 48). We will keep you posted of anything we may attempt at this end.*

That was something I hadn't thought of. By going public and causing embarrassment for the government, they could disregard my good behavior and make me serve the full sentence. That was their ace in the hole for making sure someone toed the line and they often threatened people with such ominous consequences. Charles responded to my brother with a message I was unaware of: "In my mind your request for clemency is still 'on the table' and we will raise it again as opportunities present themselves."

One of the Arabs from Jordan with whom I had become friendly was a devout Muslim. He had a book in Arabic that interpreted different occurrences in people's dreams. In Islam dreams are considered to foretell future events, so much emphasis is placed on their interpretation. I had been having some very vivid dreams during January and I spoke to him about them and asked that he try to interpret them for me from a Muslim's viewpoint. After listening to what I said, he did some reading and told me: "You will meet with success (for release) on the third attempt and the person responsible for securing your release will be a woman and someone you least suspect."

I figured that two attempts had come and gone: the attempt by my lawyer to have me freed and the efforts of the Embassy and my brother to secure clemency. So I wondered what the third major challenge would be and when it would come. I imagined that the next significant opportunity would be late in the year during Ramadan. Because there had been rumors that Shiekha Fatima, Sheikh Zayed's wife had been pushing for a few early releases, perhaps it was she who would be instrumental in having me set free.

The Embassy staff continued to work for my release, and even Ambassador Theodore Kattouf made an appeal. After a meeting with some of the sheikhs, he wrote to Sheikh Diyab:

> *It was a pleasure to see you on January 31 at the luncheon at His Highness Sheikh Hamdan's home, which again afforded me the opportunity to thank you for your invaluable support for our recent privatization conference which we believe was a great success.*

I would like to take this opportunity to raise again the case of Mr. Paul Ciceri, an American citizen who is presently incarcerated at Al Wathba Central Prison. I was unable to discuss this matter fully with you on January 31, but understand from my Special Assistant, Richard Olson, that you requested some additional information.

Mr. Ciceri was residing in Abu Dhabi as an English language teacher at ELS. In October 1998, while arriving home from Canada and his mother's funeral, Mr. Ciceri was arrested at Abu Dhabi airport. Based on physical evidence and drug testing, he was charged with the possession and use of narcotics. Mr. Ciceri was tried and convicted in May 1999, receiving a sentence of 4 years imprisonment. With good behavior he is due for release in October 2001.

In October 1999, in your role as Chairman of the Presidential Diwan you were gracious enough to meet with the Embassy's Consul, Mr. Glatz and with Mr. Ciceri's brother Richard. Richard conveyed to you his family's plea for clemency for his brother and explained that the entire Ciceri family, as well as their close friends, believe that Paul's involvement with drugs was totally out of character. Furthermore, they are convinced that Paul has been and will be a good son, a dedicated father, and a contributing member of society. Richard asked the Diwan to consider particularly that their father is elderly and has a delicate heart condition. Paul's father would like Paul at home during his final years.

I do not seek here to minimize the seriousness of Mr. Ciceri's offense. The UAE's efforts to combat drug use are consistent with U.S. interests. I would note, however, that Paul and his family, working through the Embassy, have chosen to approach UAE authorities in a quiet, diplomatic manner, to acknowledge the wrong Paul has done, and to ask for clemency.

I respectfully ask that you review the matter of clemency for Mr. Ciceri in the hope that you can find a positive decision appropriate in this case. I am grateful for your attention to this matter.

The reference to the approach taken by us in seeking clemency was obviously done to show that we did not want to embarrass the UAE government as Ian Bamling's family had done.

In early February I felt it was time to send another note to those on my e-mail list, so I contacted my friend Rick Crocker to send my message that talked about the Christmas and New Year's happenings and generally described the routine that we had all settled into:

> To pass the time I continue to read, study languages (currently German and Arabic) and keep statistics on the major sports based on reports in the newspaper. Most evenings several friends gather and we talk about everything from movies to music to law to just useless trivia of all sorts. The setting is minimalist in nature so we do the best we can. All in all, with people from many cultures and each with his own story I feel like I'm earning a PhD in humanity!

I wrote a facetious letter to my father and step-mother on February 10 that summed up my feelings at that moment:

> *Sixteen happy months of vacation have now passed at this desert resort. While I would rather have spent my vacation windsurfing, getting some sun on a Caribbean beach, hiking some mountain path, or touring the countryside I must admit that the cost of food and lodging here is very affordable. My little place of heaven for sleeping and my belongings is four feet by six feet of two-blanket thickness over a concrete floor. My ten roommates and I all get along fortunately because we're all side by side and have to walk through each other's space to get to our own. Heck, I've even gotten used to the snoring. My roommates include one Brit, two Filipinos, two Pakistanis, two Iranians, one Moroccan, and two Indians—our own little United Nations. Language is a little bit of a barrier but all the important things get communicated to everyone.*

One of the Russian prisoners was telling me about his imprisonment in Brooklyn, New York for two years. He was describing how they had television and radio, a gym, a grocery store, access to the outdoors every day, full use of a research library, beds with mattresses, conjugal visits with wives, and all kinds of games. We have none of those things as we just do the best we can. So far I've read over 100 novels, devoured any other books I've found (advertising, psychology, aeronautics), have studied some languages, and have tried to keep physically fit through aerobics and stretching (Yoga). I tend to spend a lot of the time with my British roommate, a Sri Lankan, and an Indian in talking about just about everything from music to television, radio, exercise, geography, trips, food, etc.—nothing is off limits.

Everybody in my block is here on a drugs case and all are non-UAE citizens. They (Emiratees) are kept in a separate block. But it's easy to realize that we are at the bottom of the food chain here—rapists, murderers, and child molesters are treated better and have better accommodations. But in all things you can find some good—some guys have been here for ten years and some still have up to nineteen years to go. October 2001 is just a heartbeat away by comparison. So I don't complain about the time to go. I do know though that of all the drug cases I was convicted of possession of the smallest amount.

I've made my concerns known to prison management and this past week I was called to the office to go over my claims. Then yesterday Charles and Jamal from the Embassy met with the manager to discuss them further. You'd think that since I am the furthest from home (of any prisoner in Al Wathba) that they'd just let me go! And besides they really don't need the U.S. government complaining to them all the time about the treatment of the sole U.S. prisoner here. And that also goes for my British roommate—his government has been complaining as much as mine. We are lucky because most guys have been ignored or abandoned by their embassies.

> For now I've got a full tube of toothpaste, a good toothbrush, a few good bars of soap, some warm clothes, and some books to learn Italian, German, and Spanish—so I am content! Things could be a lot worse!
>
> The manager has approved visits for me from a member of one of the local churches so that will be a good chance for me to have contact with someone outside of these walls.
>
> The weather here has been close to what Miami has been having. It does get 'coolish' at night but after the blistering summer heat there are no complaints here.
>
> With three Florida teams in the playoffs for the Super Bowl I was hoping that one might get to the final game. Regardless, from what I read in the newspaper the game was one of the most thrilling in years. I've been following the hockey and basketball too—looks like the Toronto teams are providing lots of good entertainment for the fans this year.
>
> I hope that spring comes early for you this year—I'm sure that the warm weather will help cure some aches and pains. I think of you two every day and I pray for your good health. It'll be so nice when we get to visit again. Somebody asked me the other day what food I would like when I get out. At the top of my list right now would be authentic fish and chips and a juicy hamburger with fries and a beer.
>
> Easter will soon be here and in case I don't get to you earlier I'll wish you a happy and healthy Easter now. Maybe a miracle will happen here—all is possible!

A week later in a letter to my friends Jim and Paul in Orlando. I wrote much of the same but also included news about an important milestone:

> Time's a marchin' on and here I am at day 500 (February 18th)." And there was a comment about something I wouldn't tell my parents: "I'm being a really good boy here—keeping out of harm's way and minding my own business. I was only in one fight some time ago and thankfully, for the most part, the prisoners

aren't hard-core criminals like you'd find in most American prisons. But then, 90% of us wouldn't be in jail, let alone prison, back home. But there are flare-ups and with so many nationalities represented here anything minor escalates into an Iran vs. Afghan, or Pakistan vs. India, etc. thing.

In a letter to my friend Dean in Boston a week later, I described one of my diversions:

> We have a group of cats that call Al Wathba home. They are well fed 'cause they all find their way to the place we eat and get a lot of scraps, plus the dumpsters are always overflowing. There are always kittens around and it's rather amusing to watch them learning from their mothers and horse playing. Some find their way into our blocks and I haven't quite figured out who is more entertained—us or the cats. Anyway, watching them and playing with them is a nice break from the boredom of this place. They come and they go as they wish because they fit between and under the bars and as you watch them you think 'Wouldn't it be nice if . . . ?' The other benefit of having them around is that they control the bugs (roaches, scorpions) so well that we rarely see one. When it comes to mice or rats I am the world's biggest scaredy cat—thank goodness there aren't any here!

In the same letter I let him know that I had my eye on the calendar:

> As you're reading this I passed the 17-month mark on March 7th—only 19 to go barring some kind of intervention! The Embassy remains positive but I just try to not think about it and have survival until October 2001 as my goal.

At the same time I wrote my friend Susan at ELS headquarters in Princeton New Jersey about one of my failings:

> My Arabic is atrocious. Every time I tried to learn I got four versions of the same word, phrase, or grammatical construction. I just gave it up but I know the

important words the police use: hurry; go; come; move; faster; nationality?; you British?; your hair needs cutting; no!.

After what had seemed a long time, the month of January finally passed and then February moved more swiftly—being a shorter month did help! And then it was on into March. Each day brought me a little bit closer to next year.

34

The Warden Hates Us

THE RATIONALE BEHIND SEGREGATING the prisoners convicted of drug-related crimes soon became evident. We had long suspected that the prison manager tried to make life more difficult for us than for other prisoners and signs to support our suspicions quickly became apparent after our move to the lowest-level blocks.

One of the things that many prisoners in our block looked forward to was getting out several mornings each week to attend classes at the school. Soon after we were moved to Block 10, that opportunity abruptly ended with the announcement that none of us would be allowed to attend classes in the future. Actually, what the order turned out to be was that none of the drugs prisoners in *Block 10* were allowed to participate; the 'local' drug cases in Block 9 were permitted to continue. The manager was apparently willing to make life more difficult for us, but was unwilling to endure the pressure from families of the 'locals'. Since many prisoners were sincerely trying to improve themselves, to be denied access to the school was devastating for them, especially when some still had ten years or more to serve on their sentence.

The Manager did make an exception, however, for those who wanted to attend the Islamic classes. I had given up those classes the previous summer and simply had no desire to go back to them. Sam, our teacher and my former roommate and exercise partner, had been released several months earlier and the quality of the discussions had diminished dramatically.

Block 10 was dimly lit and depressing. Because the upper stories kept us in shadows most of the day, only a few scattered rays of sunshine filtered into our area.

One of our small advantages, however, was that we were able to stick our arms through the small openings in the wall and feel the sun on our forearms. As little as that was, it was a wonderful sensation. Then, one morning in early March we saw indications that things were going to get worse. A team of maintenance personnel passed through our block and went outside into the courtyard. There they installed wire mesh over the few openings through which we previously had been able to stick our arms. Desperate, I thought, *My God! They are going to hem us in even more. We're being cooped up like chickens.*

At first I refused to eat lunch that day in protest, but others convinced me that such a protest would be in vain. We would have to work out another strategy to show our displeasure. Shortly thereafter, after many of us had made our displeasure known to the police and prison authorities, our block was raided by ten policemen. We were ordered to leave our block immediately wearing only what we had on, and were escorted to the cafeteria area to wait out the search of our quarters. After a two-hour wait, we knew that what we would be going back to would not be pretty. As bad as we expected it to be, we were greeted with a scene far worse than any we could have imagined. The destruction was total!

Clotheslines we had fabricated had been cut and clothes were strewn on the dirty floors. Bedding was tossed everywhere; blankets were ripped. One of the Muslim boys found his Koran torn and thrown aside, and I had to console him as he cried. Nothing had been left untouched. Letters were scattered. Notebooks were shredded. Pictures littered the floors of the rooms and hallways. It was total chaos. A hurricane could not have caused more damage! We were disconsolate, but as the grim task of cleaning up proceeded, our common will to survive resurfaced. We removed everything from the rooms and took the opportunity to clean all the floors before trying to rearrange our possessions. Some fighting ensued as people couldn't agree on who really owned some of the blankets or clothes. After several hours though, we gained some semblance of organization and once again put things in place. But the day had affected us all emotionally.

At the same time Ian Bamling, my British roommate, became angry and accused me of being insincere when I talked with him. Actually, if anything, I was feeling a lack of interest in listening to his constant bitching. He just wasn't dealing with the fact that the authorities hadn't responded positively to his family's pleas for clemency and with the reality that he was stuck in prison until released. One day he stormed out of our room and told the foreman that he wanted to move somewhere else. This request, of course, fell on deaf ears and for the remainder of our time together the relationship remained strained. Perhaps he realized that I felt some disdain for him and his family for having jeopardized my chance, as well as that of many others, for an early release.

I decided to make my feelings about life in Block 10 and the treatment of prisoners in general known to management. So I wrote a lengthy letter to the prison manager and sent a copy to the American Embassy. In that letter I detailed eighteen specific concerns I had about the treatment of prisoners, emphasizing the quality of life in Block 10. I told of the poor conditions in our block, the complete disregard by the police of our desire to be left in peace, the wanton destruction of our living area during searches, the poor quality of food and health care, the denial for people in Block 10 to attend classes, and the fact that much of our mail was not being received or sent out.

To my surprise I was called up to the Major's office a few days later to discuss my points with him. He told me that he respected my opinions and that he would take them all under consideration. I didn't trust him one iota and would not have been surprised to have been lead away to solitary confinement for insubordination.

To my additional surprise, Jamal and Charles had also read my letter. I was called to the Manager's office the next day where I was met by the two of them. They had been discussing my letter with the Manager and told me that they had expressed their displeasure with him. One thing I asked them to help me with was to be allowed access to some vitamins. Jamal talked with the Manager who reluctantly agreed that the Embassy could bring in some vitamins for me. They would be kept in the clinic where I could go each day to get one capsule. The Manager also agreed that I would be allowed to teach again and have access to the library. As much as I welcomed that concession, I felt uneasy about it because I was the only one in the block to be granted such privileges. I knew this would arouse some animosity towards me. The Manager also indicated that we would be moved from our block to another block once renovations were completed. That definitely lifted my spirits because it meant we would be moving to the top floor again to the block that faced out over the side of the prison where the highways and the lights of small towns could be seen.

I shared the information with my block mates, though we remained extremely skeptical that any of those things would ever come to be. To our surprise, a few days later, the police told us that we would be allowed to leave our block and move to the courtyard for an hour each day so we could get some sun and fresh air. That was a godsend and almost everyone took advantage of the opportunity. It was the first time most of us had been outside in many months and had had a chance to see the sky. There was a general lifting of spirits and the air was upbeat for a time. For those few precious minutes, one could dream of being at the beach on some secluded Caribbean island with the sun's rays beating warmly on the body.

I was jubilant at the chance to see the sunshine and I wrote my brother on March 3:

> *Since your visit they (the Embassy) have been more attentive to my needs and concerns. When I ask for something I get it next visit and even the visits have been a bit more frequent. During the last visit Jamal showed me a letter from the Ambassador to the person you visited (Sheikh Diyab) reiterating the request. Let's hope this second request results in some response. Four of us have been getting into exercising again and the results are beginning to show. On average I was getting a cold every 4–6 weeks but I haven't had one for 3 months now so something is happening for the better health wise too! Jamal got me books on Spanish and Italian. I've got the German grammar under control now but no one to talk to. The Spanish is coming and there is a guy here from Lebanon who has a Spanish girl friend so he's helping me out.*

Several persons in the prison were diabetics and had to go to the clinic twice a day to receive their insulin shots. It was decided that I would go with them on their evening trip to receive my vitamin pill. That was a welcome idea since it gave me a chance to leave the block and helped pass a half-hour each evening. Two men in our block were diabetic, so after dinner I accompanied them to the clinic. At first the guards at the checkpoint were surprised that I was among the group, but after a few days my presence became routine. Even though all the police knew that the diabetics were scheduled to go to the clinic each day, a few delighted in making it difficult. Some nights we stood at the front gate and would have to ask time and time again to be taken for our medication. This added to the frustration of the whole experience, so after a month of hassles in obtaining a single Centrum vitamin pill, I told the nurses simply to put the bottle of capsules on the cart that they took to the blocks each day. I would get my pill there. Reluctantly they agreed, but in the end this caused another problem.

Picking up my pill when the nurses came to the block elevated the visibility of The American getting some kind of special treatment. Now others decided that they too wanted to have vitamin pills. First Ian Bamling made a big issue of it, and to upstage me he had to have a couple of varieties of pills for himself. Then some of the Arabs decided that they too wanted vitamins and asked their embassies to bring them. I knew that each case had to be approved by the prison manager, and I suspected that before long he would decide that the whole process was too much of a hassle. Soon he would prohibit any of us from having pills brought in from the outside.

In a letter to my friend Dean in Boston I wrote:

> *Whether or not they [the vitamin pills] help me physically, and I'm sure they do, there is also a positive psychological stimulus in just knowing I'm doing something to help my body. I haven't had a cold for 4–5 months now. I was getting one every 4–6 weeks during the first year here. I think the stress of the trial process and letting my frustration and anger work on me were part of that too.*

One of the men in the diabetic group was an Egyptian named Mohammed. Unless he received his injection twice a day he would have a serious problem with his health. One night the guards decided that they did not want to bother taking us to the clinic, so we had to stay in the block. Later that night I heard screams from the room next door where Mohammed slept. I rushed over and there, surrounded by several of his roommates, was Mohammed convulsing on the floor. The foreman, I, and two others decided we had to get him to the clinic fast for treatment. Now Mohammed weighed about 270 pounds so it was a struggle for the four of us to lift him. We got him to the front gate where others had already alerted the guard that we needed to move him out of the block immediately. He concurred and the four of us, with our adrenalin pumping, struggled to carry him up four flights of stairs. At the security desk on the third level we were directed to put him on the floor and leave him. We told them we wanted to move him on a stretcher to the clinic. "Go back to your block, we'll take care of him," they told us again. Totally exhausted we did return and waited to see how Mohammed would fare in their hands. We received our answer in about fifteen minutes when

Contraband

Mohammed walked back to the block looking as if nothing had ever occurred. He had gotten his injection and later confided that the convulsing was an act to give the impression that he was a serious diabetic case. We were all angry with him, but later had to laugh about the incident even though all this had taken place about 1:00 in the morning. Fate would not be so kind to him, however. His diabetes was not treated properly and within six months he had to have one of his legs amputated. Subsequently, he was released.

In mid March, something really neat happened. I was surprised one Friday afternoon when I was told that I had a visitor. All sorts of things ran through my head. Maybe it was someone from ELS. Perhaps someone from the Embassy had come, and if that were so, then there must be some extraordinary news.

Who else could it be? What else?

I got dressed quickly and headed up to the visiting room along with the others who expected company that day. I knew then that whoever was coming to see me was not from the Embassy because I was led to the place where prisoners received their family and friends. So I expected something good to happen and my anticipation heightened by the minute. I wasn't disappointed. When my name was called I was ushered into a room where prisoners faced their visitors through a wire mesh. Immediately a gentleman approached me, and as soon as he spoke, I knew that he was an American. His name was Tom Hennessey and he had been living and working in Abu Dhabi for many years. He had heard about me through a member of his church who came to see Ian Bamling. He had decided that it would be a nice gesture on his part, and witness to his life as a good Christian, to visit me. I wrote to Dean:

> *I had a visit from a fellow from a local Christian church. There are about 350 Americans attending there and they got wind of my being here. Although visits are limited to 5–10 minutes it was nice to talk with an American (he's from New Hampshire). He was kind enough to bring me some toothpaste and stamps.*

For the rest of my time at Al Wathba Tom would be my most important link to the outside world and especially to my family.

35

My Guardian Angels

FOR MANY MONTHS PRIOR TO MY first visit from Tom I had received letters on a regular basis from someone I had never met. Mary McGuire lived coincidentally in the city where my father resided, and she had become good friends with Emmy, a long-time family acquaintance who was hospitalized with a terminal illness.

In the course of her daily discussions with Emmy in the hospital, Mary learned that her family and mine had been neighbors in the northern Ontario city of Sudbury, and that I had been imprisoned in Al Wathba. One day Mary helped Emmy send me a message of support and she, knowing relatively little about me herself, began to write as well.

Those letters would continue even after Emmy's death until the time of my release. Almost weekly I would get a four to six-page letter from Mary telling me about her experiences as a psychic, spiritual advisor, and life facilitator. She also encouraged me with passages from Scripture that helped keep me focused on survival and good mental health. She supported me in my efforts to meditate and learn yoga. Frequently her letters included pictures of animals, nature scenes, or angels accompanied by appropriate poems. I truly cherished these enclosures as they were such diversions from the boring day-to-day life in Al Wathba. Sometimes without explanation the pictures of the angels were seized by the translator prior to giving me the letters, but by reading her explanations I could still conjure up in my mind what the pictures must have been like.

Mary encouraged me to focus on several passages in Scripture and the one I will never forget was the 91st Psalm. In that psalm David wrote;

> Because you have made the Lord your refuge,
>   the Most High your dwelling place,
> no evil shall befall you,
>   no scourge come near your tent.
> For he will command his angels concerning you
>   to guard you in all your ways.

Mary kept me focused on the fact that I could survive in appalling conditions by using the inner strength with which I had been blessed. Her unflinching support helped me throughout my darkest moments to believe that I had good times to look forward to after serving my sentence.

Around that same time Tom came into my life. He and his wife, Jan, were members of a local Christian congregation that included many British and American nationals. Every Friday morning in church the congregation prayed for those who needed God's special help and blessing and my name was included. Because of this, many members in the church had followed my incarceration closely.

Tom's day off from work was Friday, but it was also the only day set aside by prison officials when persons like me were allowed visits. Religiously, Tom came every second week to see me, sometimes waiting hours in the scorching sun before he was allowed inside the prison. Once inside there was another wait, again sometimes for hours, until I was brought to the visiting area. Often, because the police didn't know where a prisoner was housed, the police had to go from block to block trying to locate someone who had a visitor.

In spite of all the obstacles the prison officials put in front of him, Tom steadfastly refused to cut back on the frequency of his visits. Once he was brought into the visiting area, we knew we only had a few minutes to get in all that we wanted to say. Often we had to strain to hear over the noise of the other inmates and their visitors. Some prisoners, especially the Pakistanis and Indians, had up to seven or eight people at a time and they all tried to speak at once. Consequently, we became pretty good at lip reading.

After the allotted five or ten minutes were over, the police would nudge one of us indicating our time was up. Sometimes the guard in charge knew me, understood I had only one visitor, and would allow us to continue talking for up to one-half hour. But that was rare. To make sure our time was well spent, Tom would prepare signs in large print with scores of different sports or e-mails that he had received from my family. These he would hold up for me to see. And he would always bring me something: toothpaste, toothbrush, pens, paper, or stamps. Once he brought me a few pencils, but, because only pencils provided by officers in the school were allowed, he had to take them back with him. We still haven't figured that one out!

Tom constantly kept in touch with the Embassy and sent letters prodding them to do more for me than they did. I'm sure he became a thorn in their sides, but he was genuinely interested in doing all that he could to get me out of Al Wathba. Just seeing Tom for a few minutes every other week was uplifting. Despite the waiting and the heat, there was always a smile on his face.

On the day I was released Tom met me briefly at the Abu Dhabi airport in the presence of my guards and Jamal and Nicholas from the U.S. Embassy. It was then that we seized the opportunity to give each other a hug in front of the startled guards, our first physical contact in the eighteen months that I had known him. We vowed to meet each other again in the United States, and strange as it seems, several months after my release, Tom and Jan left Abu Dhabi and relocated to Central Florida just an hour and a half west of Orlando. It was there in early 2001 that I visited them at their home, and we cherished the ability to converse without bars between us. That was a splendid moment for me.

After my release when I asked Tom why he had spent so much time and effort on my behalf, he summed up his actions: "It was just the Christian thing to do," he told me.

36

Springtime Hopes

MANY PEOPLE COMMENTED HOW SLOWLY the month of January seemed to pass. But once we moved into February things speeded up again and quickly spring was upon us.

Already the temperatures were in the mid 90s and sometimes you could smell the freshness in the air. But we saw nothing that would visibly remind us that it was spring: no plants; no rain showers; no signs of any new life. Just the same old concrete walls.

One mail day, however, I got a note from Mary in which she enclosed some pictures of daffodils and other springtime flowers. I hung them low on the wall where I could see them when I was sitting on my bed or waking in the morning. Many times I would stare at them and think about all the happy springtime memories that I had. I wrote to a friend on March 25:

> *My thoughts have turned to spring and it looks like things are warming up a bit in your neck of the woods. Today was the warmest day in many months (95°) and was rather windy with a lot of dust in the air. But for all of the bad things in this block, we do have air conditioning and the closed rooms keep out the sand. In a letter from a friend of Dad's I got a couple of small pictures of springtime flowers and they adorn my walls to help me remember all the beauty I used to take more or less for granted.*

Early springtime also brought hope that I really was going to survive my time in prison. April 6 was the first day of the Islamic

New Year and the day after marked the half-way point of my sentence. I wrote:

> Today is the first day of the Islamic New Year—one that is based on the comings and goings of the moon rather than the sun. Tomorrow marks the half-way point of my sentence and I'm not sure what I feel. Perhaps melancholy is the best choice. Although I do feel some relief that I've gotten this far it is somewhat overshadowed at the moment by frustration over the fact that I'm still here, and at times, feelings of helplessness over the time I'm wasting in my life by being here. I have learned though, that when those latter feelings arise, I have to just stop them dead in their tracks and shift focus. Otherwise those can lead to depression. So I shut them off and turn my attention to other more positive thoughts and that's why it's so important here, especially when any form of entertainment is forbidden, to find ways to keep busy.
>
> I remember from my readings of first-hand accounts of the Vietnam War that (American) soldiers said that for the whole time they were there they were in a trance-like state brought on by the enormity of the stress of the situations they found themselves in. Their bodies reacted instinctively even though their minds seemed to be in some kind of discombobulated state—a state brought on by stress so intensely foreign to their experiences that their minds became numb to processing all the information spewing forth around them. It's actually one of the human mind's abilities to preserve life. It shuts down in some regards in a defensive and preservation mechanism.

Knowing that I had passed the halfway point in my sentence did wonders for my spirits. Even though previously unimaginable things had transpired and I had experienced much mental trauma, I knew that I had survived pretty well, that I was intact mentally, and that the last half would be easier than the first. That didn't make being in Al Wathba any easier, but way down the road I could now see a bit of light at the end of the long black tunnel.

Easter is one of my favorite times of year. Reminiscences of spring flowers, warmer days, sunshine, and great music passed through my mind and I was upbeat as Easter approached. One of my favorite hymns is "Jesus Christ is Risen Today" and over and over I sang it to myself. The sounds of the wonderful music that accompanied the Easter morning church service echoed through my mind and with it I gained renewed energy.

Several cards arrived just before Easter and in a reply to my father I wrote that I had a lot to be thankful for at this time.

I give thanks for:

- Easter—Several of us fasted on Good Friday.
- My best friend [*Horace*] got released this week after 5½ years (5 for smoking marijuana and 6 months for being in possession of a Playboy magazine.
- We got to go outside this week for two 20-minute sessions. Those plus once last month were the first times in 1½ years.
- The weather is getting hot and we have air conditioning.
- The Embassy staff (Charles and Jamal) visited for an hour yesterday.
- A colleague from ELS HQ in the United States sent me some English books to use in my classes.
- I got some language books that Richard sent and the book on consulting.
- I got a recent Newsweek magazine from ELS too.
- My health is good and now I get my vitamins that the Embassy brought delivered with everyone else's medication to the block each night instead of having to argue with the police to go to the clinic each day.
- I got a letter from each of two good friends that I'd lost contact with when I came here.
- The fellow from the church says he will come to visit me every week now that his wife has returned to the U.S. for 3 months.
- I haven't lost my reading glasses yet. Unfortunately I lost the screw holding one of the arms to the frame but my resident wizard Uti fixed it using a piece of plastic strand from a broom.
- and . . . I survived another 7 days here!!!
- **AND . . . I know you all care

In my meeting with the Embassy staff the day before, I was told that there had been no response to my family's pleas for clemency and that none was expected. I had accepted that to be the case long before, and had come to the conclusion that being told this by the Embassy staff would give it a sense of finality.

With the outlook grim for an early release I had looked into the idea of working on an MBA via correspondence. The warden had given the okay for me to receive texts and study materials and had assured the Embassy staff that my reports would be sent back to the school. Tom did some checking for me, and after reviewing the alternatives, I decided that the Edinburgh Business School offered the best opportunity for me. Their programs were offered through a local college and my information to and from the school would arrive in a timely fashion. After some checking, though, it turned out that the cost was over $11,000. That was far more costly than I expected, and it wasn't an expense that I wanted to incur especially since I had no income at the time.

The newspapers the previous week had been full of exciting events taking place in Dubai. The world's richest horse race—a $4 million dollar purse—had been held, attracting a record crowd. The world's tallest hotel, a marvel of architecture, had opened. Shaped like a huge sail it boasted an underwater restaurant that could be reached by submarine, a fleet of seven white Rolls Royce limousines for picking up patrons from the airport, and palatial rooms offered at upwards of $5,000 per night. In addition, one of the most successful month-long shopping festivals had just been completed, and the government had recently announced that within eighteen months all governmental agencies would be online, enabling most departmental transactions to be handled online.

And all that was happening just seventy miles from here! Like night and day!

On a whimsical note I told my father about an article that had appeared in the last issue of the local newspaper. It described the prison in Monaco. Cells had cable television, radios, and refrigerators. Each had a view of the Mediterranean Sea, there was a complete gym for the inmates, and the kitchen boasted four qualified chefs.

I asked, "Can you get me transferred there?"

One letter I received that week was from Susan at ELS HQ in Edison, New Jersey. In it she told me about a normal week and what had been happening back home. Tongue in cheek, I wrote back describing one of my typical days:

> Those of us who didn't participate in the Fajr (dawn) prayer were awakened by the sweet sounds of a Beethoven classic played over our block's loudspeakers. Once we were all up we proceeded to the dining hall for our usual feast of varied omelettes, fresh fruit juices, cereals, breads, and pastries. After that nice leisurely breakfast we returned to our blocks to read through an assortment of newspapers. Typically that would include the Herald Tribune, Washington Post, The Times (London), Pravda, and Le Soir all flown in early in the morning just for us. A few hours later the coffee trolley came by with not only the usual array of coffees of the day but mimosas and Bloody Marys. Whoever said that this wasn't a caring country? Then, after that we had a nice leisurely lunch of meats, some Asian dishes, and fresh pies. On the return to the block many turned in for an afternoon nap but I had to get up to the Administration office where I give a presentation to senior staff every Thursday. Yesterday's topic was a continuation of my five-week presentation on fiscal responsibility pertaining to prisoners' well being. I focused yesterday on my idea for the new health spa and mineral hot springs. Next week my topic will be firing squad etiquette. At mid-afternoon we all gathered for tea and pastries in the courtyard. This is a dress-up occasion every day so everyone had clean sandals and toenails. In our little group we discussed the art forms of Renoir and El Greco with emphasis on how the moods of the paintings were reflective of their own personal struggles. Dinner of course was an elaborate array of hot dishes representative of nationalities amongst the inmates. This is the only meal where they let us use the official state cutlery and dishes all embossed with the royal seal of course. The evening presentation in the recital hall was a videotape featuring Tim Allen. His topic was "Life after Prison" and how you too can have your

own television show and make millions! It was good but he didn't have to show us all of his tattoos from his prison days. Next week's program will be even better—a live version of Jesus Christ Superstar presented by the players of the royal court. When we got back to the block, as is the usual custom for a Thursday night, our bedrolls were all folded neatly and a nice chocolate was on each pillow compliments of His Royal Highness Sheikh Zayed.

So you can see why Friday is a quiet, reflective day. Thursdays are exhausting!

I also gave my opinions on several current news items and rated their importance:

- The Pope's visit to the Middle East—** Wow! He was apologizing for everything but it fell mostly on deaf ears. Typical!
- The U.S. Presidential race—* They keep tripping over their own mouths. Boys, boys, boys grow up! There are issues!!! And, Al, the Cuban boy isn't really one of them. I will get to vote by absentee ballot—goody!
- Janet Reno's handling of Elian's case—***** Bravo! Let's show the world we stand for law and order.
- Bill Clinton's video showing how he's spending his time missing Hillary and being a lame-duck president—**** Too cool, Billy! Hilarious stuff."

All through the spring, things remained routine for me: spending some mornings in the library; teaching English to the younger male prisoners and to a second group of 'over 21' prisoners; exercising with the men on my block; studying Spanish, Italian, and German; reading; keeping track of the major sports results from the U.S; playing chess and dominoes; going over in my head the music and words of my favorite hymns each Sunday morning.

I created a diversion for myself in the library by getting permission to label all the English books along the book spines. Most of the books were well-used and the lettering along the spines was often faded or worn as a result of the books being constantly handled. Everyone who came there pulled them out to see what was on the cover. By allowing me to mark the spines, people could scan the books a lot easier and there would be a lot less wear and tear on them. It was pretty simple stuff, but it was something to keep me busy for a few weeks.

Every morning before breakfast I would awaken early and work on my languages. To reinforce what I had studied, I transcribed the grammar for the languages into my own words and created a side by side comparison of English, Spanish, French, and German relating to all aspects of the grammar. I thought that someday I could possibly get it published.

In May I read in the local paper that the sponsors of the Desert Classic, a major golf tournament in Dubai, were trying to lure Tiger Woods to play in the event. I knew that he lived in Orlando and what importance the people of Dubai gave to his participation in their event so I asked Susanne to contact his agent and ask him to mention my predicament to the sponsors in the hope that they could help get me released. It may sound like a pretty hokey thing to do, but at the time I would leave no possibility for release unexplored. Nothing came of it. But we tried.

May 26 was my father's 88th birthday. I so desperately wanted to talk with him sometime between then and Father's Day! I made a request to the Embassy that they try to arrange a phone call and they indicated they would. All telephone calls from prisoners sentenced on drug cases were forbidden, so I knew that what I wanted was likely not to happen. On one of their visits, however, they did bring me a telephone card. Jamal had friends who worked at the prison and he attempted to get one of them to help in arranging the call. On that visit when he brought the telephone card, he also had his friend stop by so I would recognize him later. He gave his friend the card and the friend said he would call me to the office within a few days to make the call. He was very nervous and I knew he was taking a risk in trying to help me. The days passed but I was not called.

I learned later that the prison authorities got wind of what was happening and refused to let me make the call. I do not know what happened to Jamal's friend.

37

God Bless Sheikh Mohammed

IT WAS JUST ANOTHER ROUTINE MORNING at Al Wathba prison. Breakfast as usual that Wednesday morning consisted of two hard-boiled eggs and a piece of bread. Although we didn't have much time to eat before the police began blowing their whistles and yelling for us to get back to our block, we ate as slowly as possible and enjoyed looking out through the wire mesh to see a patch of blue over the top of the third-level blocks. As usual the sky was mostly cloudless and you could tell that it was going to be another warm day. People were beginning to stir in the other blocks as they anticipated their turn for breakfast. For some reason that was never explained to me our block was usually called first for breakfast. Perhaps it was the warden's way to further punish us by having us wake up first. If you missed the slight window of opportunity you were given to get out and move to the eating area, you wouldn't have any food until lunch time.

Once back at the block, I showered and worked on my lesson preparation for that day. Most everyone else went back to sleep. About 8:30 the few of us going to the school met at the gate for the police to come and escort us to our destination. There was a time when they would have merely opened the gate and let us go on our own, but rules had become more strict and now everyone needed a police escort to go anywhere.

In the school area the others went to the classroom where they were being taught about Islam and I headed to the library to do some reading and kibitz with the few other prisoners who also had library privileges. When I walked in that morning, I was greeted by those already there and then by the librarian, Tarek, who shook my hand as he usually did and grinned as though he had something he wanted to tell me. The policeman in charge of the library was standing beside him and was also smiling as I shook his hand. As I was about to ask him what was up one of the others called, "It looks like you're going home."

That caught my attention. Definitely.

"What are you talking about?" I asked with excitement in my voice.

The other inmates were well educated and spoke English as well as they read and spoke Arabic. Several had PhDs, one was a medical doctor, and another was a professional engineer. They smiled and looked at me as if I had just won the lottery. They gathered together looking at the morning's Arabic newspaper.

What's going on?

On the front page of the Arabic paper was the story that Sheihk Mohammed of the ruling family of Dubai had announced that drug offenders should not be treated as criminals and should not spend time in prison. That revelation hit me like a hammer.

Incredulously I asked, "What?"

The news indicated a major rift in policy between the ruling family in one Emirate and a leading political faction in another. Each Emirate had its own ruling family and they were able to make some of their own rules and laws. Usually, however, they followed the lead of whatever Sheikh Zayed, the ruler of Abu Dhabi and President of the UAE deigned to be the law of the land. Several years earlier, deviating from the constitution of the country, he had decreed that the minimum prison sentence for drug offenders would be four years regardless of the severity of the crime. Now here was a much more forward-thinking and liberal highly-respected leader saying that that policy was wrong. Unheard of!

The article went on to say that all drug users would be freed from the prisons in Dubai. Offenders from outside the UAE would be deported and inmates from the UAE would spend time in a rehabilitation center until they were declared eligible to return to their families. This would begin immediately.

Everyone was dumbfounded by this news. The consensus in the room was "God bless Sheikh Mohammed."

We talked about the article. We read it and re-read it. But there was no mention of any response from Sheikh Zayed. There was no mention whether the policy would apply to other emirates as well.

We speculated.

We played devil's advocate.

We sat in disbelief.

Still I felt upbeat that something like this could happen in a country like this. And I had no answers. The police knew nothing more than what was in the article. I couldn't wait for the next visit from the Embassy. My mind raced with excitement.

That morning my class was all abuzz over the news. No one in my class was in prison because of drug use, and I was the only one allowed in the school from our block except for those studying Islam. But everyone wondered if this could be the beginning of reforms that included the easing of penalties for all prisoners. News spreads like wildfire in prison. Sometimes a guard who had read the morning paper would tell one person, and anything significant like this would be broadcast throughout the entire building in a matter of minutes. They had heard the news already; they all thought I would be going home soon and that maybe some good news would be in store for them too.

When I got back to the block everyone was waiting for me and expected that I would have some more information. They had been told nothing beyond what was in the paper. Lots of questions. No answers. No one slept much that morning and the mood was upbeat. Lots of talk. Lots of speculation. Everyone had an opinion.

The early afternoon passed slowly as we waited for our runner to be allowed to go upstairs to get our supply of daily newspapers. He was the most popular person in the block that afternoon, and when he returned, the papers were given out quickly so we could retreat to our cells to read the articles and talk about the issues. The English language newspaper carried the article on the front page, and inside it showed a picture of the completed rehabilitation center that was ready to accept local prisoners prior to their being released to their families. It was immense and beautiful with large grounds; nice housing, an Olympic-size swimming pool, and the freedom to roam the acreage. This wasn't just a spur of the moment decision on Sheikh Mohammed's part. This had been long planned and he was ready to act!

There was no reaction in the press from the ruling family of Abu Dhabi. Not that day, nor the next. They had to be pissed off! For the next several days, however, I heard over and over again the mantra: "God bless Sheikh Mohammed."

What happened was the main topic of my letters to family and friends that week. In one letter I wrote:

> *Just down the road (80 miles) in Dubai there was some terrific news. The leader of that Emirate made an announcement that it was time to stop treating drug users as criminals and there will be no more jail sentences for users. Then he summarily freed 500 prisoners and the 300 foreigners will be heading home this coming week. He has made Dubai a leading tourist attraction and hub of commerce in the Middle East. He is rich, educated, and merciful and loved. The people here have the first trait. Anyway it is encouraging and perhaps that momentum will carry to here. Put the bubbly on ice—you never know.*

"God bless Sheikh Mohammed!"

Tom came to visit me that Friday and he was full of questions too. He wondered if I had heard any more information, and I was wondering the same of him. All we both knew was what was written in the newspapers. After seeing me he wrote an e-mail to my family:

> It appears that the Emirate of Dubai, which is the neighbor to Abu Dhabi, has recently passed legislation that will release 'drug takers' for deportation as a new program that they are undertaking. Drug dealers will still be incarcerated. Although there is a world of difference between Dubai and Abu Dhabi, and never the twain shall meet, there is a ray of hope that it may trickle down to the Al Wathba prison. Obviously, it has been quite the

topic of conversation at the prison and has raised the hopes of those there for that reason. We hope and pray that it will happen and not be just another source of disappointment for them. Paul seems to be taking a 'wait and see' attitude and is not trying to get his hopes too high. I told him I hope he is not there when I go to visit him mid-July.
"God bless Sheikh Mohammed!"

38

Contact with my Father

MY FATHER'S BIRTHDAY HAD COME and gone and my much anticipated telephone call to him had never materialized. My brother had sent me a letter indicating where my father would be for that day and the days surrounding his birthday. This way I would know precisely where to reach him. But despite the best effort of U.S. Embassy personnel, the prison authorities did not grant me permission to call him.

My father had just turned eighty-eight, and based on the demographic studies I had seen of the UAE, that would put him in the one percent of the country's population who were over eighty-five. All through the Middle East and the Islamic world, emphasis is put on the reverence that is bestowed upon the elderly. As the patriarchs of the family, elderly males are cherished and it is customary on either Thursday or Friday of the week for families to gather at the home of the senior family members. When I was in Kuwait, I had been given the honor of joining one family for their regular Thursday afternoon get-together at the senior parents' home. All the male members of the family gathered in one room while the women and children gathered in another part of the house. It was the men who discussed family problems and set the policy of the extended family. Such gatherings had their roots in the tribal customs that surrounded those nations.

But for all of the rhetoric, I was still denied the privilege of talking with my father. I was a drug user and this was part of my punishment.

It was a surprise when, a few weeks later on June 14, I was called to speak to one of the prison guards and he asked me what time I wanted to make my telephone call. It took me a few seconds to grasp what he had said because I had dismissed any notions of making that call to my father. I quickly ran through the options and decided that about 6:30 at night would be the best. I knew that my father had recently begun sleeping-in later in the mornings and had given up on his trips to swim and exercise at the YMCA. I guessed that after lunch he and my stepmother would go out for some afternoon activity. So 6:30 p.m. Al Wathba time would equate to 10:30 a.m. where my father lived.

All day I thought about what I would say to my father. More of a concern, though, was the fact that I knew I would only be able to make one call and it had better be to the right place. I had memorized all the telephone numbers my brother had sent me and concluded that my best chance was to call my father at his home. It was an anxious day and I wasn't able to eat much at any meal. I compared it to going to a job interview where I knew I would have one chance to impress someone with my credentials, knowledge, and personality. I was going to have one chance at 6:30 and I had better not blow it!

I was ready at the front gate at 6:00 because I didn't want to miss the guard who was coming to get me. There was a clock by the gate and I watched it slowly tick from 6:00 to 6:30 to 7:00. As the minutes ticked by I knew that the window of opportunity for reaching my father was closing fast, just as a launch at Cape Canaveral had to occur within a certain timeframe to satisfy all the requirements of the mission. Gradually I began to feel that my call had again been disallowed.

And then at 7:15 the guard arrived to escort me to make my call. I expected to be led upstairs to the few pay telephones that prisoners involved in financial cases used to make their calls. But we didn't head in that direction. Instead, I was ushered downstairs, out across the prison grounds, and into the administrative offices at the entrance to the prison. There at the reception desk I faced the officer in charge of the evening duty and was told to sit. Six or seven guards, some of whom I knew understood English, stood watch. It was immediately apparent that they were there to ensure that I spoke no ill of the prison; obviously they were prepared to separate me and the telephone at the slightest hint that what I was saying didn't meet their standards.

The officer in charge handed me a telephone calling card still encased in its plastic wrap. Nervously, I fumbled with the card while he pushed the desk phone in my direction and told me to dial. It was overwhelming to have all those people staring at me, and to make matters worse, I had forgotten to bring my glasses. I couldn't make out the small numbers that I needed to activate the phone card. All I could read on the card was that it was a ten-minute international calling card. I wanted to cry.

Mercifully, the one in charge understood my dilemma, dialed the number for me, and when the connection was made, handed the handset back to me. Carefully I dialed my father's home telephone number that I had committed to memory. I waited without breathing, I think, while the call went through and I heard the first ring.

I had rehearsed what I would say. There would be no whining. There would be no begging for help. There would be no crying. There would be no theatrics. I took a deep breath and the phone rang a second time.

I would be positive and upbeat and my voice would be strong. I didn't want to add to the worries my father had about my well being. The phone rang a third time.

Please God, let them be home.

And then the telephone was picked up. It was a woman's voice. "Hello."

"Hi, is this Adele?"

"Yes."

"This is Paul in Abu Dhabi." No response on the other end.

"This is your stepson, Paul. Harold's son." Since she and my father had married a year after I had arrived at Al Wathba, we had never met or talked before.

"Oh, my goodness! Where are you? How are you?"

"Adele, I'm fine. I am still in Al Wathba prison and I have been given just a few minutes to talk. Can you get my father? Please."

I was not in that prison room at that moment. I was oblivious to the guards around me. *Oh, please God, let the answer be 'Yes'!*

"Yes, he's sitting right here."

Then I heard her excitedly call to my father, "Harold, it's Paul."

In the background I heard my father say, "Who?"

Louder she said, "It's Paul." I knew that he knew who it was. What I also knew was that he didn't have his hearing aid in place. I heard him say, "Let me get the other phone."

In a matter of seconds he picked up.

"Dad, it's so great to hear your voice." There was no response. "Dad, are you there? Dad, can you hear me?"

He couldn't.

I heard him ask Adele to hang up to make the connection stronger. I could hear him call my name.

"Dad, can you hear me?" I was pleading now. Still no response. Then I realized his hearing aid wasn't working properly. He asked if I could call back in a few minutes. My parents had always had trouble with their hearing aids while using the telephone and this was proving to be no exception.

Oh God, please let his hearing aid work.

My father began to cry, "This damn hearing aid. Oh, no! Oh, no!"

I kept repeating, "Dad, can you hear me?"

Finally after several minutes he said, "OK. I hear you now."

But our valuable time was running out.

"Dad, I am fine. The American Embassy got permission for us to talk. I just wanted to wish you a happy birthday and a happy Father's Day. I think about you all the time and I appreciate all you have done for me in drumming up support for my release."

"It's so good to hear you. How are they treating you?"

My voice broke, but I took a deep breath. There were things I wanted to tell him but this was not the time.

"Dad, I'm fine. I'm eating well. I'm sleeping well. I'm still exercising just like always."

"We have been so worried. Tom has been keeping in touch with us."

"I know. He is a God-send. Some great things have been happening in Dubai. I hope some of that spills over here and I get home soon."

"I'm sorry I couldn't come to see you."

"I know. It's better you take care of yourself."

I heard a beep on the line. I assumed the call was being monitored.

The connection sounded different.

"Dad, are you still there?"

No response.

"Dad, can you hear me?"

The line was dead. Then I realized that the beep I had heard a few seconds earlier was a warning that my ten minutes was almost up.

He was gone. I put my head down and sobbed.

One of the guards at the end of the table saw my distress and said to me, "This will be over soon." The officer in charge took the phone and in Arabic ordered a guard to take me back to my cell.

I was terribly upset but at the same time happy. I had talked with my father. I had spoken with a strong and positive voice and I hoped he felt that I was okay.

Thanks God. You never abandoned me.

That night I cried. I suspected that that call might be the last time I would ever hear my father's voice. And it was.

A few days later I wrote a Father's Day note in which I told my dad:

> "When I graduated from college over 30 years ago you gave me a card. The verse was 'If' by Rudyard Kipling—words to inspire and guide a young man facing all of life's challenges. I've kept those words close to me all this time because I found strength and comfort in them. But more importantly, it was you who nurtured me to become who I am.
>
> You instilled in me a love for nature, animals, sports, and travel. Rather than try to make me what you wanted me to be you let me be what I wanted to be and you encouraged me. You demonstrated an honest and positive work ethic. You showed me how to use my hands to create things. You trusted me. You demonstrated the power of unconditional love. You shared

your God with me. You showed me how to be authoritative without being an authoritarian. You showed me that friends are important and you respected my choice. You were there for me when I succeeded and when I failed. And you taught me that love of family transcends all. Because of those and many more my life is rich—and I am still learning from you.

I have thanked God every day of my life for you.
You are my hero!

39

A Tough Summer

THE MAIL THE FOLLOWING WEEK brought bad news.

For over eighteen years I had shared many good times with Rick whom I had first met in Orlando. Subsequently he had moved to Denver, back to Orlando, then to Columbus, GA, and later to Atlanta. I had visited him often and always went away with the peace and reassurance that only good friends can bring to one's life.

During my ordeal at Al Wathba, Rick had served as a focal point for relaying news about me to my friends. I would send him a letter and he would pass it on via e-mail to a list that had grown lengthy over the months of my incarceration. We communicated regularly and I was surprised by early June when I hadn't received any correspondence from him for several months.

On June 22 I found out why.

In my mail that day was a large envelope from Rick's sister. My first thought was that she had decided to write to me and I was anxious to read what she had sent. The first sentence was devastating: "Paul, I know of no other way to break the news to you than to tell you directly that Rick has died." I went numb. Rick had died six weeks earlier from food poisoning. A voice in my head wailed, *Oh, God! No! Don't let it be true!* But it was.

In the mail the following week was a lengthy letter from Rick's cousin Rita. She knew how close Rick and I were, and she detailed how she was the one who had been with Rick the last few hours of his life. She had been the one who had to make the gut-wrenching decision to take him off life support.

Rick was the center of a wheel whose spokes represented the many diversified groups of persons who considered him a friend. He was someone I truly cared about and being confined to prison only intensified my frustration and loneliness. I cannot describe the feeling of helplessness that I experienced when dealing with his loss. To this day that emptiness over his loss has not diminished. Rick was the eighth friend or family member who had died during the time I had been in Al Wathba prison.

Shortly after I learned of Rick's death, a newspaper article announced that Sheikh Zayed had traveled to the United States for medical treatments. That was not an unusual occurrence, since he yearly went either to London or somewhere in the U.S. for medical consultations. This time, however, there were hints that something was more serious than just a routine check-up. I was more determined than ever to get out of Al Wathba and I resolved to try a new tactic.

The newspaper gave no indication which medical facility Sheikh Zayed had gone to and even contacts in the American Embassy did not know. So I made an assumption that he must be in the Mayo Clinic in Rochester, Minnesota, since he had gone there before. In a letter to my brother Richard I asked him to have the family send letters to Sheikh Zayed seeking clemency for me. My assumption proved to be wrong, however.

On the next visit from Tom I asked him to get in touch with my family right away and have them contact the UAE embassies in Washington and Ottawa in an effort to track down exactly where Sheikh Zayed was hospitalized. Tom and I were both perplexed as to why the American Embassy could not tell us the Sheikh's whereabouts. Surely, the State Department would know exactly where any foreign head of state could be located when in the United States!

Adding to my frustration was the fact that I had not had a visit from anyone in the American Embassy in ten weeks. I knew that Charles Glatz had been transferred to the embassy in Riyadh, Saudi Arabia and it appeared that I had been forgotten. So, it was up to Tom, me, and my family to track down the Sheikh.

Several weeks later, I saw a newspaper article that mentioned that Sheikh Zayed was in the Cleveland Clinic in Ohio. After many tests it had been decided that he would receive a kidney transplant at the clinic. Tom immediately got word to my family and asked them to contact the *Cleveland Plain Dealer* newspaper. We hoped that they would find my story interesting and timely since I was the only American being held in Al Wathba prison, and the ruler of the Emirate was a short distance away receiving the best medical attention that money could buy. What a great human interest story! The newspaper, however, declined to run it. Damn it, damn it, damn it! Something didn't add up. Had they been bought off? Or had the paper been silenced by the State Department? I never have found out why my request was refused.

Soon after this, a story ran in the local paper that Sheikh Zayed had met a little boy in the hospital and was so touched by him that he donated $30,000 to the boy's school for new computers. How nice! Fluff! More frustration.

Through Tom I learned that Sheikh Zayed wasn't receiving any mail at the clinic and all questions to him were being referred to the UAE Embassy in Washington. So I decided to have my family send flowers to the clinic with a note attached. Susanne, who is a florist, made arrangements and saw that the floral display was accompanied by a letter that my daughter Jennifer had composed. On the other end the florist in Cleveland helped out by assuring us that the flowers and letter had been delivered.

Jennifer wrote:

> *I'm sending these flowers on behalf of my father and our family in wishing you a speedy recovery. My father, Paul Ciceri, has been incarcerated in Al Wathba prison since October 1998 for possession of a small amount of drugs. My father was en route back to Abu Dhabi from Canada after attending his mother's funeral when this incident occurred.*
>
> *My father has never been involved in any criminal behavior prior to this incident. He knows that this was a very foolish action to do, but he was very close to his mother and was deeply distressed after her funeral service. He has always been a wonderful and loving father to me. Unfortunately my grandfather has become seriously ill and is not expected to live longer than a year or so. He wants very much to see his son again before he dies.*

> *I know my father is not proud of what he was involved in and I truly feel that he is very repentant of his actions. I am appealing to you to intercede on behalf of myself and my family for clemency for my father.*

No answer or letter of thanks was ever received in return from Sheikh Zayed.

That summer was extremely difficult with Rick's passing, no visits from the Embassy, and no response to our efforts to contact Sheikh Zayed at the Cleveland Clinic.

In mid-August, for the first time that anyone could remember, Friday prayers throughout the country contained pleas to God for the good health of Sheikh Zayed. This compounded the rumors that ran rampant among the prisoners that something good would come out of Sheikh Zayed's medical treatment.

I wrote on August 19:

> *Friday prayers for the first time included specific ones for his health and safe return to the UAE. That was unprecedented and for the family to even admit his sickness indicates the severity of his problems. I hope you were able to get a request to him in Cleveland for a pardon. Firsthand I have been told that two British families did the same when he was in London last year and the prisoners were quickly freed.*

The rumors took on epic proportions when some embassies told prisoners that they would all be released when Sheikh Zayed returned to the UAE from his operation. It was customary in the Arab world that, whenever a ruler had medical treatment, he would perform some great gesture to gain favor with Allah for the good that had been bestowed upon him. Based on the severity of the Sheikh's medical treatment, great things were expected to happen.

But conditions continued to deteriorate at Al Wathba. In the visitation room, where previously there had been wire mesh between prisoners and visitors, the prison manager had Plexiglas installed. Reports from Arab prisoners returning from visitations one Thursday spoke about total chaos. Typical of the ineptitude of prison management, no telephones had been installed to facilitate conversation. Visitors and prisoners could not hear each other, so everyone shouted more loudly than usual to be heard. The next day I got to experience this situation firsthand when I was called for a visit with Tom. We tried to communicate over the shouting and confusion, but it was impossible. There was so much I wanted to ask him and he had much he wanted to tell me, but the visit ended in a frustrating waste of time. Tom was my link to the outside world. Here he was, a mere eighteen inches away from me and we couldn't communicate! I went back to the block despairing.

On August 23 I was called to the manager's office. There seated in front of the manager was an American who introduced himself as Mark Marrano, the new consular officer who was replacing Charles Glatz. Mark had recently been transferred from South America and he told the manager what a wonderful facility Al Wathba was when compared to what he had experienced in South America. What a stupid thing to say! I didn't need an American Embassy official telling Al Wathba prison management what a great place this hole in the desert was. Since I had no opportunity to talk freely with Mark, I cut the meeting short. I just wanted to return to my block.

Mark did come back with Jamal three weeks later and I indicated my concern over the decrease in the frequency of visits from the Embassy. During the same thirteen-week period, both the British and Canadian Embassy staff had visited their citizens five times.

On September 9 I waited all afternoon for my visit from Tom, but he never arrived. I learned later that he had come to the prison, but the officers had refused to let him see me. They claimed that his pass was no longer valid and that the Embassy would have to get a new letter signed by the Major at the prison.

With one bad thing after another taking place, I began to think I was going insane. I became more and more frustrated with life at Al Wathba and my inability to communicate effectively with anyone on the outside. I became more irritable and had less patience with everyone around me. I was losing my composure.

I just wanted to get out of that hell hole!

40

Sheikh Mohammed Does It Again

FROM LATE SUMMER INTO THE FALL rumors abounded about major releases once Sheikh Zayed returned to the UAE following his kidney transplant surgery. The surgery was life saving and as a result some monumental concessions were expected regarding the prisoners.

Everyone was upbeat and we watched the newspapers each day to learn the date of his return. Even the American Embassy staff felt that it was an opportune time to take the initiative and have my family once again plead for my release as part of the expected goodwill package. Jamal sent a note to my family suggesting that family members write to Sheikh Zayed and request that I be included in any amnesty that was to be forthcoming. Among the letters written on my behalf was one from my father:

Greetings to Your Highness,

My name is Harold Ciceri and during the last two years, God has given me the necessary strength to stay alive in hopes of once again holding my son in my arms.

I am 88 years old and since I have suffered two heart attacks in the past year, my health is extremely poor. I pray each day that you will see your way clear to grant my son, Paul Ciceri, an early release from prison on compassionate grounds.

This is not my first time writing to you appealing for clemency for my son, Paul. I have written often. It is two years since my son, Paul, was incarcerated. He was

> *returning to his work in Abu Dhabi after coming home to attend my wife's/his mother's funeral. Due to an unfortunate set of circumstances, he was imprisoned upon his return to Abu Dhabi.*
>
> *Those who know Paul well attest to the fact that he is of moral character and follows strict rules of good health and behavior. During the past two years, Paul has demonstrated to the world his positive attitude. He knows full well that God has a plan for his life and that the truth will come out some day. Paul from all reports has been a model and co-operative prisoner and has demonstrated excellent behavior.*
>
> *I am ever hopeful that I will once again see my son in my lifetime. Since it appears that my failing health and age indicate that I don't have many more days in this life, I beg and plead, as a father of his beloved son, for Paul's release.*
>
> *Every day I pray for his release. Hopefully, today is the day that my prayers will be answered. I know that your generous decision on my behalf will bring about clemency and an early release for my son, Paul Ciceri. Thank you for your generous consideration of my request.*

Meanwhile, throughout the cities of the UAE and especially Abu Dhabi, rumors spread about the good that would come when Sheikh Zayed returned. UAE citizens and citizens of other Arab countries were particularly hopeful. On October 10 I wrote to my friends Jim and Paul:

> *Rumors and rumors of rumors abound here about pardons, releases, amnesties—whatever one wants to call them. The leader of this country has been at the Cleveland Clinic for the past several months. There he had a kidney transplant and apparently is recovering well enough that he is expected back in several weeks. There has been an outpouring of celebration over his good health—parties, wholesale slaughtering of animals, gifts of money to all the country's widows, and even a few releases of prisoners in some prisons. Everyone hopes that when he returns that we might reap*

some of that generosity. Big things are planned including the spraying of all trees with perfume, perfumed water in all the public fountains, parades of school children, etc.

In spite of the hopeful reports, however, we still had to deal with our day to day existence and move on. So many times throughout my imprisonment rumors had ended up being just rumors. We allowed our hopes to soar only to have them dashed to the ground when nothing happened. I remained guardedly optimistic because for the first time even the American Embassy staff felt that some good would come from Sheikh Zayed's recovery. I wrote describing my routine at that time:

Exercise

> *I'm still teaching English four mornings a week so that gets me out of the block where I can meet other prisoners with varied sentences. Jennifer had sent me some books on web-page design and I've gone through them. I had a web-page on AOL before but now I understand it better as well as HTML. Now I just need to get some books for Java Script. Susanne sent me a course in massage that I've gone through—that's so I can keep my license active. People in our block have picked up on our exercise antics and now about 30 work out regularly. I just wish we had some real weights to use.*

The tensions between Israel and Palestine had heated up again, and for the first time I could remember, there had been some demonstrations against the United States in the streets of Abu Dhabi. Tom and other Americans had been warned to keep a low profile as they went about their daily affairs. On October 13 Tom wrote to my family:

> *I did go to visit Paul this morning, although I did go with a little trepidation. What with the Middle East as it is, I wasn't sure how I would be greeted. Of course they know I'm an American visiting an American—you just never know. Jan and I are a little anxious about the situation here. There don't seem to be any immediate problems, but most of the day they've had demonstration parades. We keep praying that they'll come to a peaceful solution.*

I was keeping up on the news about the Presidential election campaign. With just a few days before the election I still hadn't received my absentee ballot from the Embassy staff. In a letter to Susan at ELS on October 26 I was a bit whimsical about all that was going on:

> *By now we have a new President (by the time you read this). So I hope you were one of the minority who voted and in turn your candidate is the Pres.-elect. I'm still waiting for the Embassy staff to bring me my absentee ballot. Time is getting short and it may already be too late to have my ballot received in Orlando to be counted. It has been almost 10 weeks since I last saw*

> those people—they used to come regularly at 5-week intervals but the last two are running at 10. I'll just have to suppose they're busy running around visiting heads of state in a frantic effort to get me sprung from here. And while I'm fantasizing maybe I'll get candy for Halloween too!

On November 1 the Embassy staff came to visit me and brought my absentee ballot with them. With the ballot was a lot of information from a myriad of candidates, some of whom I had never heard about. I was rather amused when the consul, who had earlier complimented the manager of the prison on how nice his facility was, asked me if I had been following the Presidential race on CNN. Obviously, he didn't have a clue about the conditions inside Al Wathba.

We discussed the anticipated return of Sheikh Zayed to the UAE and the upcoming holy month of Ramadan. The Embassy staff had not had any comment from Abu Dhabi government officials as to whether or not they would follow the lead of Dubai and allow drug users to be set free; nor was there any word about how many prisoners might be released in the upcoming month. They did assure me that my family's letters for clemency had been passed on to the appropriate government officials.

A few days earlier the local newspaper had published an article about the recent trip Ian Bamling's mother and father had made to Abu Dhabi and their writing of letters to government officials:

> The parents of a British man jailed for trying to smuggle drugs into the UAE have made another plea for clemency. They hope that Bamling's name will be included on a list of prisoners to be released during Ramadan, a month on the Islamic calendar when mercy is traditionally shown. Robert Bamling, the ailing, wheelchair-bound father of Ian, has written letters to both Sheikh Saif and Sheikh Mansour. Ian's mother, Sally Durham, has written to Her Highness Sheikha Fatima bint Mubarak, wife of President His Highness Sheikh Zayed bin Sultan Al Nahyan and Chairwoman of the UAE Women's Federation. Ian's parents are

accompanied by Bamling's brother, Robert Joseph, and sister Sarah. On Saturday they met Bamling at Al Wathba prison.

Durham said Bamling's father could not stop crying when he visited him. 'He was not treated very well and still hopes for a show of generosity,' said Mrs. Durham. 'I have to respect their laws, but I want to have my family reunited and this will be a second heartbreaking Christmas for me. Abu Dhabi is like a fairytale place, wealthy with spotlessly clean streets,' she said. 'Then 45 minutes away in the desert is Al Wathba jail, a hell hole where my son rots.'

The prison, built for 800 inmates, houses 3000. The humidity is overwhelming as temperatures outside reach 50°C (122°F). The cell doors cannot be shut at night because too many bodies are competing for space to sleep on the cockroach-infested concrete floor. Fellow inmates are regularly flogged and Bamling has witnessed rape and suicide. The body of a young man who hanged himself was left to swing in view of other prisoners for several hours before guards cut him down. Bamling is suffering from insomnia and malnutrition and his mother fears for his sanity. 'I know that even when he gets home, Ian will never be the same again,' she said.

The UAE has a fearsome reputation for rough justice. In recent years things have gotten worse, says Amnesty, with floggings given out for speeding and begging, hand amputations reported for theft, and death sentences for drug and sex offences. Richard Bunting of Amnesty said, 'It is a bleak picture and things have been getting worse. The prison conditions are barbaric, and prisoners have been stripped and lashed in the courtroom immediately after sentence.'

A week later another article appeared in the *Gulf News*:

> The mother of one of two Britons jailed here last year for possession of cannabis had been told that her plea for clemency for her son will be considered. Sally Durham has been in the UAE to renew her appeal for the release of her son. She said the family had

written three letters appealing for amnesty to Her Highness Sheikha Fatima bint Mubarak, wife of President His Highness Sheikh Zayed bin Sultan Al Nahyan and Chairwoman of the UAE Women's Federation, as well as to Major General Sheikh Saif bin Zayed Al Nahyan, Interior Ministry Undersecretary, and to Sheikh Mansour bin Zayed Al Nahyan, Director of the Presidential Court. 'Although we failed to meet Sheikha Fatima, Sheikh Saif, and Sheikh Mansour, their offices have assured us that the letters would be delivered', she said. The letters to Sheikh Saif and Sheikh Mansour were written by Bamling, while Durham made her own clemency plea to Sheikha Fatima.

Ian did admit to us that he had written the letters. Somewhat embellished, the letters distorted the truth about prison conditions and his relationship with his father. His father and mother were not on speaking terms back in England and Ian actually despised his father.

A few days after the article appeared in the local newspaper, Tom came to visit me. He told me that rumors on the outside were that some prisoners would be released in honor of the combination of Sheikh Zayed's return to Abu Dhabi, the celebration of National Day, and the holy month of Ramadan. It was rather unusual for rumors to circulate about prisoner releases on the outside of prison, so it gave all of us hope that there was some truth to what was being postulated. Ian had told me that his Embassy had confirmed that his name was on the list of those to be released. The American Embassy had told me nothing, perhaps not wanting to raise my expectations. So often things that had been promised officially never came to fruition. And now, Americans were being told to be wary of their comings and goings in Abu Dhabi as tensions between Israelis and Palestinians continued to escalate.

The closer we got to Ramadan the more rampant the rumors became. It got to the point where everyone was convinced that as soon as Sheikh Zayed returned to the UAE, we would all be going home. Even people on the outside told stories about how they had been reassured by high authorities that this would be the case. Inside, we all waited in the throes of overwhelming expectation as Sheikh Zayed stopped in London on his way home from the United States. He was expected in Abu Dhabi any day.

Tom came to see me just before Ramadan and he wrote to my family after our visit:

> Went to see Paul today and he's doing fine. Just about all the men in his area are expecting to be released when the Sheikh returns. He is now recuperating in London and 'his return is imminent'. Ramadan starts Saturday or Sunday depending on the moon. That's when most people feel he'll be here. The city is all decorated with lights and banners with his picture on it.
>
> My hope is that Paul doesn't get his hopes too high. I think I've said that before but you can see it in his eyes—the expectation is there. Can't blame him, it's been a long haul for the guy. When I was leaving him today he said, 'I hope I don't see you again.' Of course he meant it in the best way.
>
> Our church has been lifting him up in prayer for almost a year now and I've let him know that. On Thanksgiving the pastor allows people to give testimony for things that have happened during the past year. I asked Paul if he would write a letter to the community expressing his gratitude to them. Well he sent the most beautiful letter and I read it at the service this morning. The people were quite moved by it.

A few days later Sheikh Zayed did return home to a hero's welcome. As expected, leaders of the Emirates released prisoners immediately as a sign of thanks to Allah for the safe return of the country's leader. Even leaders of other countries closely aligned with the UAE, because of their respect for Sheikh Zayed or because of the financial aid that the UAE provided to those countries, released prisoners as a demonstration of their gratitude for the safe return of Sheikh Zayed. Sheikh Mohammed of Dubai announced the release of five hundred prisoners on the day that Sheikh Zayed returned to the UAE.

Abu Dhabi released none.

Bastards! Sheikh Mohammed one-upped them again.

I had heard people say it before in whispers, but now prisoners commented openly that they wished Sheikh Zayed had died.

Perhaps that was the only way for the rulers of the Emirate to let us go.

For the next several days we waited nervously for an announcement about what would happen in Abu Dhabi. No news. No new rumors. Nothing. We were devastated. On December 2 I wrote:

> *Everywhere in this country there have been amnesties for prisoners but, so far, none in Abu Dhabi. Dubai has released almost 1000 so far this year—here there have been none. Even in grocery stores I always ended up in the wrong line!*

My only consolation was that I knew I had less than a year to go. A year from now, I would be celebrating the holidays in the United States.

41

A Year of Blessings

SHEIKH ZAYED HAD RETURNED TO Abu Dhabi. National Day had come and gone. Ramadan had begun. And there was no hint from the Royal Family that any of us would be released.

So, it looked as though we would be there for a while. Once again, it was time to get a Christmas message to my friends and family, and through my friend Jim Garrett I sent the following text:

> Although this is not as personal as individual greetings, sending an impersonal note like this ensures that I at least get to wish all of you my best for a joyous, healthy, and meaningful holiday season.
>
> Next year I will have my freedom again and now that less than 10 months remain until that happens I rejoice knowing that this time next year I will be back in the lands of the free.
>
> The stress of the first year in dealing with the courts and not knowing my fate has subsided and this year has generally been one of routine. However I have tried to make use of my time productively, in spite of the lack of facilities and support for the prisoners in bettering themselves. I count as my accomplishments this year:
>
> - *Teaching English to other inmates*
> - *Learning Spanish, Italian, German (some good, some less proficient)*

- *Keeping fit*
- *Improving my knowledge of HTML coding for web page design*
- *Completing a course to keep my massage license current*

These opportunities have been made possible through the kind gestures of family and friends in keeping me supplied with materials. Thanks Susanne, Jennifer, Elaine, Richard, Susan, and Gregory!

I have been humbled by all the cards and letters I have received and the words of support. Friends from as far back as 30 years ago have somehow learned of my situation and have contacted me, as well as several others from more recent times. Even friends of friends have written. One gentleman from the local evangelical church has been visiting me for over 6 months now and it has been a real source of comfort to me to visit with another American (He kept me up to date on the performance of my favorite sports teams). With his access to the internet I have been able to get important news to/from my family much quicker than before.

Through the assistance of the U.S. Embassy I was able to cast my absentee ballot in the November election. It has become obvious to all of the importance of voting with the closeness of the results this time, especially with what happened in Florida. VP Gore came close but I guess a few more citizens should have voted.

Most people here are from Arab countries so the Arab-Israeli conflict is uppermost in their minds. Although the U.S. is not considered an Arab ally in this problem I have not been overly concerned for my safety and have avoided, where at all possible, any discussion of the issue. U.S. foreign policy and religion are two areas I try to avoid in discussions. I learned my lesson with regard to the former 2 years ago when just such a discussion indirectly landed me here.

I have collected lots of stories to share with you at a later date, and I even have some mouth watering recipes

I'd like to try out. In the meantime I continue to read a lot, keep track of the U.S. professional sports and do crosswords and logic puzzles.

Fortunately I have been truly blessed during my stay here. Somehow whenever I have needed something it has materialized. I know that many of you include me in your prayers; some have sent me cards indicating my name is on prayer lists, and a prayer group at the local church includes me weekly in their prayers. God is with me and I could share with you instance after instance of signs He has given me in comfort.

Being confined is obviously frustrating. The hardest situation for me to deal with, besides being away from family and friends and being productive, is the death of friends and family. There is a helpless feeling that grips you as the closure process takes a longer time than normal. Thankfully I have a few friends here that have been there for me when I needed them.

Christmas and New Year's will pass as non-events here but I will think of all of you during those times. I wish you all the best in all you do. Maybe you'll even have a little snow to make it more festive!

Appreciate all that you have, especially the ones who are most dear to you.

Peace and love. Paul.

The letter was delivered on Christmas Day to all my friends via e-mail. Jim added the following to my letter:

```
After over two years, Paul still has
the inner strength to see him through this
ordeal. Think of the worst problem you had
this year and compare it to his situation.
Now is the time to pull out the pens (or
computers) and fire off a letter. It will
mean a lot to him.
```

42

The Worst Possible News

WE WERE ALL ON TENTERHOOKS AS Ramadan progressed. The rumors of a release were so rampant that speculation about early discharges nearly consumed us. News of several releases came during Ramadan and Abu Dhabi was the only Emirate that had not yet set any prisoners free in honor of Sheikh Zayed's successful surgery in the United States. The end of Ramadan was fast approaching and we all waited. More and more people joined in the five daily prayers, each in his own way praying that he would be included in any amnesty.

On December 22 news was printed in the local newspapers that a handful of prisoners would be released from Al Wathba. Just a *handful* of the prison population! Almost all were people involved in financial cases. The exceptions were the two Brits, Ian and Lynn. I was stunned. I was bewildered. I was angry. How in the hell could that have happened? I had been there longer than both Ian and Lynn and my family had not raised a ruckus in the local newspapers against the Royal Family as Ian's family had. Where was the fairness in all this?

Everyone in the block congratulated Ian on his imminent release. Ian and I had not talked much in the past several weeks. True to form, he ran hot and cold with many people and for some reason, whether it was jealousy or age or insecurity, he chose not to associate with me. But when we did meet on one occasion, I congratulated him on his new-found freedom. He beamed with the news of his good fortune and described it as though he were in a trance not quite believing that his nightmare at Al Wathba was almost over.

Tom came to visit me that afternoon and he confirmed that the news was indeed true about Ian and Lynn. We were both excited. Did that mean that I would be next? The noise in the visiting room was deafening as everyone there practically shouted in an attempt to be heard through the glass partitions. Added to this frustration was excitement about the announcement of the early releases. All of us were still optimistic that more releases would follow.

Tom tried to reach someone at the Embassy during the next few days, but in despair he wrote to my family on Christmas Eve that the Embassy was closed for the American Christmas holidays and he would not be able to reach anyone for several more days. The papers were ominously quiet after reporting news of the few releases on December 22.

Back in the block I waited for some word. Nothing. Everyone speculated that I would be going home soon. After all, how could they release the Brits and not release The American?

On December 26 Ian was released from Al Wathba. At the front gate of our block everyone hugged him including me. Regardless of our differences, I was happy for him. He assured me that he would do all he could to spread the news about the abhorrent conditions at Al Wathba. After he left, I went back to my room and sat in silence, a feeling of despair descending on my world. In our block there was one other Brit serving the first of his four-year sentence. Aside from him, I was the only Westerner left in Al Wathba; to rub salt in my wounds, I had been there longer than Ian and Lynn. Why wasn't I going home? Why hadn't the Embassy come with the news of my release? Other inmates wondering why Paul wasn't going home added to my dismay. Despite my family's diplomatic approach, efforts by Ian's parents who had raised hell in the newspapers had managed to get Ian released. Had we taken the wrong approach?

Throughout the next several days everyone in the block tried to reassure me that my turn would soon come. After Ian's release I expected that someone from the Embassy would come to tell me what was going on with regard to my status. I waited eagerly, but no word arrived. What the hell was going on? Why wasn't I going home? Why hadn't the Embassy representatives come to see me? I was lost in those thoughts without answers to shake me out of my despair. Then on Saturday morning I was called to the front gate and advised that someone from the Embassy was waiting in the office to see me.

Saturday! That wasn't the regular day for embassy visits and this was an Islamic holiday. Even the prison administration wasn't working that day. This had to be the news I was waiting for. They had come to tell me that I was going home too! Excited and upbeat, I walked down the long quiet corridors toward the place where I would meet the Embassy staff and get the good news.

When the guard directed me downstairs to the room where prisoners met with family and friends, I was a bit surprised because I figured that, with the news I expected to hear, we would meet in the manager's office. When I remembered, though, that the offices were closed for the holiday, I relaxed. It made sense to gather downstairs. Rather than get together with the Embassy staff, a Plexiglas window separating us, I was escorted into a small room where I had previously talked to Embassy personnel. When I entered the room, I saw Jamal and Nicholas Papp, the Vice Consul from the Embassy. Five guards accompanied them. I was surprised because I had never seen so many guards for a meeting like this before.

Both Jamal and Nick looked glum. Instantly I picked up that something was wrong. The sick feeling in my stomach told me that my name hadn't come up for release and that they had come to deliver the news in person because they knew I had been wondering what was going on.

Nicholas looked at me and said, "Paul, I have some bad news for you."

Here it comes, I thought. I wasn't going to be included in the releases going on right now.

"I'm sorry to tell you that . . ."

Here it comes. . .

". . . your father has died."

I wasn't prepared for the news. In utter disbelief I thought, *What? Did you say my father had died?* And in an instant it hit me. *Dad has died. Oh, please, God, no!*

All I could say was, "What?"

I had been standing and my legs almost gave out. I sat down. I couldn't think as the room closed in on me. I stared at them in disbelief. I was devastated. The same feeling I had that night twenty-six months earlier when I was arrested at the airport came back to haunt me. I felt as if a truck had just run over me.

And then I started talking.

At first the words poured out, but as the realization of what I had heard hit me, I found it more difficult to talk. First the tears came, and then I cried aloud as the words tumbled over one another and became more difficult to understand.

Oh God. Dad! To no one in particular I blurted out, "He tried so hard to wait for me. He was so brave and strong. He was my father. He was my friend. He was my hero. What happened?"

"He died in the hospital. He died peacefully. We got an e-mail from your daughter this morning telling us that he had died earlier today and she asked us to give you the news."

He tried so hard to wait for me. I buried my head in my hands and sobbed. As I did so, I saw a guard ask Jamal what was happening. He told him the news and he stood in silence.

"Paul, I know this is the worst possible news you could receive under the circumstances. I want you to know that the Ambassador is aware of what has happened and we are going to make an immediate appeal to the Royal Family that you be released so you can attend your father's funeral. The family is going to delay the funeral several days to provide us time to pursue this appeal and get you home."

"Thank you," I sobbed.

For several months I had suspected that my dad's health was deteriorating. I saw it in his handwriting as his once legible script became chicken scratch. His letters were taking him several days to complete because he had no energy. Somewhere deep inside I knew he wasn't well and that I wasn't being told how serious the situation was. Now I knew.

The walk back to my block seemed endless. The guard stayed behind not saying a word because he knew how I felt. I filled up as I descended the final set of stairs and saw a crowd of my fellow inmates there. Not wanting them to see my tears, I backed around the corner, wiped my eyes, and tried to regain my composure. Then the guard ordered me to move inside the block.

When I told Majdi, one of the leaders of the block, what had happened, he alerted everyone else in Arabic and they let me pass back to my room. I lay flat on my bed staring at the ceiling and trying to make sense of what had just happened. I felt desperately alone. *My father was gone.*

Within a few minutes others began coming into my room. Word had spread throughout the block like wildfire and they had come to offer their condolences. One by one they shook my hand and told me in their own languages that they were truly sorry for my loss. For all the differences we might have had over culture and religion and the fact that most hated the American government, they had transcended the disparity to offer me support and demonstrate that we were all part of one human family. I was grateful and somewhat surprised. Some of them sat around me, genuinely concerned that I was suffering. It was then that I realized how many friends I had made at Al Wathba.

When Jamal got back to the Embassy he sent an e-mail to Jennifer:

> I was deeply saddened to hear of your grandfather's passing. The Embassy staff would like to extend its sympathies to you and the entire Ciceri family.
>
> Vice Consul Nicholas Papp and myself made a special trip to the prison to inform and console Paul this morning. We carefully and softly broke the news and let him read your e-mail. Paul became very upset and was in tears for a few minutes but relaxed soon after. Your dad has asked that the family be informed that he will be okay.
>
> Jenny, I know this must be a bad time for me to ask but this may be important. I would like to request the family to fax us a copy of your grandfather's death record (something from the hospital would do) and a letter from the funeral home mentioning

when the funeral has been scheduled. We may wish to use these to tell local officials that Paul needs to be home soon. At this point in time no decision has been made as to how to approach this but once we do, these two documents are critical for any chance of success.

Tom got the word in an e-mail from Jennifer. He was still upset about the fact that I was still incarcerated while Ian had been released. He expressed his frustration in an e-mail to the American Embassy staff:

> I'm sure by now you are aware of the passing of Paul's father. It is really ironic that if he had been released with the other [*Ian*] he may have gotten to see him one last time. I really feel that enough was not done on his behalf to get that release. I realize I can only see a piece of the picture. It is strange that the British Embassy knew that there was a 'list' and that Ian and Lynn were on it. I think it was a case of 'the squeaky wheel gets the grease'. Is it possible that the Consul or even the Ambassador could put some pressure on someone to try a little harder?

My brother Richard was in New Zealand when the news of my father's death reached him, so my nephew Jason obtained the documents the Embassy had requested and faxed them to Abu Dhabi. Then the Embassy moved quickly to seek my release. Ambassador Kattouf wrote a letter on December 31 to Sheik Saif the Undersecretary of the Interior and one of the sons of Sheikh Zayed who was responsible for the prison system:

> *I would like to take this opportunity to extend to you and your family my best wishes on the occasion of the blessed Eid al-Fitr. Please accept my Government's*

best wishes for continued good health and success to you, your family, His Highness Sheikh Zayed bin Sultan Al-Nahyan, and to the people of the United Arab Emirates.

Your Highness, I am writing to you concerning a matter of humanitarian interest that has been brought to my attention by the family of Paul B. Ciceri, an American citizen convicted of drug use and serving at Al Wathba central prison since October 7, 1998. I understand that his scheduled release date is less than ten months away in the month of October, 2001. I have been informed, and my staff has confirmed, that Paul's father, Mr. Harold Ciceri, passed away on December 30th. It is my understanding from messages I have received from the family that a funeral has been scheduled for next Thursday, January 4th 2001.

I know that at this special time of the year it is customary to review the status of long-serving prisoners whose sentences are nearing completion. I hope that this information may be of assistance to you, should you be considering the case of Mr. Ciceri at this time.

Your Highness, I thank you in advance for your consideration of this matter. I look forward to the opportunity for continued cooperation between our Governments. Again, please accept my best wishes and congratulations on the occasion of the joyous Eid al-Fitr.

For the next several days I waited eagerly for a humanitarian release so I could attend my father's funeral.

43

England Hears about Al Wathba

ON DECEMBER 25 *The Gulf News* reported that Ian Bamling and Lynn Majakas had been granted clemency as part of the release of two hundred thirty-seven-prisoners in celebration of the Holy Month of Ramadan. Ian's family arranged for the first available flight out of Abu Dhabi so Ian wouldn't have to spend a minute longer than necessary in captivity.

> *'The best Christmas gift ever' was how Sally Durham received the news . . . Sally, who had visited the UAE and made several clemency appeals, was speechless for a moment yesterday. 'I have no words to explain my joy,' she said. 'I never dreamt that Ian would be released on Christmas Day'. Both (Ian) Bamling and (Lynn) Majakas will arrive at London's Heathrow Airport in the early hours of December 26. . . .*

Since news coverage of Ian's and Lynn's arrest and incarceration had been extensive, the media were there to cover the event in full when the two arrived at Heathrow airport early in the morning of December 26. Ian and Lynn participated in a news conference and Ian was pictured wearing the traditional head gear of one of the Saudi tribes, something he had promised to do just before he was released from the block at Al Wathba.

Both the *Times* and *The Guardian* published front page stories of the return of the two Brits. The story in *The Guardian* was titled "Jailed Drug Britons Arrive Home" with a sub title "Pair freed after two years in Middle East tell of appalling conditions." Steven Morris wrote in his article:

Two Britons who endured more than two years jailed in what they said were dreadful conditions in the United Arab Emirates after being caught with a small amount of cannabis arrived home yesterday having been pardoned.

Head teacher Lynn Majakas and social worker Ian Bamling flew back from Abu Dhabi to Heathrow airport for an emotional reunion with their families. With tears streaming down her face, Ms Majakas, 45, continued to protest her innocence. Her friend Mr. Bamling, 31, said: 'After two years and two months in inhumane conditions I want to go to sleep and spend some time with my family.'

The pair, who were next door neighbors in west London, were arrested at Abu Dhabi in October 1998 at the start of what was meant to be a relaxing cut-price holiday in the sun as officials stopped Ms Majakas as she walked through the airport smoking a rolled-up cigarette.

Officials examined the cigarette but found no drugs in it. When they searched her luggage, however, they found three grams of cannabis in a camera case. Mr. Bamling was also arrested when he intervened. Despite a sworn statement from a friend claiming the drugs were his and they knew nothing of them, they were jailed for four and a half years. They were granted a pardon as an act of clemency to mark the end of the Muslim holy month of Ramadan....

... The conditions the pair were in were terrible they said. Soon after their arrest they had their heads shaved and were forced to wear dirty prison smocks and sleep on concrete floors with a rag as a blanket. Mr. Bamling said he and his fellow inmates were treated like caged animals in a hell on earth. He heard men being beaten in the night and could not get their screams out of his head. Taking three tranquilizers a day was the only thing which kept him sane he said. He said he was fed disgusting mutton slop and pita bread. Within a few weeks he lost a stone. He was denied soap, toothpaste and razors and gave up trying to wash because the facilities were so squalid. Mr. Bamling said he had been amazed at some of the offences fellow prisoners had been jailed for. One told him he was being held without being charged because he had washed his car in the street in contravention of a by-law.

Ms Majakas, daughter of a vicar and former head of Bedelsford special needs school in Kingston upon Thames, southwest London, had to wash in showers which doubled as toilets. She spent much of her time with three or four prisoners in a small cell designed for one and infested with cockroaches.

A feature story also appeared in the *Observer* the following Sunday, December 31. The headline read *Jailed Tourist's Arabian Tale of Hell* and the sub-headline read, *Freed Briton says he was left traumatized by beatings and torture after the Foreign Office refused to intervene.* The article written by Tracy McVeigh said:

A British tourist who spent two and a half years in a 'hellhole' jail has spoken for the first time of his terrifying ordeal. Ian Bamling was arrested in the United Arab Emirates for possessing a tiny piece of cannabis and a bottle of gin.

Bamling spoke of being suspended by his handcuffed wrists from an iron railing, held in an overcrowded wire cage infested with cockroaches, given maggot-infested food and forced to sleep on concrete. The 31-year-old welfare worker has been left traumatized after witnessing frequent beatings and seeing the effects of torture on fellow prisoners.

Bamling had flown to the United Arab Emirates for a sunshine break with his friend, 44-year-old head teacher Lynn Majarkas. But at Abu Dhabi airport, a few meters from the Duty Free shop where they bought the gin, the pair were arrested for possession of alcohol. They were ignorant of the fact that local law prohibits possession of alcohol, despite its being freely available. . . .

'We were told to sign papers that were written in Arabic,' said Bamling. 'We had no idea what was going on but knew we would be beaten if we did not do what we were told.' After his arrest in October 1998 Bamling was first thrown into a dank police cell with dozens of prisoners. 'I was just violently shoved forward and all I could make out was a dozen hands reaching to grab at me in the darkness. 'The stench was unbearable, he said. He believes that only the intervention of an English-speaking prisoner saved him from being attacked.

Although the UAE authorities claimed to have assigned a lawyer to the two Britons they had no contact with him nor met anyone to discuss their defense. When the case went to court in Abu Dhabi, the frightened and confused pair had no interpreter to help them understand the proceedings. 'There was someone from the British consul sitting in court but he did not come to speak to us or help us get legal advice. Yet it must have been obvious there was a serious injustice going on,' said Bamling.

The sentence shocked and depressed him. Especially after a signed affidavit was sent to the court from a friend in London. The friend, who owned the luggage Majarkas had borrowed, admitted that the cannabis was in fact his.

But Bamling and Majarkas were still convicted on the strength of blood tests that showed they had smoked the drug in London, despite it being outside the court's jurisdiction. Bamling was sent to the notorious Al Wathba jail, a concrete complex in the desert outside Abu Dhabi city.

'When I went through those gates I knew I was entering hell,' he said.

At times suicidal, Bamling endured sweltering temperatures in wire and concrete cages built for 60 prisoners but at times holding more than 200.

Many of the Pakistani, Indian, and Filipino prisoners were there for the most minor offences, often a mask for angering wealthy Arab employers who bring thousands of poor migrant workers into the country every year. 'One man was convicted of breaking wind in an elevator,' said Bamling.

Food was shoved into the cell on a communal plate to let inmates fight over the paltry scraps. 'I really believe some of the guards enjoyed their sadistic treatment of those poor people,' said Bamling, who tried to comfort torture victims who had been strung up on ceiling hooks by their ankles or wrists or had electrodes attached to their testicles. One man he helped had had his moustache plucked out hair by hair. . . .

UAE government officials were not pleased with the negative press coverage in England. Most of what Ian and Lynn had said was true, but some discussion about the prisoners' living conditions in our blocks was exaggerated.

44

Another Opportunity Missed

FOR THE FEW DAYS AFTER GETTING the news of my father's death, I waited anxiously for news that I would be released to go home for his funeral. As the hours passed I realized that the window of opportunity for me to make airplane arrangements, cross the Atlantic, and get home in time for the services was closing. As that played out, I became more depressed and angry.

I was angry because all the time I had lived in the Middle East I had listened to the Muslims in my block talk about how forgiving and benevolent their religion was. And I also had listened to how much they respected the elders in their culture. Deep down, I knew that it was all lip service.

After Richard arrived back in Toronto, he contacted Jamal at the Embassy and inquired whether they had received any response to the petition to release me prior to the funeral. Jamal reassured him that the Embassy had made an appeal for clemency on humanitarian grounds, but they too, after hearing no immediate response, were not optimistic about my chances for release. Jamal wrote, "So far we have not heard any information regarding any early release. At this point, we are not encouraged that he will be released early."

On the day of the funeral I concentrated on mentally transporting myself to Canada and being present in spirit for the funeral and burial services. I felt that I was indeed there, and in my own way, got to say 'goodbye' to my father and feel closure on my loss. The day after the funeral I wrote to Richard and Elaine:

For a couple of months it seemed like there was a news blackout for me regarding Dad's health. Through snippets from various letters I received I knew that his health must have been deteriorating. Still, it was far from my mind the morning the Embassy came to see me last week. With Ramadan releases winding down I was just expecting them to tell me I wasn't on this year's release list—actually they did tell me that after the news about Dad. So it was really a bad day for me!

Once again you had to deal with all involved in organizing things. It seems like I'm always in the wrong place.

As much as I still want to get out of here, all the urgency has seemed to evaporate. I so desperately wanted to get home to see Dad before the end came that it seems now that all the wind has gone out of my sails. Tomorrow will mark the ¾ mark in my sentence and 9 more months should pass fairly quickly.

Tom was here today for a visit and I got a little news from him. It is so difficult to converse because they installed Plexiglas in the middle of the screening between us and there are only a few small holes and no telephones. So . . . everyone yells and nobody can be heard. Another wonderful technical achievement!

I am so happy that neither Mom nor Dad suffered for long. Fortunately for you, Peter, and me the time when they both left us was a long time in coming. There's something about having a dad that lets you stay a kid 'cause you know when you screw up he'll be there for you and for sure he was always there for me. There's a hollow feeling I have knowing I won't see them on this earth anymore.

I'm sure the impact of all this won't hit me until I get out of here and realize how much the world has changed in only a few years especially when it comes to family and friends who have died.

You know Dad always said that life is for the living and we'll all manage to go on. How lucky we are that we

> *grew up with a sense of family—our own and extended. We'll just have to make sure we keep up the tradition.*

I discussed briefly conditions at Al Wathba:

> *Things are slowly improving here. There's a new catering company starting on the first of February so the food should get better. For the last several days we've been out in the sun for 45-minute stretches and that has been a treat. I think I've turned that pasty prison white you hear about. I'm not sure I'll be teaching the next several months—if I can get a few things changed (like more administrative support) then maybe I'll continue. Otherwise I'll use the time for my own studies.*

And finally I wrote, "It's a good feeling to be able to say for certainty 'I'll see you later this year.' Can't wait!"

A week later when it was certain that no action would be taken on the Embassy's request that I be released, I wrote a letter to Nick and Jamal:

> *I wanted to thank you for your visit of a few weeks ago. I know that delivering such news is one of the downsides of your job and I really do appreciate the timeliness of the information.*
>
> *This past week seven people—drug traffickers with 0–3 months left on 10–15 year sentences—were released from my block. We have been told there will be many more drug cases being released but rather than tell us who is on the list they drag it out, and they may do so even until Eid. Assuming that my name is not on this list I can only imagine two scenarios that would justify that. Firstly, perhaps my sponsor has requested I not be released. I am aware of several other situations like that but I can think of no reason why my sponsor would do such a thing. Secondly, perhaps there is some anti-American feeling amongst those who make 'release' decisions. I can only speculate on that possibility.*

> *Looking at those who have been released and some of those awaiting release it is clear that this is not a 'good-behavior' list. Indeed, many have spent a good deal of time in solitary for such things as using and passing drugs within the prison. Even in the case of Ian Bamling, the British citizen who was released on the Ramadan list, his violent outbursts (verbal) are well known throughout the prison and for some time was taking psychiatric drugs.*

The plea for clemency because of Dad's death had fallen on deaf ears. Another opportunity to leave Al Wathba had passed. By mid January, through a lot of prayer and meditation, I had become at peace with my dad's passing and had hardened my resolve to serve out the remainder of my sentence using my time as productively as possible.

45

Light at the End of the Tunnel

AT THE PRESS CONFERENCE HELD when Ian and Lynn arrived in London, Lynn stated that all the women in Al Wathba had been glad for her release. Regardless of what they might have told her, there was much bitterness among female prisoners who had been incarcerated longer than Lynn and who felt that they should have been released before her. Some of them protested by setting fire to mattresses and destroying part of the wing in which they were housed. Those incidents were never reported in the local newspapers.

On his next visit Tom told me that Lynn had appeared on television in a half-hour feature program on BBC World. She indicated that she was having a hard time readjusting to life on the outside, and was even having difficulty getting used to her normal diet. Surprisingly, the program was allowed to be viewed in the UAE via satellite services. Within six weeks I received a post card from Ian. He mentioned that he, as well as Lynn, was having readjustment problems similar to those of other Brits who had been released earlier. Would this be a problem for me too?

I had forgotten, perhaps because of the news of Dad's death, that when Nicholas and Jamal had visited in December they had brought newspapers and magazines for me to read. On January 16 I was called to one of the security checkpoints to pick up those items that the censors had cleared. In the stack were some issues of the *Boston Globe* and copies of *Sports Illustrated* and an *Architectural Digest* that had been sent by my friend Dean in Boston. It may be hard to imagine the positive psychological impact that had on me, but it ranked right up there with being given food after having been deprived for several days.

I read the *Boston Globe* newspapers from cover to cover absorbing myself completely in their content. I had become so far removed from the reality of every day life in the United States that it was as though I were reading about another lifetime. Paradoxically, I was so homesick for some of the day to day aspects of American life that I even found myself studying the weather charts, scanning obituaries of people I didn't know, reading letters to the editor about totally mundane topics, and looking at advertisements for sales long over. I had put myself back into American life through the contents of those newspapers. I had mentally gone home.

I practically inhaled the contents of the *Sports Illustrated*, but I limited myself to just one magazine per day. That gave me something to look forward to for a few weeks and helped me get through the month of January. But it was the single *Architectural Digest* that I loved the most. The particular issue I had received showed magnificent pictures of seaside and ocean front homes in Europe and a feature on the American Ambassador's residence in Vietnam. I have a penchant for the informality of waterside living and I never tired of flipping through the pages of that magazine. I passed it throughout the block and everyone else loved it too. I also used it in my classes to enrich the students' vocabulary by having them look at the pictures and tell me what colors they saw, name the different pieces of furniture in the rooms, or describe the homes and landscaping in their own words. That one magazine brought hours of joy to Al Wathba. Unlike the newspapers and the *Sports Illustrated* magazines that appealed primarily to me, the pictures of nature and architectural design were of interest across all cultures. The words didn't matter. The pictures did.

During this period of time the local newspapers covered extensively the transition in power to George Bush's presidency. People in the Middle East were anxiously hoping that there would be a resolution to the conflict between Israel and Palestine and were looking for any indication that President-elect Bush would initiate policies to bring peace to the region.

In the meantime I was still mulling over why I hadn't been released along with Ian and Lynn. In a letter to Susanne in February I wrote:

> *I've searched my mind for reasons why I'm still here after all the appeals and the release of 3 Brits at Christmas. Unfortunately I must conclude that it is due to a bias toward our country over our perceived support of the "other" side in the Israeli–Arab conflict. Although they couldn't say as much I think the Embassy people are thinking along the same lines. Regardless the time is still moving quickly and I'm beginning to see the light at the end of the tunnel. Eight months doesn't seem like a long time when I realize 28 have already passed.*

Gradually my thoughts had begun to turn to life after Al Wathba. There were so many people that I wanted to visit and thank for their support during my incarceration. An advertisement appeared in the local English-language newspaper for Amtrak that caught my attention. Tom and Jennifer checked into it for me and Tom sent me some internet printouts from the Amtrak website. I was interested in the various passes available for using Amtrak for a fixed cost. I was beginning to think that that would be a good way not only to unwind after my stay at Al Wathba, but it would afford me the opportunity to visit several people at a good price. Thinking about that possibility was yet another way to keep my mind away from my surroundings.

Everyone was waiting anxiously for Eid to arrive in the hopes that more prisoners would be released in honor of Sheik Zayed's recovery from surgery. By early March, Eid Al Adha had come and gone and Abu Dhabi released no one. We had been confined to our blocks for the entire week of Eid with the exception of going for meals. No school. No sports. No library. The prisoners were dreadfully disappointed once again. Now the Arabs openly expressed how they wished the Sheik had died—at least then there would have been releases! This talk was most unusual because informants often notified prison authorities about such attitudes and that inevitably resulted in additional time added to one's sentence. But prisoners, because of the despair about Abu Dhabi doing nothing, were throwing caution to the wind. Adding fuel to the fire was talk about the prisoners staging hunger strikes and boycotting any sports activities. Such strikes quickly got the attention of prison authorities because word spread to the outside world and prison management didn't want to deal with the wrath of Sheikh Saif and the Ministry of the Interior. But these tactics never materialized due to new rumors of upcoming changes in the sentencing structure that included a reduction in the length of incarceration for drug possession. The rumor mill ground stronger than ever, since no one believed that Abu Dhabi would refrain from all celebration honoring Sheikh Zayed's good health.

Ian was gone, and it looked as if the rest of us would be there for the reminder of our sentences. Eventually, that frustration got to me. In a letter to Dean in Boston on March 8, I wrote:

> More than ever before I've been experiencing some bouts of loneliness for things familiar brought on I think by the rising excitement and anticipation of getting out of here, the lack of educational books to keep my mind occupied recently, and the general lack of mental stimulus provided by most of my compatriots here. The discussions around here, at least the ones I understand, are not the most brilliant and stimulating. There is only one guy in the whole block, a Sri Lankan, with whom I can have a good dialogue. He is really up on the music scene, which I am not and never will be, but he's up on science and technology issues and we get on some far ranging topics at times. We get talking about DNA, cloning, space travel, etc. so I enjoy time with him.

I had become friends with an Indian fellow, George, whom I met on our frequent visits to the library. George was the longest-serving prisoner at Al Wathba. By this time he had served fifteen years on a three-year sentence. He had been kept incarcerated because of pressure exerted on the outside by a fellow Indian who had initially pressed charges against him and did not want him released. George had endured a lot. His family had to continue their lives without him and he had not been there for the crucial adolescent years of his son and daughter. Regardless, George kept up his spirits, was a model prisoner, and had been a friend to scores of inmates throughout his prison stay. George and I shared many thoughts and he had made telephone calls on my behalf.

For over a year the new Indian Ambassador had made it his personal goal to secure George's freedom. And finally in March he succeeded. George was going home and I was losing my best friend. I was happy for George but sad for myself. We agreed to keep in touch once we were both free again and we have lived up to that promise.

Tom had become increasingly frustrated over my ongoing imprisonment. He decided to write a letter to a more senior ranking person at the U.S. Embassy. He addressed the letter to Deborah Jones who was Deputy Chief of Mission at the Embassy in Abu Dhabi. He wrote:

> *My name is Tom Hennessy, a U.S. citizen, and I work for a defense contractor here in Abu Dhabi. A friend told me that you had been responsive to his situation and I am hoping you will have the time to hear about what I am involved in.*
>
> *I have been visiting Paul Ciceri, who is in prison at Al Wathba, for a little over a year now.*
>
> *My concerns are as follows. There have been a number of prisoner releases since Ramadan and the December 2000 Eid, plus the fact that Paul's father passed away this past Christmas. Much to Paul's and my disappointment, he was not among them. I do not want to jeopardize Paul's relationship with the embassy or the prison system, nor am I trying to put down the level of attention given to Paul's situation by the Citizen's Services department of the embassy. I am quite familiar with the case of the British inmates, Ian and Lynn, who were released at Christmas time and who were incarcerated for the same offence. Their prison time started just about the same time Paul's did and their length of sentence was the same. I do realize there was a lot of publicity surrounding their case.*
>
> *Is it possible to do something about an early release for Paul? I know he has been an exemplary prisoner. He teaches English to several inmates. Lastly I can't understand why no one has visited Paul since his father passed away. I understand that he may not be at the top of the embassy's favorite people list but he is not a hardened criminal and he is a U.S. citizen.*

> As you can probably tell my reason for contacting you is because of my concern for Paul and my belief in our country and for basic human rights and needs.

Deborah Jones replied immediately and stated that the Embassy staff had been very active in trying to secure my release:

> When the Consular Section learned there might be a possibility for a few prisoner releases during the month of Ramadan, the Consular Chief went personally to see the Director of the Office of the Undersecretary for the Ministry of the Interior and urged that Mr. Ciceri's name be included on any amnesty list. In addition, the Ambassador wrote a personal letter to His Highness Sheikh Saif bin Zayed al Nahyan, Undersecretary for the Ministry of Interior, seeking clemency for Mr. Ciceri after his father passed away. Regrettably, for reasons that remain unclear to us, Mr. Ciceri was not among the few prisoners that were finally granted amnesty.

Senior embassy personnel were echoing thoughts I had raised in an earlier letter I had written to Jamal in which I had postulated a few reasons why I thought I might still be in prison. Was I still there because they had a real prejudice against the United States? I was beginning to believe that that was indeed the case. Regardless, life went on inside the walls of Al Wathba. March passed quickly and I gave Jennifer an update on life in my block:

> We are all getting along fairly well. In my room there are 3 Iranians, 2 Pakistanis, 3 Indians, 1 Filipino, 1 Brit, and me—and no one snores in our group so we get some decent sleep.
>
> They rounded up all the cats and carted them away somewhere so I miss the cute little white one that hung around our area. She got a lot of attention here.

46

My Last Easter in Captivity

ALMOST THREE MONTHS HAD PASSED since my father's death and I had psychologically set myself up to serve out the remainder of my sentence which would have been until October 6. I was approaching the six-month mark for time still to be served.

Easter, my favorite religious holiday arrived, and I wanted to share my thoughts with close friends. One of my letters was to Tom and Jan Hennessy:

> *I wanted to wish you a most blessed and meaningful Easter. As usual, this festival will pass without notice here except for those of us who hold it in our hearts and minds.*
>
> *Easter has long been my favorite of festivals in the sense that the message of Easter is basic to our faith as we are 'The Easter People'! My memories of Easter center around worship, family, and newness of life.*
>
> *Up north (in the U.S.) as you know Easter was always close to early spring and we so looked forward every year to the new growth of flowers, and the greening of lawns and trees. Easter just seemed to heighten the impact of all that as it emphasized the promise of a new life for us.*
>
> *Family gatherings were traditional and every Easter included that fellowship including the Easter meal—usually turkey or ham. And it was always so good!*

> *Worship was always as meaningful on Easter as Christmas, or even more so. My favorite hymn of all is 'Christ the Lord is Risen Today' and worship on Easter Sunday always began with that hymn whether it was the traditional service in church or the sunrise service in the church parking lot or on the beach on the Atlantic coast. But worship in church always included a brass band, and the whole energy of the moment could bring goose bumps and a few tears. I hope that some day when I am in Orlando you can join me for Sunday worship.*
>
> *I know you will have to work on Easter Day but I imagine you will find the time to celebrate the occasion with friends like you normally do. I won't see you on that day but I'm sure our thoughts will be like-minded.*
>
> *Thank you for all you do for me and in your actions I know God lives in you. I wish you the happiest of days and may God continue to bless you abundantly as he has me. Please pass on my similar wishes to those of your church and especially thank those who uplift my name in prayer. You and they are very special to me.*

My Easter letter to Jennifer and her boyfriend Don included a poem:

> *Happy Easter greetings I send to you*
> *A wonderful day is my hope 'tis true*
> *It's a special day for both family and friends*
> *And happy thoughts of spring, new life, and warming trends.*
> *Although I'm not there to share in your day*
> *I will think of you both in loving ways*
> *May the spirit of Easter abide in your life*
> *And keep you happy and safe and free of strife.*

On Easter morning I found some private space, reflected on my situation and gave thanks for all that I had. And over and over I found the words to the Easter hymn echoing in my heart. *Jesus Christ is risen today. Alleluia!* And I was uplifted and found peace in my situation.

But whatever peace I found was shattered by the brutal reality of life inside the walls of Al Wathba. Around this time there were several Russians in my block, two of whom were brothers. The Russians were housed in one room and had decorated the walls of their room with paintings of wildlife quite marvelously done. Most of these men were quiet, but one or two put fear into many hearts as they would fight with anyone over anything. In particular, one of the brothers who had been in an American prison in Brooklyn constantly stood up to the guards and spent a considerable amount of time in solitary. His last altercation where he had refused to obey orders caused the prison authorities to place him into solitary once again. During that stay I saw him once escorted by guards to the clinic to get some medicine. He was smiling and joking with the guards at the time.

Within days rumors spread that he was dead, the result of being beaten up by the guards. We all talked about the rumors, but always out of earshot of his brother who got more and more anxious that he had had no word from anyone who had seen his brother.

The brother asked the guards to look into the matter, but was told only that his brother was in the hospital. The following week he had a visit from his sister who had gone to the hospital and was told that his brother was not there. That caused more concern and he then demanded to see an officer. No one would come to talk to him about the welfare of his brother until one night, united as a block, we refused to go to have our dinner. Shortly thereafter one of the officers came and told him that his brother was ill and that he would arrange a meeting in the manager's office.

A few days later he was escorted to the manager's office and on his return he was crying. He had been told that his brother had died in the hospital from a disease and that his body would be released to the family. In the meantime, a few guards who were friendly to the prisoners told us that his brother had been murdered by the guards in his cell one night following orders of the manager to kill him.

Word got out to his sister who made an appointment with the manager under the pretense of doing a story for a newspaper. She inquired about a rumor she had heard about people dying in prison and asked about a Russian who had died recently. The manager shrugged off the incident by telling her that the man had died in the hospital and that the body had been turned over to his sister. She then seized the moment to tell the manager that she was his only sister and his body had not been turned over to her.

Dumbfounded he ordered her from his office as she vowed that the Russian Embassy would be doing a thorough investigation.

We never heard any more prior to my being released.

47

Counting Down

EARLY IN THE YEAR I HAD DRAWN UP a chart showing the number of days and months left until my release. At first I indicated the days in groups of fifteen, but once I reached one hundred, there would be an entry for every day. I always thought I would never mark the days off one at a time because I figured it would give the impression of slowing time down. Closure on the ordeal at Al Wathba couldn't come fast enough for me.

As the end of my incarceration drew near, things that I had been able to ignore in the past became more of an irritant to me. The smoking, the fighting, the yelling, the loud and disruptive talking while others tried to sleep; the lights left on late into the night while prisoners played cards into the early morning hours; the whistle blowing policemen and the ongoing destruction caused by the guards when they ransacked our rooms; the confiscation of my third chess set—all these things grated on my nerves. I missed the view of the outside world that I had previously enjoyed on the third level block, and I resented the delay by the administration in delivering books and magazines that the Embassy staff had brought to me many weeks earlier. I was annoyed at the deterioration in the quality of the food following the hoopla surrounding the change of the catering company. I seethed at the apparent neglect of the Embassy staff, the nagging speculation as to why Ian had been released and I hadn't, and the failure of the Abu Dhabi government to liberate prisoners when the other Emirates had done so. During one of our visits Tom picked up on my irritability and wrote to my family, "Paul seemed a little more frustrated with things this time." An understatement!

As I approached the end of my sentence, I also had the nagging worry that maybe my prison term had been extended without my knowledge as it had been for other prisoners. I could not bear the thought of having to stay one day beyond October 7. With the help of my Lebanese friend, Samir, I wrote a letter to the prison authorities asking for confirmation of my release date. After several tense weeks, I finally got my letter back with a handwritten note stating that my release date would be October 6. Although I was somewhat relieved, I still worried because others had had their sentences extended despite such similar acknowledgments. It seemed that anyone with influence who wanted a prisoner to remain incarcerated could arrange for that to happen. With the conflict in the Middle East between Israel and Palestine being in the state that it was, I wouldn't have been overly surprised if my sentence had been extended just to aggravate the United States for its pro-Israel bias.

On April 18 I had a visit from the Embassy staff. I had asked them to check with their contacts to see what my official release date would be. Their response satisfied me for two reasons: first, they did affirm that my release date would be in October; secondly, they told me my release date would be October 6 and not October 7. One less day in Al Wathba!

My joy, however, was tempered by another hair incident. At the time I was admitted to Al Wathba the first act of subjection for new inmates was to cut their hair close to the scalp almost to the point of shaving all the hair off their heads. That humiliation was something I never wanted to experience again, and indeed, throughout my thirty-one months in Al Wathba I had escaped further haircuts by having other inmates cut my hair fairly short on a regular basis and by some luck. Recently, though, the prison authorities had gotten stricter on their hair-cutting regulations and they stationed a barber by the checkpoint outside the visiting area. Anyone who wanted to have a visit had to subject himself to having his hair cut.

On the way to my visit on April 18 the guard in charge of the desk told me I had to have my hair cut before going for my visit. I refused. He told me I could not go for my visit.

"Fine," I told him. "I'll go back to my block. You tell my Embassy why they couldn't see me then."

He thought about it for a few seconds and then let me pass. On the way back he was waiting for me. Again he told me that I had to have my hair cut. Again, I refused and became quite agitated. He ordered me to sit down and informed me that I would have to go to solitary. I acknowledged his threat and took a place down along the wall. After making a phone call, he repeated that I had to have my hair cut, but that he would tell the barber not to cut it as short as the rest. He looked at the barber and told him to use the number 4 setting which he assured me would leave my hair longer on top than the customary 1/8 inch. I agreed to that and sat on the barber's chair which was a bucket. As soon as I did this, I sensed that the guard was motioning quietly to the barber. Suddenly, I knew he had changed the setting back to 1/8 inch, but it was too late. He had cut a swath of my hair that left me no choice at that point but to have all my hair cut.

I was furious with the guard who just smirked at me. He had won. I felt painfully embarrassed by the way I knew I looked. When I returned to my block my haircut didn't go unnoticed. There were many comments and one good friend gave me a hug because he knew how distressed I was. This provided just one more reason to feel frustrated and angry over my imprisonment.

A few days later when a guard came to escort me to the library and school, I refused to go with him. When he asked me why, I pointed to my head and he just shook his head in disbelief and left. For the entire week I stayed away from the school. I heard through my communications network, however, that all my students, as well as the other officers at the school, had asked about me. I was the star teacher and the Administration was getting restless because the school was the one place where visitors were taken to show how 'progressive' the prison was in providing a positive outlet for its inmates.

Finally, a week later I agreed to go the library. While I was there, the commander in charge of prison operations came to me and said he had heard that I was upset over having my hair cut. I told him that we had been promised months earlier that teachers would be spared having their hair cut, and I found it to be an affront to all prisoners to be subjected to such humiliation. Indeed a few years earlier one prisoner had committed suicide after having his hair cut because it went against the beliefs of his religious sect. He told me that he would give orders that no teacher would have to have his hair cut again. I acquiesced at that and agreed to go back into the classroom.

Word had gotten to my family that my October 6 release date had been confirmed and that, once this was over, I wanted to fly to Toronto to visit with my brother Richard and his family. As it turned out, October 8 was the celebration of Canada's Thanksgiving Day. What a wonderful way to celebrate my release!

48

Something's Up

THE DAYS CONTINUED TO SLIP BY and as I marked off my countdown sheet, my thoughts more and more turned to getting back to North America. On May 25 I wrote to Richard:

> *These days my thoughts drift more often to life after Al Wathba than they used to. Inasmuch as I usually focus on getting through one day at a time I've allowed myself the luxury of letting thoughts of Stateside occupy more of my time.*

I also allowed myself to take up the issue of having my airplane ticket ready to go for my flight out of the Middle East.

> *I'm sure that Tom has passed on that my release date has been confirmed as October 6th which means I'll be free to leave here anytime after 12:01 a.m. on the 7th. That confirmation has only been given orally but even if it were in writing it wouldn't make it any more official based on my experiences here. As little as I count on the embassy for anything, it is in this issue that I expect them to be firm. Not a day more should be their stand.*

At the same time the State Department announced that Ambassador Khattouf would be leaving Abu Dhabi to assume his new position as Ambassador to Syria in Damascus. He had come to Abu Dhabi shortly after my arrival at Al Wathba and I found it somewhat ironic that his tenure coincided with my stay in that facility. His last days were hectic as the UAE government became more vocal in its condemnation of the role of the United States in resolving the Israel–Palestine conflict. Several times in May, Ambassador Kattouf had been summoned by the Foreign Ministry to receive admonitions demanding that the U.S. government step up the pressure on Israel to make peace with the Palestinians. This ongoing anti-American sentiment made me feel that I would indeed be staying the full term of my sentence. I also feared that the prison administration might tack on additional time to my sentence to spite the United States government.

On May 25 the son of one of the Pakistani prisoners had married and we gathered that night to celebrate the event. We squeezed together into one of the larger rooms in the block to be entertained in song and dance by other prisoners. We devised make-shift music by banging on pail bottoms to accompany the performers. Most notable among the entertainers was one Filipino who had performed in drag at night clubs in Japan, Thailand, and in other Far East countries. He sang several numbers from the cabarets in which he had previously performed. Not long after this event, he was granted an early release amid rumors that he had become an informant for the CID. Many fellow Filipinos had told me earlier that they suspected he had been responsible for their arrests and this made the rumors credible. Indeed, some newly-arrived prisoners had mentioned that he had been spotted close by when they had been arrested. One always wondered who informants were among the prison population, because when the police raided specific cells they always managed to find some contraband like drugs, radios, or other things prohibited in prison.

In late May the police initiated a new policy regarding what visitors were allowed to bring for the inmates. In an effort to stem the smuggling of illegal items into the prison, the authorities decided to institute a chit system whereby each prisoner could set up a cash account that would be drawn down as items were purchased. Once cash was deposited into an account, chits were issued in various amounts that the prisoners could use to buy necessities such as toothpaste, towels, flip flops, envelopes, stamps, pens, paper, clothes, and cigarettes. Such a program had been tried before, but each attempt had ended in quick failure, since those responsible just couldn't handle the administrative work involved. But this time it seemed to work. A few inmates from each block were chosen to collect a list of orders and were subsequently escorted to a supply room where they would gather up the items for later distribution. Actually, it seemed to work well and we were told that if we cooperated with the plan, the administration would broaden its scope.

Yeah, I'll believe that when I see it! I thought.

But I was wrong. Within a week the program had been extended and we were now able to buy juices and sodas when we ate our lunches.

You would have thought we'd struck gold! I hadn't tasted a soft drink in almost three years and I savored every drop as I sipped my Pepsi Cola during the first lunch that drinks became available. There were men who hadn't tasted a soft drink in almost fifteen years, and they screamed and yelled in celebration of this phenomenal addition to prison life. The talk in the block that first afternoon centered around our disbelief that the warden had actually let us savor a bit of the "good life" within the walls of Al Wathba.

What would come next? Chocolate bars? Biscuits?

The next thing happened to be razors. For all the time I had been at Al Wathba, we had been issued plastic disposable razors every two weeks. After a few days they would be collected, and the same number that had been initially distributed had to be returned. Otherwise, intrusive searches would be conducted randomly throughout the blocks. With the cooperation of some guards, however, we had always managed to stash a few away so that one or two were always available at a price.

Normally there would be a rush to shave right after the razors were handed out. In the Muslim tradition no one shaved his moustache, but other facial hair, underarm air, and much pubic hair was routinely shaved off. More importantly, the razors were used for shaving heads or providing hair cuts. The plastic protective pieces along the sharp end of the razor blades would be cut off, and with a comb that someone had smuggled in or had made from a plastic pail, it was the best way to get a haircut. Many people were neophytes at head shaving, and if they used a sheer blade, bleeding heads were an inevitable result of the process.

Had the prison officials gone mad? These acts of kindness were so unlike what we had experienced over the years that something had to be up. But what?

My Indian friend George had recently been released after fifteen years. Somehow, I thought that maybe he had a hand in all that had recently transpired with regard to our 'supermarket' of goodies. On many of those mornings before he left, we had talked in the library about his status with the prison authorities, a position that had risen as he became the longest-serving prisoner at Al Wathba. He showed me letters he was writing to the prison manager and wanted me to review them to see that they were written correctly. In them he thanked the manager for his previous generosities and considerations, but, more importantly, he asked that all the prisoners be allowed to purchase some foods like crackers and sodas. That availability, he felt, would raise the level of good will and substantially reduce smuggling.

A wave of euphoria swept through the prison as items previously banned became available. The response to the new program was phenomenal. Inmates were drinking four or five sodas for lunch and ignoring their food. Even for me, that first drink of Pepsi had brought back thoughts of life outside the walls of Al Wathba. A little bit of hope had crept into our lives after so many months of deprivation. A can of Pepsi. A container of yogurt. A glass of milk. Things that had once been taken for granted and then removed, were now ours again.

There was a new excitement in the air.

I couldn't help but wonder what the ulterior motive was. After witnessing the prison authorities' actions for thirty-two months, I just didn't believe that the new procedures were born out of a desire to make our lives easier. What were they up to? There was a grander scheme in all this.

I wouldn't have to wait long to find out.

June 6, 2001

I AWOKE TO SHOUTS OF EXCITEMENT that Wednesday morning and I could sense the upbeat mood to the conversations. I thought that maybe I had slept in and this was the usual conversations after breakfast.

The news had circulated throughout our block, and indeed, throughout the entire prison that Sheikh Zayed had announced the release of six thousand prisoners in celebration of his recovery. The prison guards had spread word that the lead story in the newspapers that morning had been about the releases.

Six thousand! Six thousand! That was a huge number considering that only a handful had been released at any one time over the thirty-two months I had been at Al Wathba. Euphoria filled the blocks as everyone speculated as to what was going to happen and how fast.

I couldn't wait to get to the library that morning and discuss with my friends what the Arabic papers had said. Everyone was all smiles and talked animatedly as I walked into the library and greeted the others. Even the police guards seemed upbeat and shared with us what they thought was going to happen. The newspapers had talked about a general amnesty that applied to everyone except murderers and child molesters. There was no mention of anyone else. It didn't mention drugs cases.

It didn't mention drug cases. That must mean we're included, I thought. *Oh God I hope it's true.*

My Arabic friends read the article in the Arabic press over and over as we dissected every sentence making sure we understood what had been written. Repeatedly we came back to the same statement, 'Six thousand prisoners will be released from Abu Dhabi's prisons, but the release will not include those sentenced in murder or child molestation cases.'

Six thousand was everybody. And that included all of us. We were all going home!

But, yet, we were afraid to believe it. Then a policeman came in and an excited buzz filled the room. I didn't have a clue as to what was being said. *What's happening? Tell me what's going on!*

I was told that all the locals were being released that very day.

We sat in shocked disbelief. Nothing like this had happened before at Al Wathba. It was beginning to sink in that, indeed, this was really going to happen. It wasn't rumor. People were actually being released as we excitedly talked about the news.

Thank you, God, I breathed.

We were anxious to return to our blocks and see what was going on. We wanted to be available if the police came looking for us to tell us we were going home. Thus, after an hour of rehashing the news, we asked to be sent back to our blocks. Teaching that day did not figure in importance.

As we returned, we noticed a flurry of prisoner activity in the hallways. Something major was really going on. When I neared my block I heard cheers, whistling, shouting, and laughter. Just across from my entrance was Block 9 where all the local people involved in drug cases were housed. The block door was open and prisoners were being led away by guards. I realized that everyone from that block was being released that day. A few months earlier, in an effort to reduce some of the overcrowding in our block, Arabs from other Middle Eastern countries were moved to Block 9 where the Emiratees were being held. And they were all going home too! All the Arabs were going home!

That day! I was astounded! My heart beat faster and I too was caught up in the jubilation. What was happening seemed so incredulous. All my Arab friends were leaving—the Saudis, the Bahrainis, the Emiratees.

Our turn had to be next.

By 4 p.m. Block 9 had been emptied. In less than twelve hours of getting the news, hundreds had been released from Al Wathba. Incredible!

The police told us we would all be going soon. All of us! I so wanted to believe it, but I just didn't. Daily prayers were jammed that day, and I said my own prayers of thanksgiving too. Even if I weren't going home, I was glad for my Arab friends who had left.

That night we went to bed hopeful that tomorrow would bring our turn. June 6, 2001 was a day I wouldn't soon forget. My mind raced as I lay in bed. I thought about all that I had accomplished during my stay at Al Wathba: all the books I had read; the Spanish, Italian, and German grammar I had learned; the book I had written comparing English to Spanish, Italian, and German; the poems I had written; the students to whom I had taught English; the exercise program we had set up. I thought about the numerous volleyball games we had played; how I'd relearned the game of chess; and made new friends from all over the Arab world and Asia. I even thought about all the rice I had eaten. But I also remembered the harassment and torture of prisoners by prison authorities and the fighting among the inmates. I remembered those who had committed suicide. And the Russian boy who had been murdered by the prison guards.

Then my thoughts turned to home. Was I really going to be there soon? That was my last thought before saying a fervent prayer and slipping off to sleep that night.

The next few days I wrote several letters anticipating that these would be the last I would write as a prisoner in Al Wathba. They all carried the same message:

> *Today is my birthday (June 8th) and there is a lot more than usual to celebrate. Just 36 hours ago a general amnesty was announced (except for murderers) for over 6000 prisoners here. It took us all by surprise and everyone is reacting in his own way but all are very happy. Some people are just days short of completing 15-year sentences and some are just beginning 25-year sentences but we all share one thing in common—We are going home!*
>
> *It is yet a strange feeling. After all the up and down roller coaster rides we've ridden the last few years with so many rumors that left us high with expectation and low with disappointment we are still processing what*

we have now been told. It, by far, exceeds anything expected before. When we were all initially arrested our mind and bodies became numb as a protection I guess about the unknown and the fears. That numbness has returned. Although all the 'locals' were released within hours of the announcement we haven't quite processed the fact that this will all soon be over. However, seeing the announcement in the newspaper yesterday has helped to make it all believable.

Maybe we feel like so many others before us have felt when they were released from bondage or how those boys in war felt when the surrenders of the opposing forces were announced. It is a strange feeling and I'm sure the 'fuzziness' will wear off over the next days as the releases become reality and real excitement will bubble over.

As happy as I am, I think how close I came to seeing Dad again—less than 6 months! It will be different and the reality of all those who have died during my stay here will become more acute over the next several weeks.

There is no way I can express the gratitude I feel toward people like yourself who have stood by me unconditionally these past many months. Perhaps when you hear the truth of all that precipitated this you will know that your faith was not misplaced. I will carry the warmth of your love with me all my days.

Tom had just returned from the United States late on Friday evening, so we didn't have a chance to meet on the one day per week set aside for visits to non-Arab inmates. But he did immediately call the Embassy to find out what they knew about the releases. He wrote to my family, *I called the Embassy and Jamal said they have been on the phone this morning (Saturday) trying to get more info on who it is that are getting released. I'll let you know as soon as I find anything out.*

A day later an article appeared in the local English-language newspaper that Mr. Ansar Burney of the Ansar Burney Welfare Trust had sent a congratulatory note to Sheikh Zayed for his humanitarianism in announcing the release of six thousand prisoners from Abu Dhabi's prisons. Tom seized on the opportunity to request their assistance in securing my release.

Everywhere in the block people were laughing, joking, hugging, giving 'high fives,' washing their clothes, getting their belongings in order, cutting hair, and doing whatever they could to get ready for their releases. We were going home.

Or were we?

50

The Agonizing Wait

THE PRESS REMAINED STRANGELY silent over the next few weeks about news from Al Wathba. Every day new rumors surfaced. Everyone seemed to know someone on the outside who had heard that the releases were imminent. But nothing happened. The locals had been let go. The euphoria of June 6 had subsided and the continued wait had created tense days, sleepless nights, and short tempers.

Tom reported in an e-mail to my family after our visit on the 22 of June: *I think knowing they are going to be released and it not happening has had an effect on all. He said there was a lot of bickering going on in the cells and everyone was on each other's nerves.*

Still the Moslem participation in the daily prayers was considerable and competition to lead these prayers increased. In Islam people earn "points" for good deeds and that included leading prayer. Thus, prisoners vied for the opportunity to be the local 'imam.' That rivalry lead one night to another inmate's entering our room while everyone was asleep and trying to stab the man next to me with a handmade knife. Fortunately, he was caught in the act but the struggle awakened everyone. Those in the block who were considered the most astute religious leaders quickly brought the parties together and diffused the situation before more harm could come to anyone. After an eruption of shouting and arguments, the block calmed down and the incident was not reported to the police. The bottom line was that everyone was getting so uptight that a few were starting to act irrationally. Still, no one wanted anyone sent to solitary, a situation that might have excluded him from the releases.

The pressure got to me, too. For so long I had been able to block out the noise and confusion in my room, but after a few weeks of constant talk and the stress of waiting for our releases, I became annoyed by people who talked too loudly. One was a Pakistani, a nice fellow who had led a sheepherder's life, but had come to the UAE to drive trucks. His staunchest defender was Rana, a young burly Brit who had shared my room for the past several months. Rana was born in England to Pakistani parents and considered himself more of a Pakistani than a Brit, although he used his British citizenship to good advantage as needed. He tolerated the Pakistani's loud talk, defending his right to do so because that was how men communicated over distance in the Pakistani countryside. One morning as I was reading the previous day's paper, I remarked in a low voice to the person next to me, "Man, can he possibly talk any louder . . . ?" My head was buried in the paper, but out of the corner of my eye I caught sight of Rana getting up from where he was sitting. I thought nothing of it. A few seconds later he socked me in the head and sent me spinning; since he caught my glasses, I had a gash just above one eye.

Rana was a big man who had put many a prisoner in his place, and this morning he was in a rage. For several weeks I had sensed his hostility toward me as our releases supposedly neared. I looked at him and saw murder in his eyes. Everyone in the room stopped talking and immediately tried to diffuse the situation. I was frightened not only about what Rana might do, but also because I was an American and a non-Muslim. Up until the time of the announcement of the releases everyone had counted on me and the American government to ensure that nothing grave happened to us in Block 10, but now that we were going home that protection was not as crucial as it had been before. Over the past weeks I had sensed open hostility building against me.

Ignoring calls to let the incident go, I contacted my Lebanese friend who accompanied me to the front gate of our block. He explained to the guard in Arabic what had happened and within minutes more guards arrived and escorted me and Rana upstairs to the security table. There I explained what had happened and Rana concurred with my version of events. We were ordered to sit on opposite sides of the corridor and a few minutes later I was escorted to the clinic to have a dressing put on my head wound.

Upon returning I was again seated opposite Rana and he apologized for what he had done. From his explanation it became clear that he was angry at me for not having shared my home address and telephone number with him as I had done with some other non-Western friends. Rana was only about twenty and I explained that we had practically nothing in common. For us to remain friends after leaving Al Wathba wasn't a likely thing. But I took him at his word and approached the guard to tell him I wanted to let the incident go and that we just wanted to go back to our cells.

He told me it was too late. The warden had been advised and he would be meeting with us very soon. There was nothing I could do about that, but perhaps I could use the chance to find out what was going on with our releases.

After a while we were escorted up to the Captain's office. I was escorted in first to meet with Captain Ali who was responsible for prisoners' well being. He and I had talked at other times and his command of English was very good. I explained what had happened and then I told him I had forgiven Rana and didn't want anything to happen to him that might jeopardize his chance at a release. I was led from the room and then it was Rana's turn to tell his story. When he was finished I was escorted back in. Captain Ali told me that Rana concurred with what I had said, and although I had requested leniency, Rana had to be punished.

Captain Ali also told me that all the prison administrators liked me because I had been a model prisoner and that they knew I wasn't at fault in the incident. I used the opportunity to ask him what was happening with our releases. He was the pivot man who handled the discharges, and as if to prove the point, the floor in his office was covered with prisoners' files. Candidly he told me that only four hundred would be released.

"What about the six thousand?" I asked incredulously.

"I don't know. That is what I have been told."

"Is my name on the list?"

"I don't know. But I hope so. Jamal has called me several times for updates and I haven't been able to tell him with any certainty that your name is on the final list. I should have the definitive list within days."

I thanked him for his candor and left with Rana to head back to the block. At the security desk we were stopped and searched and I was told to go back to the block. They told Rana he was going to solitary. I knew that wouldn't make me popular among the Muslims back in the block, but I also knew that the police had been given orders to watch out for my safety.

After I returned, I was greeted coldly by several of the staunch Muslims. A rumor had spread that I had defamed Islam and Rana had responded to that. As I had often experienced during my stay at Al Wathba, the Muslims used their religion as needed to make a point and create a rallying cry among those like-minded. To some in prison, and even to some on the outside, the Muslim religion was all they had to cling to for security. Whenever the need arose, rather than trying to determine the real reasons behind the aggression, they created a defense based on a challenge to their beliefs.

Most of the others in my room were cool to me also, so for the next few days I kept to myself. Whenever I moved about the block, however, I felt all eyes on me. I was the evil American who was now responsible for putting one of their kind in solitary.

Please God, get me out of here before something serious happens to me.

About the same time, the Embassy staff was in communication with UAE officials in an effort to secure my freedom. Theodore Kattouf wrote a letter to the Minister of Justice, His Excellency Mohammed Nukhairah Al-Dhaheri on June 24:

> *Thank you very much for the opportunity to meet with you on Saturday, June 23rd. It was a pleasure to exchange viewpoints with you concerning issues of mutual interest to our Governments.*
>
> *I would again like to applaud His Highness, President Sheikh Zayed bin Sultan Al-Nahyan's humanitarian act of pardoning and releasing 6000 prisoners from UAE prisons. This act indeed reflects His Highness' true spirit and character.*

> *Your Excellency, as we discussed, I am attaching herewith a list of the names of the American citizen prisoners who are currently incarcerated in UAE prisons for committing various crimes. As I stated in our meeting, if foreigners are being considered for pardons, I would ask that these incarcerated Americans be given consideration so that they can return home to be with their families and start a new chapter in their lives.*
>
> *Your Excellency, once again I take this opportunity to thank you for the continued support the American Embassy receives from the Ministry of Justice.*

Other friends in the Arab world were trying to find out about my status. My former secretary, Belinda Campos, wrote to my brother Richard on June 25 to inquire if the rumors of my release were true. Rumors, even on the outside, were rampant!

Friends in the United States contacted Tom to find out what he knew. On the 26th one query resulted in the following reply from Tom:

> *Wish I had some news. I look in the paper every day and there hasn't been anything regarding the release. The Embassy just says they're optimistic; that's the most I get out of them. Feels like my hands are tied. Can't really accomplish much, just visit when I can. Will sure be happy when he's out.*

Confirming that the Embassy had tried to intercede on my behalf, Richard wrote to Tom on the 27.

> *Embassy informed me that they have had discussions with Diwan re Paul but I have not heard anything further. Have you heard anything?*

Everyone, both inside and outside the prison, wondered what was going on. Inside though, nerves were frayed. Fights were a daily occurrence now as tempers grew short from the stress of not knowing our fate and rumors, both good and bad, continued to abound.

On the 28th Tom tried again to get some information. He wrote to Richard: *Sorry I have no more info than you have. It's quite frustrating. I called Jamal yesterday and he was off for the day.*

On Saturday the 30th Tom wrote again:

I wasn't able to visit Paul this week, but if he's still there next Friday I will definitely go. I can't imagine how he must be feeling. I still haven't heard anything about the release. There was an article in yesterday's paper that said 300 were being released this week, but they only talked about those in for financial reasons. And the list of countries represented did not include USA.

We had read the article too. It was always the same—locals and financial cases. I was coming to the realization that the six-thousand figure given in the press was for propaganda purposes only; it was just another scam on the government's part to give the impression that they were humanitarians. We had gotten word that several thousand persons who had finished their sentences were still being held in the "out-prisons," and that that was where the bulk of the six thousand was going to come from.

But something else started happening. Inmates began to arrive from other prisons to be housed at Al Wathba. They had been told nothing except to gather their belongings and board the buses. We quizzed them hoping for the smallest glimmer of new information that might give us a clue as to what was happening. But no one could figure it out. Even the police claimed ignorance.

On June 30th in reply to a query from my daughter Jennifer, Jamal wrote:

While it is true that 6000 prisoners (including UAE nationals) have been ordered released by the President, Sheikh Zayed, nobody is certain that non-UAE citizens incarcerated for drug offenses will be included in the pardon. We have however witnessed UAE citizens involved in more serious drug cases pardoned and released. We are keeping our fingers crossed and hope that Paul will be released. Last Saturday, June 23rd I was present in a meeting between U.S. Ambassador Theodore Kattouf and UAE Justice Minister, Mohammed Al-Dhaheri. The Ambassador raised the prisoner issue and the Minister asked for the names of Americans incarcerated in UAE jails. Your father's name was on the list provided the Minister.

Only one hundred days to go! And each one was moving slower than the one that preceded it.

51

Day 1000

THE LAST HUNDRED DAYS OF ANY prisoner's incarceration pass slowly as the anxiety of being released builds. As I crossed that threshold, I marked off the days on my calendar one by one.

What I didn't know was that Richard and the Embassy staff were trying to obtain seats for me on flights from Abu Dhabi to Toronto. Often people from the Middle East, including local Arabs, leave for the summer and either return to their permanent homes or vacation in cooler climates. As a result flights are generally filled on outbound legs from Abu Dhabi.

It had now been almost a month since our 'local' brothers had been released from Al Wathba, and yet none of us had gotten further word. As the days rolled on we began to accept the fact that the news of the six thousand releases was another propaganda effort on the part of the UAE. Throughout the prison now you could hear talk of "I wish Sheikh Zayed had died. At least then we would have stood a better chance of getting out of here." Caution was being thrown to the winds in the bitterness that the prisoners felt toward the country's leadership. Prisoners risked severe punishment and extended detentions if such talk were ever linked to them.

In our discussions in the library and in my classes the speculation had died down, and once again we turned our attention to learning English. But just in case there were spur-of-the-moment releases, my students from Syria, Iran, and Egypt gave me their home addresses and told me to visit them some day when this was over for all of us.

That's how the morning of July 3, my one thousandth day at Al Wathba, began. As usual I returned to my block about 11:45 and had a chance to rest before lunch. When the call came, we routinely fetched our water or juice coupons and headed toward the front of the block to line up for the walk to the eating area. As I left carrying my glass of water, a policeman said to me, "You are Paul, the American?"

"Yes."

"You must come with me. The Captain wants to see you in the office."

Everyone around me stopped and collectively assured me that I would be getting some good news. They were excited because perhaps it meant I was going to be released. And if I got released, then maybe they would be released also. Word spread quickly in the dining hall that The American had been summoned to the administration area. Lunch was downed quickly that noontime, as everyone wanted to be back in the block to hear what had happened.

I didn't know what to expect; therefore, I didn't allow myself to get excited. So many times I had made that trip and each time I had met with disappointment. This time, however, I allowed myself to think, *Maybe this is it. Maybe I'll get some good news this time.*

The walk seemed endless. We had to stop at the security check point where I had had my hair cut just a few weeks earlier. I still felt the tension build in me. I knew there were some rogue policemen working at this checkpoint who would love to demean any American and would risk the wrath of their superiors to do so.

Thankfully, we were waved on after a quick search and headed down the long corridor and up the stairs to the administrative wing. There the policeman instructed me to wait in the hallway outside the warden's office as he went in. I couldn't see into the room and I didn't hear any talking.

"What the hell was going on? What did I do now? What had happened?"

In a short time the policeman returned and motioned for me to move into the office. As I stepped inside, I saw Jamal and Nicholas Papp, the vice-consul of the American Embassy talking with the warden. When they saw me, they both turned in my direction and Nicholas started moving toward me.

Without hesitation he said, "Paul, I know that in the past we have come here with a lot of bad news. But now I've got some good news. You're going home tomorrow."

Shock. Disbelief. But most of all relief.

I embraced Nicholas and breathed, "Thank you!"

At that moment I felt the tension drain out of me. I had never noticed that I was so up tight until that instant when a surge of hope raced through my entire being. As tears came to my eyes, all I could do was repeat over and over, "Thank you."

When I gained my composure, I said to Nicholas and Jamal, "Do you know this is day one thousand for me here and tomorrow is July the 4th? How significant this day will be for me for the rest of my life."

Nicholas showed me the airplane ticket he had procured and as he did so I thought, *"This really is happening. I'm going home."* I was numb. I was speechless. *"I'M GOING HOME!"* I shouted over and over in my head. I must have looked like a complete idiot as I stood there without further comment. What had happened caught me so off guard that I didn't know what to say or do. Whatever it was, I didn't want to jeopardize what I had just been told, so I thought, *"Don't say anything. Wait."*

Jamal asked me if I had something to wear for the trip home. I told him that I did—in my suitcases—but that most likely everything was quite musty by now. In Arabic he asked the warden if it would be possible for me to get clothes from my suitcases and have someone wash them. He nodded in the affirmative.

Jamal and Nicholas told me that my passport would be in order and would be given to me as I boarded the aircraft. They also assured me that they would meet me at the airport the following night to turn over a few things to me. I asked that they contact Tom and have him join them, if possible.

Shortly thereafter, another policeman, whom I had met several times before, was summoned by the warden. When he arrived, I was escorted to the area where I had put my street clothes into a gunny sack the first morning of my stay at Al Wathba. The officers had already found my bag and they handed over the pants, the shirt, and the socks that I was wearing the night I was arrested. It was like being reunited with old friends.

From there we went to the area where inmates' suitcases were stored. Mine were coated in sand and dust from the many sandstorms we had had over the time I was incarcerated. I went through them, selected some clothes, and then we moved on to the laundry where the people told us my things would be washed by noon the following day.

The policeman who escorted me back to my block was very talkative, telling me over and over that he wanted my help in getting to America. This was an officer who had never before shown any touch of civility toward me but who now, like many other policemen, wanted to be my best friend. Back at the block several awaited my return and were eager for any news that I might have for them. When I told them I was going home, word spread like wildfire. A breakthrough. Someone was going home. And, thank God, *I* was the one!

The emotional roller coaster was at work again as everyone speculated as to who would be released next and how many would follow. Would it be everyone? Would it be drug dealers as well as drug users? I didn't tell anyone that only about four hundred would be released from the entire prison.

My Lebanese friend Samir, who had several months earlier been sentenced to fifteen years for possession of a large quantity of drugs with intent to distribute, came to me and asked what I knew. Deep in my heart I thought that he likely wouldn't be released, but I couldn't tell him that. All I could do was say that I didn't know any details and I gave him a hug for comfort. Knowing that I was leaving, he cried.

The rest of that day and evening I spent organizing my papers, clothes, and books. I gave my magazines and some other books to friends, and exchanged addresses and telephone numbers with those with whom I would like to keep in touch. Some of the people with whom I was closest still had ten or more years to go on their sentences.

I had been told that my flight would leave about 1:30 a.m. the following morning and that the guards would come for me right after dinner to process me out of the prison. That gave me time to go to my class and to the library where I got the chance to say goodbye to my friends and students. It was July 4, 2001 and many who were aware of the significance of that day for Americans commented about the irony of the timing of my release. There were some very sobering moments as we hugged and wished each other well, fully knowing that we likely would never see each other again.

After lunch I couldn't sleep as I normally did in the afternoon. I took my last shower at Al Wathba and then put on blue jeans and a button down shirt—things I hadn't worn in almost three years. It was all so American. Many of my block mates commented on my attire and I felt like a new man. I'm sure the change in appearance wasn't just the effect of a change of clothes, but went far beyond to my facial expression that must have registered genuine relief.

I began the long wait for 6 p.m. when I expected to be escorted to the administrative area for release processing.

52

Goodbye to Al Wathba

AT 3 P.M. ON JULY 4, I GOT WORD that the police were waiting at the front gate to escort me to the holding area pending my release. I gathered up my belongings and tied them in a bed sheet. Some of my cell mates carried my things to the front for me, and as soon as my blankets were rolled up, there was a shift in sleeping positions. My spot was immediately claimed. I had had a coveted corner, and there had been jockeying for my place in the room ever since the announcement of my release. Usually choice locations were given by seniority and not by length of sentence.

As soon as I could, I visited the other rooms to say a personal goodbye to those who were closest to me. There were hugs, some tears, and well-wishing on both sides. Any joy I felt at leaving Block 10 was mitigated by the sadness I felt at leaving my friends behind. I prayed that their release would soon follow.

I was escorted downstairs to turn in my four blankets and the two sets of prison garb that had been assigned to me when I had checked in to Al Wathba. Coincidentally, the policeman in charge of the counter that afternoon was the one who had checked me in thirty-three months earlier. Mohammed, a Mauritanian, was regarded as one of the nicest policemen at Al Wathba, and he and I had had conversations in French on numerous occasions during my stay. I wished him well.

From there we crossed the courtyard that separates the prisoner wings from the main administration area. I was escorted for the last time to the front desk where a security guard checked my belongings. Again, I was extremely fortunate because the person doing the check was a Filipino whom I had come to know over the years. It was he who most often had checked us on our way to the visiting area and when returning to our cells after meals. He had never found anything on me, and as a friendly gesture, he merely glanced at my books and notes knowing full well that there were likely things in them that should have been censored. What I had expected to be a difficult part of the release process was not a problem. I was one step closer to going home.

Next, I was escorted into the room where my suitcases were stored and where I had handed over my personal belongings. Foreign currencies, my wristwatch, a ring, my wallet and credit cards were handed over to me. My American and Canadian passports were given to the policeman who stood watch over the proceedings. Another step closer to home!

I was then taken to a large holding room for those going to the airport. I met a few other people who had already been processed, and over the next couple of hours our group grew to a total of seven. I used the time to repack my bags, and fortunately, all my books and notes fit into them. Once that was done, I sat and waited hoping that the rest of the night would go as smoothly.

Everyone else in the room was shackled and handcuffed, but I was neither. Once more I was fortunate because I had earned a good reputation while at Al Wathba. I had met most of the guards on duty that night several times during my stay, and for whatever reason, they decided I was not a security risk.

Damn right I wasn't! Why would I flee? Who in their right mind would want to run away and hide out in Abu Dhabi? I was going home to my version of civilization and I wasn't going to do anything to jeopardize that.

After several hours, the heavy outer door to the room swung open and we were told to bring our things and follow the guards. This was it! I was leaving Al Wathba! *Oh, God, please don't let anything go wrong.*

We were escorted to a waiting police bus at the curb in front of the administrative wing. There were already several Filipino women prisoners and female guards on the bus, so altogether it looked as if there would be thirteen of us making the trip to the airport. I decided to head for a back seat and took a place in the last row.

Eventually everyone and his baggage was loaded on board and we proceeded to the front gate. After some minor scrutiny by the guards we were given the nod to head to the airport. It was now very dark in the desert as we pulled out the front gate. I was ecstatic knowing that I was going home, but anxious that something still could go wrong. As we pulled out onto the highway and started down the hill from Al Wathba prison, I turned to get one final glimpse of the place where I had spent the last thirty-three months of my life. I was stunned at what I saw.

I will never forget that image. There, sitting low in the sky directly over the foreboding desert fortress with all its floodlights and sentry lookout stations, was one of the beautiful full moons that had been so meaningful to me during my stay. Tears came to my eyes. It was God's way of telling me that He had indeed been with me during all the trying times, and that much goodness would come my way. *Thank you, God.* After staring in stunned silence and recording that image in my permanent memory, I turned toward the front of the bus and the future that awaited me.

Tom had gotten word of my release and was hoping to meet me at the airport with the Embassy staff. He had written just a day earlier to my family:

> *Praise the Lord! It finally is happening. I did get a call from Jamal informing me of Paul's release on the 4th. He did say I would be able to go to the airport and at least wave him good-bye (a brotherly hug would be better, but we'll see). Will write more when I hear more.*

At the airport we disembarked the bus and were ordered to put our bags in luggage carts for the walk to the check-in area. The women had the biggest bags and boxes, so I helped load their belongings onto the carts and guided them the three hundred yards to the check-in. This was a special area not used by the public, and one by one, our bags were tagged and placed on the airplanes along with those of the other passengers. I was at the end of the line because my flight was scheduled to be the last to leave. Everyone else was heading East and their departure would be within a few hours. Flights to the West usually left after midnight to connect with early morning flights in Amsterdam, London, and Frankfurt.

When it came time to check my bags, I was informed that my flight wasn't confirmed yet, and that I would have to wait. Everyone else was escorted to the two holding cells: one for the women and one for the men. One guard stayed with me until my bags could be checked in. When that was accomplished without a hitch, I was led to the holding cell where three other men released from Al Wathba remained. They told me that their plane would be leaving within the hour, and they were soon called for their flights and led away. I was by myself and my plane wasn't scheduled to leave for three more hours.

I couldn't sleep. I couldn't sit still. And the concrete benches were hard and uncomfortable. While I waited, I couldn't help thinking about a story that one of my friends from the library had told me. Apparently, he had been waiting for his flight home when a guard came to inform him that he would not be leaving. He was returned to Al Wathba to serve more time. And I still wasn't out of their jurisdiction.

About 11 p.m. a guard came to the door and motioned for me to follow him. It was too early to go meet my flight, so what was happening? I was escorted out into the parking area and there I was greeted by Tom, Jamal, and Nicholas. There was nothing between us but empty space, and I ran to give them all a hug much to the surprise of the guard. My longest and hardest hug, however, was for Tom, my angel. It was an emotional meeting insofar as I would not be seeing him for a while and there were so many things for which I wanted to thank him.

Jamal handed me some letters and notes that were in my file and I thanked him and Nicholas for standing by me for those thirty-three months. Those moments in the parking lot seemed surreal because I was leaving one world and soon would be entering another. My emotions were heightened by the fear that something could yet go wrong and I would be heading back to Al Wathba.

After my friends left, I was escorted back to my cell by the guard. On the way he asked me if I remembered him. I didn't. He told me he was the guard who had taken me in the truck to the police station the night of my arrest. Then it hit me that he was the bastard who had taken me on that ill-fated ride that first night. I had come full circle in this ordeal. I said little to him and was put back in my cell to continue waiting.

Time moved slowly. The hour for my flight had come and gone. Had something gone wrong? Eventually the guard came to my cell and told me he had bad news for me.

Oh, God! Please don't let them take me back there flashed through my mind as I waited for the news.

"Your flight has been delayed one hour. I will come for you in a few minutes."

The plane is late. That's all it is. I'm still going home. I breathed a sigh of relief as my heart raced with expectation.

A half hour later the guard returned with the key to my cell. He motioned for me to come and bring my bag. I followed him through the underground labyrinth of the Abu Dhabi airport and eventually we climbed a stairwell. At the top of the stairs we passed through a door into the concourse of the airport with all the other departing passengers. He motioned for me to follow him and we headed toward the gate for the departing KLM flight. He pushed to the front of the queue for check in, and abruptly thrust my boarding pass at the check-in clerk demanding a receipt to give his superiors. Everyone was stunned at his rudeness and must have been wondering why I had a police escort. We proceeded down the gangway to the aircraft, again bypassing those waiting in line to board. At the doorway to the airplane the flight attendant verified the information on my boarding pass and passport. The policeman turned to me, gave me the documents, and motioned for me to get on. I didn't argue. As I entered the aircraft, I looked back and saw him standing there to ensure I didn't walk away. Fat chance!

The 747 appeared to be taking on a full load that night. From seat 14H my mind flashed back thirty-three months to the last time I had seen 'regular' people traveling. None of those on the plane tonight had a clue about what I had just gone through.

I stowed my bag, took my seat, fastened my seat belt, and held my breath. I was still under the jurisdiction of the Abu Dhabi police so anything could happen. Eventually, though, all the passengers were on board and pre-flight announcements were made. I didn't comprehend any of it. Then we began to move. Slowly we backed up, and once the tug was removed, we began to taxi forward. My heart again started racing.

We stopped.

It's okay, Paul. They're just waiting for clearance to the active runway.

Then we moved onto the runway and with all engines at full thrust we taxied down the runway. And then rotation. We were off the ground. It was 2:28 a.m. local time.

On monitors in the front of the cabin passengers could watch the progress of the flight as we flew through Saudi airspace and westward toward Amsterdam. At 2:57 a.m. we crossed out of the UAE. I was actually on my way home!

53

Freedom

BECAUSE WE WERE FLYING EARLY IN THE morning, most people took the opportunity to sleep in preparation for what lay ahead after arriving in Amsterdam. But sleep was not something I wanted to do. Just as I had needed to pinch myself after being arrested one thousand and one days prior to this flight, I now had to do the same as I headed away from Abu Dhabi. Several hours earlier I had been locked up in a cell; here on the plane I was still cramped in a small space, but no guards watched my every move.

I stared out the window, anxious that at any minute the airplane might bank and head back to Abu Dhabi. There was nothing to see in the night sky but blackness. I watched the monitor at the head of the cabin where the location of our aircraft was tracked on a map. As much as I wanted to believe that what I was watching was real, I had a gnawing suspicion that this was all a hoax, not unlike stories I had seen on "Mission Impossible." Yet, as the flight continued, my anxiety lessened.

Eventually the cabin lights came on and a breakfast was served. This was my first non-prison food in thirty-three months. The usual bland airline orange juice tasted like nectar from the gods and I savored every sip. What was served afterwards I don't remember because I couldn't eat it. I struggled with the uneasy feeling in the pit of my stomach that something could still go wrong and I might end up back at Al Wathba. *Would there be police waiting to arrest me at Schiphol? Would the plane still turn around?* Those feelings may seem absurd now, but, after having been confined for so long a period, my fears didn't go away quickly. I trusted no one but myself.

Finally, the pilot announced that we were to prepare for our landing in Amsterdam, and as the morning light filtered across the sky, I could see that we really were near this wonderful city. The fleeting thought crossed my mind that it would be truly ironic if the freedom for which I had waited so eagerly would be wiped out by a crash landing and my death.

As we taxied to our gate I still harbored the fear that there would be police waiting for me. I joined the crowd filing off the plane and anxiously walked up the ramp to the terminal. As I approached the waiting area, my eyes scanned the crowd like a spy taking in his surroundings. There were no police! There were no guards!

I walked onto the concourse and stood for a moment. I was on my own. There was no one to tell me what to do. People scurried in every direction. I heard announcements for flights to worldwide destinations.

Paul was free! Paul was free!

Thank you, God.

Although we had left an hour late from Abu Dhabi, we arrived in Amsterdam less than twenty minutes behind schedule. This left me with about seven hours before my flight left for Toronto. I walked through the concourse slowly taking in the everyday scenes around me: mothers tending cranky babies; couples eating in the restaurants; people shopping at the various stores and kiosks; electric carts ferrying passengers to their gates or transporting luggage to its destination; businessmen racing to catch their flights. The airport was throbbing with people coming from and going to all parts of the world. I saw a computer bar where you could log on to the internet, so I took the opportunity to send one e-mail to my friend Dean in Boston. I knew he would forward it to everyone else. At 7:04 Amsterdam time on July 5 I wrote:

```
"Arrived Amsterdam Schiphol a few min-
utes ago. Very tired but glad to be out of
that place. Will call you soon."
```

I wanted to be outside in the open air, so I decided to catch the train to Central Station in Amsterdam. I stowed my carry-on bag in a storage locker and walked to the concourse where trains departed. In a way I was not sure that I could cope with all that was happening. After all, I had been told what to do day and night for thirty-three months. There were no shouts of "Yalla, Yalla." (Arabic for "Come, come quickly.")

I had been to Schiphol many times before and my first impression was that nothing had changed since my last visit several years earlier. Everything was just where it always had been. Even the trains! I boarded my train to Amsterdam and took a window seat facing in the direction that I was traveling. I wanted to see everything coming and had no interest in seeing where I had been. This was a new era in my life and I intended to absorb each moment in its entirety.

The fifteen-minute ride to Central Station was uneventful. For most others the activities outside our train were likely a repetition of what they experienced every day. But the passing glimpses of traffic, people, buildings, and sky were breathtaking for me; I was like a blind person whose sight had been restored and was seeing every movement for the first time.

Shortly, we arrived at Central Station and I joined the throngs of people heading up the stairs toward the daylight. It was a bit reminiscent of the crowds at Al Wathba lining up whenever we went for meals or other organized activity. But there were no guards shouting orders or giving directions. I reached the top and headed toward the exit to the street.

In seconds I was outside. There was activity everywhere. But I was alone under the sky and I could do whatever I wanted. I was free!

Thank God Almighty. I'm free! I'm free!

In front of me was downtown Amsterdam, a place I had visited many times. But this time it looked more enticing than it ever had before. I was on my own and had about five hours to do anything I wanted.

So I began to walk. I looked at the people around me more intently than I ever had before. Every shop window caught my interest. Every sound and smell and sight was exhilarating. My senses were vibrant, drinking in my surroundings. I felt taller. I felt alive—as if I had come back from a living death. I walked and walked, crisscrossing the heart of the city as if I had never been there before. At one point I stopped at a little bakery and bought a cappuccino and a ham and cheese stuffed croissant. While I watched the sights and people pass by, I savored every sip and bite. The realization that I was free of my shackles was awesome.

Periodically, I caught myself looking back over my shoulder just to make sure there weren't police stalking me. It surprised me to know I was still paranoid about that. I was also surprised to realize that, despite the circumstances, I felt ashamed that I had spent time in prison. But as the morning wore on, I began to wear my new-found freedom like an old familiar shirt, and though I hadn't slept for more than twenty-four hours, I felt more and more energized as the day wore on. Mentally I kept repeating, *Paul, you are free. You are free!*

The hours passed quickly and soon I had to get the train back to Schiphol. I allowed myself a little extra time so I could take a shower before boarding my plane for Toronto. The shower was a catharsis as I scrubbed and scrubbed the years of grime and grit from my body. Every step I took that day brought me closer to a normal life. I was able to do those things that had been denied, and to push thoughts of Al Wathba to the back of my mind. I began to look more and more to the future as I let the painful past slip away.

The flight to Toronto was packed, and since my reservation was booked at the last minute, I ended up sitting on an aisle seat right next to one of the galleys. My aisle mates were two women; one going to visit relatives in Toronto and the other an employee with the Canadian Department of Defense. Both were very friendly and it wasn't long into the flight before the conversation got around to my incarceration. They both found my story fascinating, and in telling it to them I found myself better able to deal with the fact that I had been put away for thirty-three months. I have found that talking about what happened to me has helped me deal with the injustice that I suffered.

Coincidentally, the lady from the DOD was a psychologist who worked with returning service men and women after six-month stints outside of Canada. She explained that most persons needed some counseling to help with their readjustment to re-entry into a former life after being away for long periods of time. That surprised me because I felt okay with what had happened to me. A long time earlier I had accepted my ordeal as a part of my life, and had learned valuable things from it. I didn't feel that I needed any counseling, but she reassured me that it would be perfectly normal if I felt a need to seek it after my return. Once again, I believed that the hand of God was at work in my life, for on my own I couldn't have orchestrated such a perfect traveling companion for that portion of my return home. The more I talked the more my self esteem improved and I felt confident about getting back to the 'real' world. Sleep eluded me as conversation and thoughts of the future flashed across my mind. As the distance between the plane and Abu Dhabi increased, so too the tension I had felt decreased as we neared my destination. I relaxed more and more. I now looked forward to seeing my brother Richard and his family in Toronto.

The flight to Toronto went smoothly and we landed at Pearson Airport at 4:10 in the afternoon. As usual the lines to clear immigration and customs were long. As I waited with my American passport in hand, I wondered what questions I would be asked and what I would say. Since I had been deported from the UAE, there was supposed to be a cancellation of my visa, but I couldn't find that anywhere on my passport. My ten-year UAE visa was unmarked so perhaps they had not blacklisted me at all. Perhaps there was another mark known only to customs officials. If so, I was afraid that they would see it and start asking questions that would delay my entry into the country.

But everything went smoothly and I was admitted into Canada. After clearing customs, I moved to the area where arriving passengers were greeted by friends and family, and as was the case whenever I had arrived in Toronto, there was a mob pressing against one another, trying to get the first glimpse of loved ones. As I searched through the crowd, I saw Richard's son waving his arms frantically. I headed in that direction.

Richard and his wife, Elaine, and their children, Jason and Andrea, were there to greet me. Elaine handed me flowers and I was smothered with hugs and kisses. This was an emotional time and it felt wonderful to be back among family. I could tell that they were somewhat surprised at my appearance. Because I had lost weight and had the chalky-white look of someone who had not been in the sun for a long time, I did look emaciated and drawn. Otherwise my spirit was strong and I looked forward to catching up on all that had happened during the past thirty-three months.

Without incident we drove to their home. My journey back to normalcy had begun.

I was free. The ordeal was over.

Thank you, God.

Tom wrote his last e-mail to Richard informing him of what had happened the evening of my departure. Entitled "Thank God" he wrote:

> This will be my last paragraph in the 'Paul in Prison' chapter of our lives. Future chapters will be brighter, I'm sure. Thank God, again. There was no way I wasn't going to be at the airport regardless of whether I got to see him or not. I got there about 3 hours prior to flight time and then called Jamal and he said they would be there in 30 minutes and I could be with them when they brought Paul out of the holding cell to give him money, etc. That part worked just fine.
>
> I was able to greet him with a big hug and did converse for about 10 minutes. It was one of the highlights of the year for me. I was never so happy to see someone leave this place.
>
> It has been a blessing that God has given me to be able to fill you in on Paul's happenings and to relay to him all that is going on in yours and the extended family's lives. I probably know more about your family than I do my own.
>
> God bless you all.

And God bless you, too, Tom!

54

The Journey Back

RICHARD AND ELAINE WERE MOST gracious in allowing me to stay with them as long as I liked. I didn't know where I would live or what I would do, and it would take me a while to sort that out in my mind. Before I did anything, however, I had two objectives: to thank those who had stood by me during my ordeal, and to try to help a few of my friends still in Al Wathba.

One of my first calls was to Mary McGuire, who had done so much to lift my spirits during those dark days in prison. Although she thought she had done little, the goodness and thoughtfulness she demonstrated throughout that time was in total contrast to the way the police and prison officials dealt with those of us in their charge. She seemed surprised that I had contacted her and felt she simply had carried out a mission to help me, even though we had never met. We never did get together because she neither wanted, nor expected, any thanks. Her reaction was just like Tom's: "It was the Christian thing to do."

How she and Tom came into my life still amazes me. No one pushed them into doing what they did for me. I will never forget these wonderful people who stood by me!

Susanne and Jennifer were next on my list, and it was wonderful reconnecting with both of these women who are so important to me. I knew all along that during ordeals like this, it is often more difficult for those who care about you to weather the storm, since they can only imagine what living under such horrible conditions must be like. It was a tearful reunion over the telephone, but

I assured them I was okay and told them how much I appreciated their support.

Once word of my release became known, Jim Garrett sent out an e-mail to my friends and acquaintances to let them know the good news:

> GREAT NEWS!! Paul Ciceri is out of prison and with his brother in Canada. For whatever reason, the powers that be in the UAE decided to release Paul early (three years would have been in October).
>
> Evidently Paul did not know he was getting out until near the first of July. The authorities are so fickle that he was not sure until the plane actually departed. According to Paul people have been released only to be dragged back from the airport! I understand a guard actually told Paul that he had bad news . . . but the news was that the plane was an hour late leaving.
>
> Paul is probably going to sleep a couple of days to allow his body (and head) to recover from the long plane trip. I am sure he will start contacting everyone. His plans are uncertain at this point as you can imagine.
>
> I have no further information but we need to start thinking about the BIG welcome home party when Paul gets back to Orlando. Please spread the word about Paul's release.
>
> I'm sure he will have a lot of interesting stories to tell . . . including a lesson on what freedom should mean to all of us. Somehow his getting out on the 4th of July seems really appropriate!

There were so many other people to contact that I chose e-mail to make the fastest connection:

> On July 4th I received a special gift—my freedom! I am in Toronto and will be here for a while working on keeping some promises I made to help some of my friends still in Al Wathba prison.
>
> You people are incredible—it was a long 33 months—1001 days to be exact—all that you did to keep up my spirits and support me through a difficult time will never be forgotten.
>
> It is a rather strange feeling—the one of freedom—but I think I'm doing okay readjusting to life here again. There are so many stories to tell and things to do. . . .
>
> This is rather generic but I will be in touch with as many as possible personally over the next several weeks.
>
> My love and heartfelt thanks to all of you.

After the first week I made a visit via Amtrak to see my friend Dean in Boston. It gave me an opportunity to personally thank him for his support during the many months I had been at Al Wathba. I had never spent any time in Boston and enjoyed walking the downtown area and visiting some of the historical sites with him.

After I returned to Toronto, Richard, Elaine and I went to Windsor to visit Ann and Lloyd Fox. They were dear friends of our parents and had been very supportive of me during my ordeal. To my delight my older daughter, Jennifer, met us there and we had a wonderful reunion. Richard and Elaine returned to Toronto and I went with Jennifer to her home in Indiana. This gave me the chance to get my car that Jenny had taken care of while I was away.

Then it was back to Toronto for another visit with Richard and Elaine. I stayed there until early August when we had a family picnic for all the relatives on my mother's side of the family. That gave me a chance to see many people at one time and thank them all personally for their encouragement and support.

At this point, I had decided to head to Florida to see Susanne and all my friends there. My first stop, though, was to Edison, New Jersey to visit with Susan and Charles, executives with ELS Language Centers. They too had supported me throughout my prison ordeal and I wanted to express my thanks personally. Then I meandered down the east coast taking time to see the Atlantic shore at Rehoboth Beach and then on to Atlanta. I visited with Rita Holt, a cousin of my good friend Rick who had died while I was in Al Wathba. She had taken in Rick's cat, "Ralph," keeping a promise she had made to Rick some time earlier. Strangely, when Ralph saw me, it was as though he knew who I was. I really believe that Ralph, did remember me, and in his eyes I saw hope that maybe I had brought Rick back with me. All during my visit he watched my every move and stayed close beside me.

Eventually I made my way to Orlando and a tearful reunion with Susanne. Even though we had been divorced for almost twenty years, we had remained good friends and had always been supportive of each other. She had done much to bolster my spirits during my incarceration that I will never be able to forget her love and support. I stayed with her for a few weeks while I visited with other friends in the Orlando area.

After a while I accepted an offer from my friend Jon Reames to share his home. Jon and his new friend Juan Carlos made me feel comfortable and accepted, and again I realized how extremely fortunate I was to have such good friends. It was during this period that I placed an ad in the local newspaper for my massage services so I could earn some money to support myself.

By now Tom and Jan Hennessy had relocated to Florida only a few hours west of Orlando. One Sunday Susanne and I drove over to meet them for a wonderful day recalling all that had occurred the previous few years and the happenstance that had brought us together. What a special reunion that was!

Three months had passed since my release from Al Wathba and I felt that I needed to move on and fulfill several resolves to properly put closure on that time. One of those was to write a book about my experiences. But where? Orlando? California? Canada?

Key West! I had visited there many times and was always taken by its laid-back charm and its attraction to artists and authors, most notably Ernest Hemingway and Tennessee Williams. I would never be in their class, but perhaps their influence might rub off on me. So I headed to Key West, the end of the U.S. Highway 1 and the southernmost point in the continental United States. There I found a quaint, comfortable place to stay, a perfect spot to contemplate and pursue my writing.

Key West has remained my home and now that my book is complete my thoughts turn to my next adventure. Will it be here, on the high seas, or somewhere else in the world? Only time will tell, but wherever it is I am content to know that my thoughts are on paper and the time spent in prison fades into the shadows.

The first spring after my release I attended a Marlin's baseball game in Miami. It didn't have the hype or the last-inning heroics of that Yankees–Pirates game years earlier, but I was participating in life again and it was wonderful!

Addendum A

Photographs and Documentation

Addendum A: Photographs and Documentation 337

Paul Ciceri at ELS Language Centers

Susanne and Jennifer

Left to right: Tom, Susanne, Jennifer, and Jan

Paul in Athens, Greece

ADDENDUM A: PHOTOGRAPHS AND DOCUMENTATION 339

Left to right: Paul, Richard, Dad, Peter

Receipt from Athens, Greece hotel

Boarding pass for the flight home

" بسم الله الرحمن الرحيم "

دولة الإمارات العربية المتحدة

وزارة العـــدل والشؤون الإسلامية والأوقاف

دائرة القضاء الشرعي

محكمة أبوظبي الشرعية الابتدائية

" بــــــــم الحكــــم "

الصادر في يوم ١٥ من شهر محرم ١٤٢٠ هـ الموافق ١ / ٥ / ١٩٩٩ م

نحن قضاة دائرة الجنايات الشرعيــة ـــ بمحكمة أبوظبي الشرعية الابتدائية

١) القاضي : عبد المعز أحمد إبراهيم — رئيساً ومقرراً

٢) القاضي : محمد عبد الرحيم خوري — عضواً

٣) القاضي : علــي الشـــاعــر — عضواً

قد نظرنا القضية رقم : (٧٠٦٧ / ٩٨) المقيدة في : ١٣ / ١ / ١٩٩٩ م

بحضور السيد : محمد صقر — وكيل النيابة

والسيد : علي عرفه — أمين السر .

الشاكــــــي : النيابة العامة :

المتهـــــــم : بول بــراين سيسـري / أمريكي

التهمــــــة : جلب مادة مخدرة (كوكايين + ماريجوانا) وحيازة مادة مخدرة (حشيش + ماريجوانا) .

الوقائــــع والأســبـــاب والمنطوق "

بعد الإطلاع على الأوراق وسماع المرافعة والمداولة :

اتهمت النيابة العامة :

بــول براين سيـــسري / أمريكي الجنسية / ٥٣ سنة / موقوف :

لأنه من يوم ٧ / ١٠ / ١٩٩٨ م وتاريخ سابق عليه بدائرة أبوظبي : ـــ

١- جلب مادة مخدرة [كوكايين + ماريجوانا] لداخل الدولة بالمخالفة لأحكام القانون .

٢- حاز مادة مخدرة [حشيش + الماريجوانا] بقصد التعاطي بالمخالفة لأحكام القانون .

- وطلبت عقابه طبقا لأحكام الشريعة الإسلامية الغراء والمـواد ١ ، ١/٦ ، ٣٩ ، ١/٤٨ ، ١/٥٦ ، ٦٣ ، ٦٥ من القانون الاتحادي رقم ١٤ لسنة ١٩٩٥ في شأن مكافحة المواد المخدرة والمؤثرات العقلية والبنديـن

يتبع ص ٢

List of Charges, Page 1

دولة الإمارات العربية المتحدة :
وزارة العـــدل
محكمة أبوظبي الشرعية الابتدائية :
دائـــرة الجنــــــايات :

" تابع الوقائع والأسباب " ص ٥ ....
في القضية الجنائية رقم : ٧٠٦٧/٩٨ م

وبالتالي فإنه لا يلزم لأجرائه أدلة كافيه أو إذن سابق من سلطة التحقيق أو رضاء به ممن يحصل تفتيشه [محكمة التمييز — دبي — جلسة ١٩٩٢/١١/١٣ الطعن رقم ٩٠ لسنة ١٩٩٣ (جزاء)] ــــ .

وقد ثبت للمحكمة من إطلاعها على محضر إثبات الحالة المحرر بدائرة الجمارك أنه أثناء النوبة الليلية يوم الأربعاء ٩٨/١٠/٧ وأثناء قدوم طيران الخليج رحلة رقم ٠٠٢ القادمة من البحرين وعند التفتيش على المسافر (المتهم) وجد بحوزته المضبوطات الآتية .

(١) عدد واحد زجاجة صغيرة بنية اللون بها مادة بيضاء يشتبه بأنها كوكايين الوزن الإجمالي للزجاجة مــع المادة خمسة جرامات وقد وجدت بداخل حقيبة أدوات الحلاقة .

(٢) أدوات التعاطي وهي أـ أوراق لف ب ــ سكين عليه أثر حريق ج ــ عدد ١ شمعة د ــ عدد أنبـــوب صغير يستخدم للشم .

(٣) عدد ٩٥ حبة دواء مشتبه .

(٤) عدد ٣ علب بها سائل متعدد الألوان مشتبه به .

(٥) عدد ١ جواز سفر كندي غير مستخدم .

ملاحظة : س ما هي المادة التي تحملها ــ ح ــ هي مادة الكوكايين . ..

وبوصف المضبوطات بمعرفة قسم الأدلة الجنائية فرع السموم والمخدرات ــ وبفحصها :

(١) عدد ١ جراب جلدي رصاصي اللون بداخله زجاجة بنية اللون صغيرة الحجم ذاتـــه غطـــاء بلاستيكي أسود اللون له مشبك أسود اللون على شكل ملعقة صغيرة وبداخل الزجاجة مسحوق أبيض اللون يــزن صافياً [٠,٦٥ جرام] فحصت مخبرياً واستهلكت بأكملها في الفحص هـو عبـارة عـن مسحوق الكوكايين المخدر .

(٢) شفره معدنية ذهبية اللون مدون عليها باللغة الأجنبية عبـــارة [MADE IN U.S.A] تـم فحصـها مخبرياً ــ عليها آثار لمادة الكوكايين المخدرة .

(٣) أنبوب معدني ذهبي اللون ــ عليه آثار لمادة الكوكايين المخدرة .

(٤) سكينة سويسرية حمراء اللون متعددة الأغراض على نصل أحدهما أثار عليها آثار لمـادة الحشيش المخدرة .

يتبع ص ٦ ...

List of Charges, Page 2

LETTER		PRONOUNCIATION		FIRST	MIDDLE	LAST	
ﺍ		A	ALIF	ﺍ	ل	ﻼ	ى
ب		B	BAA	بـ	ـبـ	ب	ب
ت		T	TAA	تـ	ـتـ	ت	ت
ث		TH	THAA	ثـ	ـثـ	ث	ث
ج		J	JIM	جـ	ـجـ	ج	ج
ح		H	HAA	حـ	ـحـ	ح	ح
خ		KH	KHAA	خـ	ـخـ	خ	خ
د		D	DAL	د	د	د	د
ذ		TH	THAL	ذ	ذ	ذ	ذ
ر		R	RAA	ر	ر	ر	ر
ز		Z	ZAA	ز	ز	ز	ز

Learning Arabic

Possessive	Français		Español		Italiano		Aleman	
	m	f	s.	p.	m.	f.	m./n.	f./plu.
my	mon mes	ma mes	mi	mis	mio miei	mia mie$	mein	meine
your (f.)	ton tes	ta tes	tu	tus	tuo tuoi	tua tue	dein	deine
your (p.)			su	sus	suo suoi	sua sue	Ihr	Ihre
his	son ses	sa ses			suo suoi	sua sue	sein	seine
her							ihr	ihre
our	notre nos	notre nos	nuestr(o/a) nuestr(os/as)		nostro nostri	nostra nostre	unser	unsere
your (f.)	votre vos	votre vos	vuestr(o/a) vuestr(os/as)		vostro vostri	vostra vostre	euer	eure
your (p.)			su	sus			Ihr	Ihre
their	leur leurs	leur leurs			il loro i loro	la loro le loro	ihr	ihre

To avoid am-
biguity can use
de él, ella, -os
-as, Vd., Vds.

Su amigo =
El amigo
de ellos.

All preceded by
article except
member of
family singular

loro always
has article.

Language Book

> 16/5/99
>
> سورة الكهف
> SURAT AL-KAHF
> (The Cave)
>
> [Arabic verses 1-8 from Surat Al-Kahf]
>
> 1) Praise be to Allah who has sent down to his slave the book and has not placed it in any crookedness.
> 2) Straight, to give warning of a severe punishment from him and to give good news to the believers who do righteous deeds that they shall have a fair reward.
> 3) They shall live therein for ever.
> 4) And to warn those who say Allah has begotten a son.
> 5) No knowledge have they of such a thing, nor had their fathers. Mighty is the word that comes out of their mouths. They say nothing but a lie.

Islam Class Example

بسم الله الرحمن الرحيم

امتحان للطلبة المسلمين الجدد

الاسم : PAUL CICERI .... الجنسية : U.S.A. AMERICAN .... الدرجة : ....

السـؤال الاول : –

س١ : عدد أركان الاسلام الخمسة ؟
1- SHAHADA - ONLY ONE GOD (ALLAH) * MOHAMMED IS HIS MESSENGER
2- FIVE MANDATORY DAILY PRAYERS
3- FASTING (RAMADAN)
4- ZAKAT (CHARITY)
5- HAJJ (PILGRIMAGE)

س٢ : عدد اركان الايمان الستة ؟
1- ONLY ONE GOD, ALLAH
2- ALL THE MESSENGERS
3- ANGELS
4- HOLY BOOKS (QURAN, TORAH, NT, PSALMS OF DAVID)
5- JUDGEMENT DAY
6- FATE (GOOD & EVIL)

س٣ : ماهي مكانة النبي عيسى عليه السلام في الاسلام ؟
IN ISLAM, JESUS IS A MESSENGER OF ALLAH. HIS BIRTH WAS DIVINE (NO EARTHLY FATHER) AND HE HAS NOT DIED BUT IS IN HEAVEN. HE WILL RETURN TO JUDGE US. HE DOES NOT RULE WITH ALLAH NOR HE IS THE SON OF GOD.

س٤ : ماهي اوقات الصلاة في اليوم الواحد ؟
FAJR, DHUHUR, ASR, MAGHRIB, ISHA

اقلب الصفحة . . .

Islam Test Page 1

السؤال الثاني : –

اختر ثلاث اسئلة واجب عليها :

س١ : اكتب حديث مما تحفظ ؟

THE PROPHET MOHAMMED (PBUH) SAID " WHEN ALLAH DIVINED THE CREATION HE PLEDGED HIMSELF BY WRITING IN HIS BOOK WHICH IS LAID OUT BEFORE HIM ' MY MERCY PREVAILS OVER MY WRATH '."

س٢ : لماذا لعن الله سبحانه وتعالى اليهود ؟

WHEN THE JEWS, LED BY MOSES, FLED PERSECUTION FROM THE PHARAOH AND HIS SOLDIERS, GOD PARTED THE RED SEA TO PROVIDE THEM ESCAPE. THEN, WHEN THEY WERE SAFE THEY COMPLAINED THAT GOD LED THEM INTO NODE →

س٣ : وضح معنى السنة النبوية ؟

SUNNAH IS THE TEACHINGS, DOINGS, SAYINGS, AND HABITS OF THE PROPHET MOHAMMED.

س٤ : اذكر اسماء الكتب السماوية . . وعلى من انزل كل منها ؟

١- QURAN – MOHAMMED ✓
٢- TORAH – MOSES ✓
٣- NEW TESTAMENT – JESUS ✓
٤- PSALMS – DAVID ✓

اشراف : الانشطة الدينية

ع ص ...

Islam Test Page 2

(Relative Pronouns)
① Referring to persons or things, subj. or obj.
   que (who, which, what)
      The girl who...   La chica que...
      The car (that) he drives... Le coche que conduce.

     after a prep. refers only to (things)
      The house in which we live. La casa en que vivimos.

   quien, quienes (who, whom) ≡ only to (persons)
     after prepositions: The teacher with whom I study.
                      El professor con quien estudio.
                        The man for whom he works.
                        El hombre para quien trabaja.

     after "to be" + noun   It is Maria who has to write.
                             Es Maria quien tiene que escribir.

     after "to be" + pronoun It is he who is to blame.
                              Es él quien tiene la culpa.

   el que, la, los, las que   } (who, whom, which, that)
   el cual, la, los cuales, las cuales |
     after prepositions:
      The woman with whom he is speaking. La mujer con la que está hablando.
      The bus in which I travel. El autobus en el que viajo.
      The friends of whom we were talking. Los amigos de los cuales...

   (el que, la que, los que, las que)
     ≡ he who, she who, those who, the one (ones) who)
      The one who has just arrived is his son.
      El que acaba de llegar es su hijo.

      Those who have come are all students.
      Los que han venido son todos estudiantes.

② Referring to clause or idea
   lo que, lo cual (what, which)

   I don't understand what he says. No comprendo lo que dice.

   He hasn't arrived yet which surprises me. No ha llegado todavía
                                          lo cual me sorprende.

Spanish Grammar

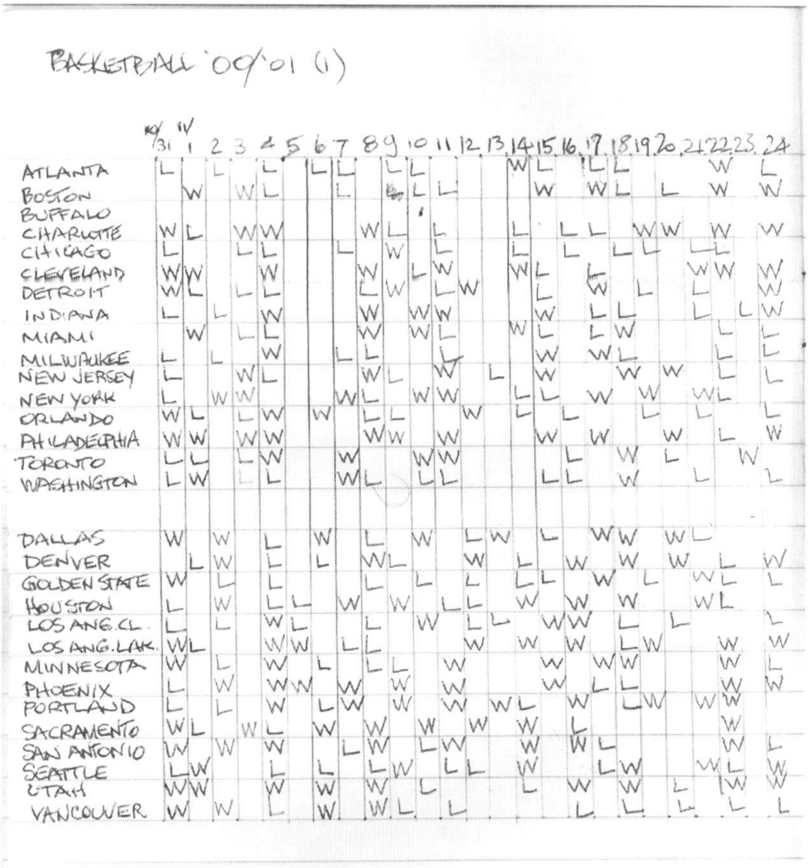

Basketball Results

Embassy of the United States of America

Abu Dhabi, United Arab Emirates

February 8, 2000

Letter from Ambassador Theodore H. Kattouf to His Highness Sheikh Dhiab bin Zayid Al-Nahyan

Your Highness:

It was a pleasure to see you on January 31 at the luncheon at His Highness Sheikh Hamdan's home, which again afforded me an opportunity to thank you for your invaluable support for our recent privatization conference, which we believe was a great success.

I would like to take this opportunity to raise again the case of Mr. Paul Ciceri, an American citizen who is presently incarcerated at Al Wathba Central Prison. I was unable to discuss this matter fully with you on January 31, but understand from my Special Assistant, Richard Olson, that you requested some additional information.

Mr. Ciceri was residing in Abu Dhabi as an English language teacher at ELS. In October 1998, while arriving home from Canada and his mother's funeral, Mr. Ciceri was arrested at Abu Dhabi Airport. Based on physical evidence and drug testing, he was charged with the possession and use of narcotics. Mr. Ciceri was tried and convicted in May 1999, receiving a sentence of four years imprisonment. With good behavior, he is due for release in October 2001.

In October 1999, in your role as Chairman of the Presidential Diwan, you were gracious enough to meet with the Embassy's Consul, Mr. Glatz, and with Mr. Ciceri's brother, Richard. Richard conveyed to you his family's plea for clemency for his brother and explained that the entire Ciceri family, as well as their close friends, believe that Paul's involvement with drugs was totally out of character. Furthermore, they are convinced that Paul has been and will be a good son, a dedicated father, and a contributing member of society. Richard asked the Diwan to consider particularly that their father is elderly and has a delicate heart condition. Paul's father would like Paul at home during his final years.

His Highness
   Sheikh Dhiab bin Zayid Al-Nahyan
     Chairman, Presidential Diwan,
      Abu Dhabi.

I do not seek here to minimize the seriousness of Mr. Ciceri's offense. The UAE's efforts to combat drug use are consistent with U.S. interests. I would note, however, that Paul and his family, working through the Embassy, have chosen to approach UAE authorities in a quiet, diplomatic manner, to acknowledge the wrong Paul has done, and to ask for clemency.

I respectfully ask that you review the matter of clemency for Mr. Ciceri in the hope that you can find a positive decision appropriate in this case. I am grateful for your attention to this matter.

With best regards and wishes,

Sincerely,

Theodore H. Kattouf
Ambassador

ON OCTOBER 5, 1996, LATE IN THE AFTERNOON, I RETURNED TO ATHENS AND MET UP WITH MY FRIEND. SINCE WE ONLY HAD TWO DAYS LEFT IN ATHENS, HE WANTED TO GO OUT ON THE TOWN IN ATHENS. I WAS JET-LAGGED AND EMOTIONALLY TIRED FROM MOTHER'S FUNERAL. HE OFFERED ME THE REMNANTS OF SOME COCAINE HE HAD. STUPIDLY, I ACCEPTED IT. ALL THAT WAS LEFT WAS A SMALL GLASS CONTAINER WITH SOME PARTICLES ATTACHED TO THE SIDE. HE WAS GOING TO CLEAN IT BEFORE GOING HOME.

THE NEXT DAY, WE HAD A MAJOR DISAGREEMENT OVER U.S. FOREIGN POLICY RELATIVE TO THE MILITARY ACTION THE U.S. TOOK IN RESPONSE TO THE EXPLOSIONS OF OUR EMBASSIES IN AFRICA. I WAS VERY VOCAL BECAUSE I WAS UNDER THE IMPRESSION THAT A CONSULAR OFFICIAL I HAD KNOWN DURING MY DAYS IN KUWAIT HAD RECENTLY TRANSFERRED TO NAIROBI AND HE AND HIS SON WERE KILLED.

WHEN I ARRIVED AT ABU DHABI AIRPORT, THE CUSTOMS OFFICIAL SELECTED A SPECIFIC BAG OF MINE, OF THE THREE I HAD, AND WENT SPECIFICALLY TO A PLACE IN THAT BAG AND RETRIEVED THAT GLASS BOTTLE. I SUSPECT WITHOUT RESERVATION THAT MY FRIEND PUT IT THERE AND NOTIFIED THE AUTHORITIES.

SUBSEQUENT TO MY ARREST, THERE WAS AN ILLEGAL SEARCH OF MY APARTMENT DURING WHICH THE POLICE CLAIMED THEY FOUND MARIJUANA AND HASHISH. THE POLICE WOULD NOT LET ME LOOK AT THE MARIJUANA TO LET ME VERIFY THAT IT INDEED WAS MARIJUANA. THEY COULD NOT TELL ME WHERE THEY FOUND IT. THEY HAD NOT FINGERPRINTED THE CONTAINERS TO VERIFY I HAD TOUCHED THEM.

FROM THE BEGINNING, I DENIED THAT THE DRUGS WERE MINE AND I CONTINUE TO DO SO. MY CONVICTION IS BASED SOLELY ON THE POSSESSION OF 2.159 GRAMS OF COCAINE. THE SENTENCE OF FOUR YEARS IS BY FAR THE HARSHEST OF ANY GULF COUNTRY FOR THESE CIRCUMSTANCES AND THE SENTENCE COMES DIRECTLY FROM SHAYKH ZAYED, THE RULER

OF THE COUNTRY. THE JUDICIAL AND PENAL SYSTEM OF THIS COUNTRY ARE PERVERTED. I WILL ELABORATE MORE ON MY RELEASE.

I APOLOGIZE FOR ANY EMBARRASSMENT I HAVE CAUSED TO MY FAMILY AND I APPRECIATE YOUR CONTINUED SUPPORT. MY LAST TEN LETTERS TO MY FAMILY AND FRIENDS HAVE NOT BEEN SENT BY THE PRISON AUTHORITIES BUT PLEASE BE AWARE THAT I HAVE WRITTEN YOU. I KEEP YOU ALL IN MY PRAYERS AS I KNOW YOU DO ME.

AT THIS TIME, I THINK OUR BEST COURSE OF ACTION IS TO SEEK CLEMENCY. THE APPROPRIATE WAY IS TO SEND LETTERS TO HIS EXCELLENCY THE PRESIDENT SHAYKH ZAYED BIN SULTAN AL NAHYAN, PRESIDENT OF THE UNITED ARAB EMIRATES, THROUGH THE U.S. EMBASSY IN ABU DHABI. IN THESE LETTERS, YOU SHOULD EMPHASIZE DAD'S ADVANCING AGE, OUR FAMILY CLOSENESS, THE FACT THAT I HAVE NEVER BEEN ARRESTED FOR ANYTHING IN MY LIFE, AND - FROM JENNIFER - THAT I HAVE BEEN A FAITHFUL, HONEST FATHER FOR HER. PLEASE EMPHASIZE THAT I AM REPENTANT AND, WHILE IN PRISON, I HAVE BEEN TAKING ISLAM CLASSES FOUR TIMES WEEKLY.

Message Home

I HOPE TO SEE YOU ALL SOON. MY PRAYERS ARE WITH YOU.

FOR FUTURE MAIL, I HAVE BEEN MOVED TO BLOCK 8 IN THE PRISON.

END MESSAGE.

Prison ID

ADDENDUM A: PHOTOGRAPHS AND DOCUMENTATION

UNCLASSIFIED

Department of State

INCOMING TELEGRAM

ACTION

PAGE 01 ABU DH 06856 258856Z
ACTION NEA-01

INFO LOG-00 UTED-00 H-01 TEDE-00 ADS-00 NEA-00 OCS-05
     VO-03 SAS-00 /009W
     ---------------79A309 258856Z /38

R 258833Z OCT 98
FM AMEMBASSY ABU DHABI
TO SECSTATE WASHDC 9832

UNCLAS ABU DHABI 005856

A PASS

E.O. 12958: N/A
TAGS: CASC, TC (CICERI, PAUL BRIAN)
SUBJECT: CONGRESSIONAL INQUIRY

REF: CONGRESSMAN BARNEY FRANK'S LETTER DATED 10/20/98

TO: THE HONORABLE BARNEY FRANK
    MEMBER OF CONGRESS
    29 CRAFTS STREET
    NEWTON, MA 02458

DEAR MR. FRANK:

THANK YOU FOR YOUR OCTOBER 20, 1998 LETTER REGARDING THE ARREST IN THE UNITED ARAB EMIRATES (UAE) OF MR. PAUL BRIAN CICERI, A FRIEND OF YOUR FRIEND, MR. DEAN BAUER. MR. CICERI HAS SIGNED A WAIVER OF HIS RIGHT TO PRIVACY THAT ALLOWS THE EMBASSY TO PROVIDE YOU WITH INFORMATION CONCERNING HIS INCARCERATION.

MR. CICERI WAS ARRESTED AT ABU DHABI INTERNATIONAL AIRPORT ON OCTOBER 7, 1998 ON NARCOTICS CHARGES. MR. CICERI'S BROTHER, RICHARD, WHO RESIDES IN CANADA, INITIALLY REPORTED MR. CICERI AS MISSING WHEN HE WAS UNABLE TO CONFIRM THAT MR. CICERI HAD ARRIVED SAFELY BACK IN THE UAE FOLLOWING A VISIT TO CANADA. THE EMBASSY SPENT SEVERAL DAYS LOOKING FOR MR. CICERI BEFORE BEING NOTIFIED BY UAE AUTHORITIES ON OCTOBER 12 THAT HE HAD BEEN ARRESTED. A CONSULAR OFFICER VISITED MR. CICERI ON OCTOBER 14 AT AL WATHBA CENTRAL PRISON, ABOUT 25 MILES EAST OF ABU DHABI CITY. MR. CICERI WAS IN GOOD CONDITION PHYSICALLY AND EMOTIONALLY. HE DID NOT ALLEGE ANY MISTREATMENT BY THE UAE POLICE.

THE ABU DHABI PROSECUTOR'S OFFICE HAS CHARGED MR. CICERI WITH THREE CRIMES: POSSESSION, IMPORTATION, AND USE OF COCAINE. THESE CHARGES ARE BASED ON A POLICE REPORT THAT MR. CICERI WAS FOUND TO HAVE 5 GRAMS OF COCAINE IN HIS CARRY-ON LUGGAGE, AS WELL AS THE RESULTS OF LABORATORY ANALYSIS OF A URINE SAMPLE TAKEN FROM MR. CICERI BY THE UAE AUTHORITIES.

THE MINIMUM POSSIBLE SENTENCE FOR THESE CHARGES RANGES FROM 6 TO 12 YEARS OF IMPRISONMENT, PLUS A HEAVY MONETARY FINE. THERE IS NO EXTRADITION TREATY BETWEEN THE UAE AND THE UNITED STATES. IF MR. CICERI IS CONVICTED OF THESE OFFENSES, HE WILL HAVE TO SERVE A PRISON SENTENCE IN THE UAE.
NO TRIAL DATE HAS BEEN SET. IT TAKES APPROXIMATELY ONE MONTH FOR THE ABU DHABI PROSECUTOR AND THE POLICE TO COMPLETE A NARCOTICS INVESTIGATION OF THIS NATURE AND TO SCHEDULE A TRIAL. IN ADDITION, MR. CICERI'S CASE WILL BE SUBJECT TO REVIEW BY THE UAE PRESIDENTIAL COURT PRIOR TO THE BEGINNING OF A TRIAL.

THE EMBASSY ABU DHABI STAFF CONTINUES TO FOLLOW MR. CICERI'S CASE AND WE ARE IN CONTACT WITH HIS BROTHER, RICHARD, IN ONTARIO, CANADA. AS IS CUSTOMARY IN AN ARREST CASE, WE PROVIDED MR. CICERI WITH THE EMBASSY'S LIST OF LAWYERS. HE HAS SELECTED ATTORNEY IBRAHIM AL TAMIMI OF ABU DHABI, TELEPHONE: (971 2) 224-488 OR 215-588, AS HIS LAWYER. WE UNDERSTAND THAT MR. CICERI'S BROTHER, RICHARD, HAS BEEN IN CONTACT WITH MR. AL TAMIMI AND THAT

MR. AL TAMIMI IS OBTAINING A COPY OF THE CASE FILE FROM THE PROSECUTOR'S OFFICE FOR HIS INITIAL REVIEW.

PLEASE BE ASSURED THAT WE WILL FOLLOW CLOSELY MR. CICERI'S CASE, VISIT REGULARLY WITH HIM IN PRISON, MONITOR HIS HEALTH AND WELL-BEING, AND ASSIST HIM IN MAINTAINING CONTACT WITH HIS FAMILY AND HIS LEGAL COUNSEL. IF I MAY BE OF FURTHER ASSISTANCE IN THIS OR ANY OTHER MATTER, PLEASE DO NOT HESITATE TO CONTACT ME.

SINCERELY,

CHARLES L. GLATZ JR.
CONSUL
AMERICAN EMBASSY
ABU DHABI, U.A.E.

JONES

RECEIVED
OCT 26 1998
Barney Frank, M.C.
Washington, D.C.

UNCLASSIFIED

Message to Barney Frank

Hidden Information

Addendum A: Photographs and Documentation

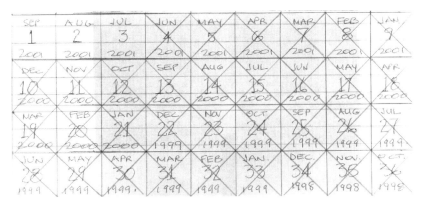

Counting Down Months

Counting Down Days

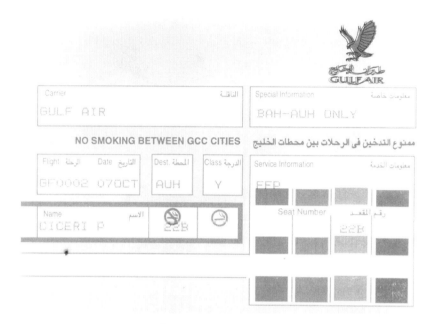

Bahrain to Abu Dhabi

Ticket Home

Addendum B

Poem: A Better Person

MORNINGS WERE A TIME OF RELATIVE CALM in the block as many people went back to sleep after breakfast. I used the time to read and study and to do some writing. Amongst my writings was a poem addressed to my family and friends that gave my feelings about my life at Al Wathba since October 7, 1998.

(Authored by Paul Ciceri, March 26 1999)

(1)

Through the bars I see the stars
  that you see
And the sun and the moon
  sometimes I see
  easily
Sometimes I strain and crane
  my neck
  to catch a glimpse
  of what I took for granted
  once
Sometimes I stare
  thinking
  maybe you are watching too
  your morning sun and my
  evening
And for a moment we are one
  again
But the patch of sky
  that I can see
I know
  is not yours to see
And then I feel alone

(2)

When I want my space
  I seek a place
  that is mine alone
but there is none
  unless I make it one in mind
  and shut the others out
Then I read
  and write
  and think
  of you and family and
  friends
And wonder why
  this is my life
But I am not alone
  the boy and youth I was is
  here
  and the man I was
  and am
  and all the memories
And I close my eyes and
  dream
  happy thoughts

(3)

Why I am here is still not
  clear
  because
  a friend does not do
  what one did to me
When I look back
  it was a simple talk
  perhaps an argument
  over why we bombed
  them
  when they blew up our
  embassies
  in Africa
  and killed a friend

Revenge he got
I am here
  he is not
  because he set me up
God says
  "The truth shall set you free"
And I am
  and will be

(4)

I think ahead with some dread
  of what could be
  but just for a moment
Because I know
  there is a reason
  for this
God knows
  and I ask
  and He tells me in His way
  to teach by example
  to be a friend
  to use all I have learned
  and to learn some more
And I am

(5)

Some people here are
  quite sincere
  but most
  are not
They yell
  and scream
  and talk too much
  and rudeness is their norm
And the nice ones
  are quiet
  educated and not
We talk and laugh
  about our lives
  the world
  our dreams
  the law
  and provide
  comfort
And when they move on
  we cry a little
More will come
I hope

(6)

From the West is to be
  blessed
  in others' eyes
  and mine
They seek me out
  and ask
  I take them home
Our place is best
  they say
  Arabs, Asians, Russians,
  all the freedom
America, America
  number one they say
  you are so nice
  and friendly
  and kind
  and honest
But that is not
  their way
They bring me tea
  I do no work
  out of respect they say
  and we are friends

(7)

Books I read fill a need
  to escape
  from here
  to another place
Where I want to be

    like Paris, like Rome
      and home
Where I am free
    to walk the streets
to have some fun
    and thrills
    and to a place
    I can be me
They come alive
    and in a way
    are more real
    than here

        (8)

To receive some mail
    here in jail
    is such a gift
I savor the moments
    of hearing from family
    and friends
    about love
    and caring

And I cry a little
    because I know what once
    was
    and then I smile
    because I know
    how blessed I am
    to have you

        (9)

But when I pray
    that is to say
    talk with God
I feel okay
    and protected
    and confident
    because He is here
    with me
And I will be home soon
    with you
    He tells me
A better person than before

Addendum C

A British View of Things

Addendum C: A British View of Things

MY BRITISH FRIEND JAMES OAKES was released from Al Wathba during the summer of 1999, and after his release, he expounded on his feelings about the UAE and life at Al Wathba in a fax that he sent to Richard Branson, the Chairman of Virgin Atlantic Group. James had met Mr. Branson and was now appealing to him for any assistance he could provide.

James wrote, in part, on August 9:

> "Approximately 40 minutes out of Abu Dhabi Al Wathba prison is in the desert on top of a hill. It was built by the Germans to accommodate approximately 900 prisoners - it actually houses about 2000. In every sense this is a Top Security prison with 3 outer perimeter electrified fences, flood lights and cameras. The construction of the prison is basically steel sheets covered in concrete. The whole complex is open to the elements.
>
> I was arrested after I left the employment of the Al Muhairy Group to go to work for another company. At the time of leaving I was in theory in debt to the company for Dirhams125,000 (Sterling 20,000) of which Dirhams 70,000 had been given to me to help pay for my eldest son's education and the loan was to have been repaid once the Franchise actually started which of course in the end it did not. The Company agreed to accept that the repayment was really a legal matter to be resolved so I agreed to give them signed checks as a guarantee on the basis that they could be used only with my authority. The Chairman, having agreed to this, then left on a shooting hunt with the Sheikhs and was involved in a car accident which resulted in a long-term stay in a hospital in Germany. In the meantime the Financial Controller of the Company, who knew the situation, decided to play a particularly vicious game and issued the check for the full amount. Under Sharia/UAE law, the fact that the check and signature were both mine was the substance of the case even though it was very obvious that I had not completed the date, payee, or amount. When the check bounced the CID were informed.

I was arrested on March 23rd and after 3 weeks in the Mina Prison I was transferred to Al Wathba. Upon arrival you are given 4 blankets and a dark blue uniform with a red stripe. Your head is then shaved and you then go through the registration procedure—ID photographs, finger prints, etc. In effect they set out to make you LOOK like a criminal even before you have been sentenced. When your ID is ready you are given it to wear. It states your name, nationality, and type of crime.

The first night at Al Wathba is spent in a transit cell which for some odd reason has 4 permanent residents already there—all are convicted transvestites/sex offenders. The following morning you are taken to one of the main blocks. I was sent to Block 3 which was very dirty with broken plumbing, cockroaches, etc. Block 3 housed 250 prisoners—it was built to house 80. There were two showers, four sinks and toilets Arabic style only. There was no air conditioning and it was already 120 degrees Fahrenheit.

I was in Block 3 for about 5 weeks before I was given a final sentence of one year after which I was moved to Block 4 in a gray uniform as a sentenced prisoner. Block 4 was much cleaner—they say because it is a permanent block that prisoners take more of an interest.

Whenever you go to the Sharia courts in Abu Dhabi you have to assemble at 5:00 in the morning prior to leaving about 8:00. You are bodily searched—leaving nothing to the imagination—and you are chained up in leg shackles prior to being driven in an open truck covered in wire. Upon your return you are then again thoroughly searched and then you have to crouch down in the mid-day sun while drug-sniffing dogs are brought out for a 'final' search. If you have to go to court after sentencing again you are chained both hand and foot to another prisoner.

The food in prison is very bad and below subsistence level for anyone normal. I could never eat the lunch which was rice with a piece of black fish or a large lamb bone with no meat that actually stank. The evening meal was things like dhal with Arabic bread which I could eat. All meals are served in an open central area. The food is put onto stainless steel troop trays and you have to eat with your fingers. Finding dhal rather difficult to eat like that a fellow prisoner made a plastic spoon out of a small piece of plastic he removed from a bucket. You are again bodily searched after every meal and during the meal the prison staff are constantly shouting and blowing whistles to hurry people along. There is a black market of exchanging food for Winston cigarettes where if someone needed cigarettes they would try to smuggle out food getting past a body search — the only way to do this which was risky was for the chap to put a piece of Arabic bread or an apple for example in his underpants. Needless to say I didn't get involved but many did. Tea was put in the block twice a day and in the evening it contained a sedative. Water was the only other drink available. You sleep on the concrete covered steel floor which is like sleeping on a radiator due to the day's sunshine which heats the walls and ceilings as well.

There is painfully little to do in Al Wathba and the only facility they had was a limited library and they allowed daily local newspapers. Radios etc. are banned and so are games but some of the more talented prisoners could make chess sets from Arabic bread (ground to a paste and then shaped into chess pieces). They also make hand-held fans from card, cloth, and cut down broom handles. The other occupation is for non-Muslims to attend Islamic classes which I did as it is a good way to meet other Europeans in the prison and exchange information. You can also get some preferential treatment from the officers if you have any special request or need some particular help. The Islamic teacher is an Irish passport holder—Iraqi father and Irish mother. Hussein (Sam) is 23 years old and in November he will have completed 4 years for a drug offence—taking hashish. He will be deported. He has 'rediscovered' his religion. Quite often in the evenings the local Abu Dhabians would start a singing session using upturned buckets as drums—I must admit to enjoying them as despite their individual problems it was a way for people to take their minds off things.

Telephone calls—locally - are permitted for 'check cases' only twice a week and you have to apply for this through the prison office. Other than probably a couple of calls for myself I spent most of my time calling for other prisoners who were not allowed access.

There are several prisoners who have been prescribed heavy doses of Valium—particularly amongst the long-term prisoners. One nicknamed "7 Up" is a walking zombie and I have never seen anyone that thin. He is serving 10 years for a minor stealing offense involving robbery.

Sending and receiving letters is allowed but all incoming and outgoing mail is censored and all letters should be in Arabic or English. All the Indians/Bangladeshis that received letters one week just got empty envelopes with the words "Write in English" on the empty envelope. In my case most of my mail never arrived—even post that was handed over by the Embassy. The one letter that did get through to me was from a London based organization called "Prisoners" of which you are a patron which I found quite ironic. In this country NO such organization—even Amnesty is allowed to interfere.

With the exception of drug related cases—who are only permitted Embassy visitors- prisoners are allowed to have visits from close family only. Women can visit you on a Monday and men on a Friday.

Each prisoner is given one bar of cheap soap each month and one small packet of Tide for the whole month's washing of clothes. Once a month you are given a disposable razor that you have to return the next day. Other than that shaving is not allowed and clean-shaven prisoners are often stopped by the prison staff and taken to solitary confinement for breaking prison rules. A visit to anywhere in the prison—clinic, library, etc. could result in you having your head shaved again—another way to degrade and humiliate.

There are 3 air-conditioned blocks in Al Wathba. In the hot summer months they try to move all prisoners into air conditioning but I opted to stay where I was as I wanted to stay in daylight and get more access to showers.

The prison warders are mostly from Morocco and Mauritania and on the whole I have to say that most were not unpleasant. They have to work in non air conditioning too so often tempers were frayed. There were of course a few extremely unpleasant ones of a sadistic nature. I quite often saw some unpleasant scenes where a Muslim was being searched and didn't like where fingers were being put and got angry. I found that I was never searched with much fervor - probably because of my age and nationality.

There is a Women's block in Al Wathba mostly for drugs and prostitution cases. There is also a block where mothers with children are held—usually for a case where both the husband and wife have been arrested. They only get to meet each other during court appearances and both are chained up separately. One of the women is English—she visited Abu Dhabi 9 months ago on her way back to London from Thailand—she was carrying drugs and will get a 4-year sentence.

The British Embassy visit once every two weeks and usually have to face abuse from one or more of the prisoners on the basis that as a tax payer the Embassy was not doing enough to help the individual. In fact, the Embassy has no budget, little resources and it seems very little clout in the Ministry of Interior who runs the prison. They also have little knowledge of the local law which is hardly surprising because it changes so often. On the whole they did a good job for me and I certainly appreciated the cigarettes but they should acquaint themselves more with the law for each case they are faced with although the problem with this is that the law seems to change so often. I believe also that they should find a way to discreetly warn visitors to Abu Dhabi about the drinking laws—even advising that taking Al Ghazal and not local taxis every time you go out would be a good idea as not only are they ensured they are very unlikely to take you straight to the police station if they pick you up and smell alcohol late at night. The other local taxis do when they feel like it AND they get a reward. A couple of British people were in the prison for a month for drinking and one was only in the country on business.

Regarding the legal system itself, the critical time in any case seems to be when you are first arrested and make a statement to the police. It is this statement that can get you into serious trouble. In my case I told them the truth—that was a mistake. As for using a lawyer from what I could see in the court I believe that it is a waste of time and money. The lawyers seem to have no say in front of these Judges. In my case I was told by other prisoners that I had the worst Judge dealing with my case and they were right. A combination of him and the Al Muhairy lawyer got me a 1-year sentence.

One positive thing about this experience if there is one is that I met a lot of genuinely good people in Al Wathba. There is no segregation of prisoners so you mix with murderers, sex offenders, etc. There are a lot of very sad cases and cases where people just simply should not be there. A few examples:

- The Mansoori Family—9 men all from the same tribe—ALL in for LIFE—that means for ever. The crime was a tribal murder. Each day one of them has to go out in chains to water some trees with buckets of water.

- A young Bedouin Saudi caught smuggling 500kg of hashish from Saudi Arabia—he will get over a 20-year sentence if not death. He had been badly beaten up to get other names but had not given in. He was a typical Bedu often sitting alone chanting.

- 2 Indians were working for a cleaning company on a project in the city. They were accused of trying to steal a cleaning machine worth about Sterling 1000 and were sentenced to 5 years each. This particular case sickened me because I have a strong feeling the accusation was false and in fact they were beaten up to get a confession.

- Paul Ciceri, a 54 year old American who was living in Abu Dhabi was given a 4-year sentence for drugs. A very nice chap who has made a mistake. Hopefully the US Embassy might be able to do something. His family is doing all that they can. Paul is remarkable in the way that he keeps his spirits up and helps other people—including me when I first arrived. I am now in e-mail contact with his family and friends and can contact Paul through second hand telephone messages from the prison.
- 2 Bahraini flight attendants who I had met before on Gulf Air's London flight were also in prison—another drugs case. They will also get 4 years.
- Ahmed Al Moheirbi—from one of Abu Dhabi's richest families is also in for drugs. An extremely pleasant person to talk to—unfortunately he is in for drugs. He is a heroin addict but was arrested on hash which he was smoking in Dar Al Shiffa hospital where he was recovering from having an operation for the removal of tattoos. I asked him why he had taken drugs when he had so much going for him in life but he didn't really have an answer. Whenever he is released he will be leaving for Europe and probably back to his habit.

Of the above cases I agree that so many have committed real offenses but it is sad to know that there are so many who have not and there are so many whose sentences were totally excessive for the crimes they have supposedly committed. I also hope that some day this changes and that some organization is set up to counsel prisoners once they have been released.

In general what surprised me most about Al Wathba was the amount of locals in there and the amount of locals there for drugs. The nephew of the ruler of Ajman—Sheikh Ali Al Nuami was given a 4-year sentence while I was there. So many of them were in there because of informers—someone gets caught and gives names.

The other thing that surprised me was that there was hardly any violence amongst prisoners. Obviously there was the odd situation where prisoners lost their tempers but from what I have read about US and UK prisons there is no comparison. The only real fighting would be when a group of non-Saudi Arabs would take on the Saudis and a bad situation could happen and did. The other rather sad thing is that there were far too many people with mental illnesses who should have been in special care—most were ragged by the other prisoners which really did infuriate me and they knew it.

Most people think that Saudi Arabia's national sport is flogging. Al Wathba is a flogging factory—all prisoners—both men and women—of any nationality - but with the exception of check cases are given a minimum of 80 lashes with a cane. This is done just outside the interior prison's main entrance every Sunday and Wednesday. A Koran is supposed to be lodged under the arm of the hand holding the cane but this does not happen. I estimated they get through 30 prisoners every session.

As a general comment, I have lived in Abu Dhabi for many years and I have seen some good and some bad and I would have to say that for a country with its wealth and genuine charitable help to other countries in need that Al Wathba is incongruous. Having said that I do not believe that the Royal Family of this country is in any way aware of the conditions in Al Wathba and other prisons and that if they did action would be taken to stop it happening.

On the 16th of April this year I was taken to the appeal court where the Egyptian judge told me that he had read my case and that reading between the lines I knew that he knew I had been tricked and that 1 year was far too much. One week later I was released having lost over 12kg which I could ill afford to lose as it was. My health in general was poor and on reflection the whole experience was very traumatic.

I really do appreciate the fact that you have taken the time to read this. . . .

Addendum D

Poem: The Noise

INSIDE PRISON WALLS there is noise.

Always.

During the tense times of going to the court house for my trial the noises around me seemed amplified. One morning in April 1999, just before my sentencing, I wrote down how I felt:

> *The noise*
> > *constant*
> > *penetrating*
> > *mind numbing*
> > *disabling*
> > *maddening*
>
> *No way to shut it out*
> *I'm trapped*
> > *Must live with it*
>
> *Better to*
> > *relax*
> > *concentrate*
> > *mentally minimize it*
>
> *Must survive*
> *Don't cross the line to insanity*
>
> *"Allah Al Akbar" it begins*
> *The call to Islamic prayer*
> > *resounds from every block*
> > > *Each leader trying to out shout the other*
> >
> > *the first of five times*
> > > *this day*
> > > *every day*
>
> *It's 4:30 a.m.*
> > *Lights come on*
> > *People stir*
> > *Footsteps in the corridor*
> > *Water running*
> > *Prisoners hacking and clearing their throats*
> > > *and blowing their noses*
> >
> > *Talking*
> > *Prisoners chant verses of the Koran*
>
> *The day has begun*

The metal plate on the block gate
   Kicked by the police guard
   Noise resonates everywhere
Time for the tea brigade
   to be kitchen bound

People come back from prayer
   talking
People calling for quiet
More stirring

Tea has arrived
The call "Shy, Shy" goes out
   Walking
   Running
   Fighting over who gets it first

Some settling down
   to talk
   to enjoy the tea
A bit more sleep

At 6:00 a.m.
The bathroom clean-up gang begins
   running water
   scrubbing
   brushing
   spraying
And people stir
   for more tea
Talking increases

At 7
The whistles start
Breakfast time
   Block by block
Hurry
   Don't miss your chance
   Move fast
   Like rounding up cattle
      The cowboys are police with whistles
Banging trays

Yelling to friends
  who pass by

And by 8:30 a.m. all have finished

A few gather at the block gate
  Calling for the guard
  Yelling and banging when he doesn't come
  Wanting out
    for classes
    to go to the library
    for visits with family and friends
    to see the doctor
    for twice a week's hour of sports

The general hubbub of the day begins to build
  Talking
    many languages clashing
  Yelling
  Card playing
    leading to heated
      verbal exchanges
        sometimes physical
Running and chasing
  some horseplay
  some seeking revenge
Screaming at friends
  in other blocks
  on opposite sides of walls
Loud arguments
  amongst prisoners
  between police and prisoners
The loudspeakers blare
  chanting from the Koran
And continues
  all day
  every day
  until lights go out
    late at night

"Kana, Kana" is shouted
  Indian words
  The call to lunch
Loudspeakers couldn't make more noise
And chaos erupts
  Pushing
  Shouting
  Lines non-existent
  Clanging of trays
  Fights over quantity and quality of food
  Yelling to friends
    in overhead blocks
Policemen blowing whistles
  Hurry up
  Time's up

Back from lunch
  The call to noon prayer
  The hubbub continues
  Bics flick
    as everyone lights cigarettes
      One of 30
        for each
        every day

A little quieter
  as some
    get some sleep

The afternoon call to prayer
  People awake
    and the noise builds

Water splashing
Hoses squirting
  Floors being swept
    and scrubbed
  as rooms and corridors
    are cleaned
  And the water splats
    as it drains off
      on the courtyard below

The courtyard gets swept
   and hosed
Police giving orders
Some horseplay with the water
Shouting
   Someone thinks he's working harder
     than another

The late afternoon call to prayer
People prepare
   washing
   dressing
   Like they have
     3 times already today

"Shy, shy"
   Fresh tea
   The cries go out
   Yelling
   Running
   Fighting
     to be first
   Standing on sinks
   Cutting in lines
     so there aren't any
   Chaos
   Like desperate animals

"Kana, Kana"
   comes shortly after
And the flight to dinner begins
   amidst chaos
Like breakfast
Like lunch
People fighting for food
   like there won't be enough
But there always is

Back to the block
And the bics light up again
   in unison

And the evening begins
   Card games
      more intense
      louder than before
   Talking
   Running
   Yelling
   Some singing
      accompanied by
      beating of pail bottoms
And the last call
  for prayer today

The night noise builds

And then
  Trouble!
A fight
Everyone runs
  to see
Sometimes
  the police come
Arguments
Someone is taken away
  perhaps to solitary

It's 11
  maybe 12
The lights go out
Talking drops off
  eventually
The singing stops
Talking turns to whispers
  broken by screams
  and yells
  and fights

And you are thankful
  for a little quiet
    as you pray
      and lay your head
        to rest

Almost asleep
  the evening is getting quiet

And then
  The guard dogs
    free to roam
      Bark and
      Yelp
The cats in heat
  perform their mating calls
Eventually
  they, too, quiet down

You sleep
  in peace
  for a few hours

Addendum E

Count Down

AS THE END OF MY DETENTION approached there weren't a lot of new things I could write home about, so one day I decided to simply write the details of some typical days as they unfolded. In one of those letters to my friend Dean I wrote in early April:

> Today is a beautiful day here, as most are—at least what we can see of it anyway. There has been a problem here for well over a year now that finally got resolved last night, with the result that I had my best sleep in a long time. Right outside my room's door there is an area that is more open than others in the block because that's where a set of toilets and showers are. So every night guys congregate there after the lights in the rooms are switched off to talk and play rummy (that's actually forbidden in Islam) and they are usually loud until 1 a.m. or later. Those of us in our room have been pleading with our foreman to get the police to turn off the lights in that area too—and last night they did. No crowd! No noise! A blessing. So I got a good sleep from 11 until about 5 this morning when the folks that pray came back from their first prayer of the day and began to talk while the first supply of tea for the day was available. It is brought to the block in those big urns and is dished out in two sessions—one after first prayer and then right after breakfast. Now don't go thinking it's like what you might brew at home. It's rather like a sweet caramel-like drink but it's rather tasty.
>
> So that's where my day began so let me walk you through the rest of the weekend (that's Thursday and Friday for us).
>
> One of the guys in my room takes my cup for me and brings me back my tea. He just does. I don't know why. Maybe 'cause I help him with exercising. That's about 5:50 and I cover it with a book so I can have it, maybe lukewarm, with breakfast. Our breakfast call was at 6:25 so off we went. This morning we got 1 jam (you know what you get at a restaurant when you order toast—yeah, one of those packets), 2 of those little triangular cheese pieces, and a round piece (about the size of a small pizza) of flat bread. It was tasty and I was hungry. Then by 6:45 it was back to the block and

another ½ cup of tea. Then I got another ½ hour nap and was wide awake. I read for a bit and tidied up my 6' x 4' area. Then I checked out my laundry to see if it was dry from the wash I did (in a bucket) last night. After a folding I tucked it away. Thursday mornings our mail for the week usually arrives around 9:30 so we were all kind of hanging around waiting. But it didn't come - maybe later today or tomorrow. No reason given. So back to my bed and I did some crunches using a stack of Sports Illustrateds as extra weight. Then I hung out in the corridor, talked with a friend, and stared outside for a bit. I was hoping we might get some time in the sun today but the policeman on our block today wasn't in the giving mood. So back to my bed and I did 15 minutes of some breathing (meditation) exercises. That helps keep me calm and focused. Then I began this letter and it's 11:45.

It's 2:45 and the block has come alive since lunch. Before lunch at 12:30 I played a game with those bishops and pawns. (Remember, all letters are censored and chess was forbidden.) Lunch was white rice with a piece of mutton and gravy. Also there was some grated cabbage and carrots and a 'sweet'. Not bad. I usually have some water too - yippee! Back in the block that space I was telling you about is very busy again. I like staying in my room 'cause everyone smokes outside and it's like being in a bar. I spent a few minutes reviewing a page of my Italian course. The nurse then came to our block to distribute daily doses for those on prescriptions. I got my Centrum vitamin - something I arranged through the Embassy. I've got enough left for 2/3 of my remaining time so I'm rationing the supply. The newspaper came and I glanced through it and recorded the baseball and basketball scores—the Celtics won. Scores are two days behind because of the time difference. I got a 20-minute nap and was awakened by the call for afternoon tea. This tea has no milk in it and tastes a little more like tea. I've been doing the crosswords, bridge quiz, and chess quiz in the paper - recently I've been tackling the cryptic crossword for the challenge and the best I've done so far is to get about 1/3 of it right. It really makes one stretch to figure out the answers. I spent a little time out in the corridor talking a bit and staring out at the bit of sky I can see. The mail came—got 2 letters; one from an Orlando friend and an Easter card from a lady who I've never met and writes 2–3 times a month. I'll get back to the paper and read it in depth after dinner.

I am not really encouraged for an early release when the main headline in huge letters says that this country blasts the U.S. over its bias towards Israel. Every day it's the same old issues in that regard. Does that conflict even make the front page at home anymore? I just wrote a letter for one of the Arab guys for his English girlfriend. He's not that confident with his written English so I've been doing this for him for almost two years now and she doesn't know. I feel like the guy that Steve Martin played in a movie named Roxanne where Steve Martin had a big nose too and wrote letters to this beautiful girl anonymously for a long time before being found out. I don't know how she will deal with this once he tells her the truth behind his letters.

Dinner was at 6:30 and was a serving of chick peas in a liquid plus an optional cup of soup. Not many like the chick peas so I had 2½ servings plus one of the breads like breakfast and a cup of soup—I was hungry! Back in the block after dinner I worked on Saturday's school lesson for ½ hour, read the paper in more detail (by then it had been read by about 10 others), and worked on a logic problem in a book left behind by one of the Brits. There is a lot of talking around me, most of which I do not understand, and which I am told is mostly useless anyhow. One thing about most {prisoners} here though is that they talk so loudly - that is the annoying part.

It's 9:00 now and I just finished cleaning my toe nails- you see, here we wear no shoes and socks. In the room we are barefoot and otherwise we wear flip flops so we rinse our feet more than usual. I'll be reading now until about 10:30 when I'll call it a day and try to get some sleep. I passed on the tea at 8:00 because it would cause me to have to get up during the night for a pee.

It's Friday afternoon and much of today has been like yesterday. I passed on breakfast today because it was a bean dish (much like refried beans you get with Tex-Mex) with lots of oil and raw onions. Usually I pick out the onions (raw ones I have trouble digesting) but wasn't overly hungry today to go to the trouble. Lunch was like yesterday except the meat was chicken and we had a banana instead of a sweet.

This morning I wrote a letter and then had my usual 5-10 minute bimonthly visit with Tom. It's always nice to see him and today he brought me a notebook (from which they removed the staples) and some hair shampoo. The pencils weren't allowed in. He gets ticked off when he hears how long a time there is between embassy visits. I had expected them Wednesday (that would have been 10 weeks since the last visit) but they were a 'no-show'. I guess they'll be here next week 'cause they will be bringing me my income tax form and the deadline is near. Hopefully they'll have the Sports Illustrated and computer books and then I'll have to wait some time for the censors to pour through them before I get them. Last time it took 13 weeks to get the books once the embassy brought them. Because of that, please don't send any more because I won't see the embassy again until July and I'll be lucky to see the books before I get out of here. Tom is vigilant and he has been sending communiqués to anyone he thinks might be in a position to help in this part of the world. The next target is Jimmy Carter who will be here on the 22nd to receive an award for his contribution to humanity—he has a project partially funded by the UAE to eradicate a bug in Africa that has, in the past, killed many thousands.

The rest of the day has been the usual—couple of short naps, crossword, exercise (abs today), talking, studying, and oh yeah we got 20 minutes in the sun this morning. I just lay back, close my eyes and pretend I'm at a guest house in Key West or on a Caribbean beach.

> *The rest of the week is similar to today and yesterday except that from 8–11:30 those mornings I'm at the library or teaching and then four days a week for 1 hour four of us do our exercises using our weights. So you can likely imagine how easy I will be to please after I'm out of here and after a long time of celibacy it should be interesting."*

It was time to send my friends back home an update on my status. The last time I had done that was at Christmas and fortunately it seemed that the time since then had moved quite quickly. The temperatures were starting to soar again as I looked forward to getting through my last summer in the desert. On May 4 I wrote:

> "Here's an update on prison life from fabulous Al Wathba prison in Abu Dhabi:
>
> - As of May 15 it's day 951—only 145 to go until Oct. 7. The countdown has begun!
> - Appreciated your condolences on my dad's death. May is a time of some melancholy as I remember my parents' birthdays, their anniversary, and Mother's Day.
> - Keeping healthy despite some allergies to all the cigarette smoke. Like living in a bar.
> - Following the U.S. sports. I'm over basketball since the Magic got eliminated. Good race amongst Toronto, New York, and Boston in the AL East. Poor Tampa Bay.
> - Roommates: 1 Brit, 3 Indians, 1 Pakistani, 2 Filipinos, 3 Iranians. Interesting.
> - *Lots of negative press about GWB* (George W. Bush) and American foreign policy and according to public opinion the U.S. is a very dangerous place to live. GWB needs a Secretary of Public Relations.
> - Interesting how GWB extended the tenure of Pete Peterson as Ambassador to Vietnam so he wouldn't return to Florida to challenge Jeb in the gubernatorial race.

- All of our stray cats have been rounded up and shipped out. I miss the one that used to hang around here and cuddle in my lap.
- Please send no more mags or books. Embassy visits are now only once per quarter so by the time they come and the censors do their thing I'll be ready to leave.
- Chuckled over the story of a U.S. student in Moscow getting a 3-year sentence for having a small amount of drugs. People at home are screaming about the severity of the sentence. He had 200 times more than me and I got four years. Politics, politics!
- Still teaching English—helps to pass the time.
- Java Script and HTML studies for web-page design coming along okay. I have a lot to put out there post prison.
- Summer is starting early (46°C–114°F) today. Thank goodness for the a/c.
- So bored at times that I'm doing cryptic crosswords and studying Swahili.
- I've had enough humbling and humiliation to last the rest of my life. Looking forward to coming home. Your cards and letters have been much appreciated.

Hope you all have a great summer. Keep one on ice for me!"